More Advance Praise for *The Big Stick*

"An eloquent argument for hard power's enduring importance in an age of global disorder and domestic diffidence. Drawing on his superb grasp of history, Eliot A. Cohen describes in clear and compelling detail how military force and strategy can help enable effective American diplomacy and global leadership in the twenty-first century."

— Ambassador William J. Burns, president of the Carnegie Endowment
  for International Peace and former deputy secretary of state

"A century before Barack Obama, the Nobel Peace Prize was awarded to President Theodore Roosevelt for his role in ending the Russo-Japanese War. Roosevelt's watchword for diplomacy was 'speak softly and carry a big stick.' Eliot A. Cohen has now presented the most compelling case yet for why the 'big stick' remains as essential for managing the national security challenges of the twenty-first century as it was one hundred years ago. This elegantly argued and persuasive book will be essential reading for the new president's foreign and security policy team as they tackle their new responsibilities."

— Eric Edelman, former undersecretary of defense for policy, 2005–2009

"To a people increasingly enamored with soft power and tiring of their role as 'the indispensable nation,' Eliot A. Cohen makes a cogent argument for the use of military force in American foreign policy. *The Big Stick* is the antidote to the siren song of neo-isolationism as well as to the argument that history—and warfare—have ended."

— Professor Peter Mansoor, General Raymond E. Mason Jr. Chair of
  Military History, Ohio State University

"Whither America's military? In a world of disorder and plenty of disillusion from recent wars, the question could hardly be more timely. Eliot A. Cohen has written a remarkably sensible and balanced guide. Yes, he makes the case for American military power in this uncertain world. But his advice is historically grounded and honest about American weaknesses as well as the strengths. In the spirit of Theodore Roosevelt, Cohen urges preparedness, not belligerence. His analysis is not deformed by partisanship and his prose is a pleasure to read."

— Professor Philip Zelikow, director of the Miller Center of Public
  Affairs, University of Virginia

THE BIG STICK

ELIOT A. COHEN

THE
BIG STICK

The Limits of Soft Power &
the Necessity of Military Force

BASIC BOOKS
New York

Books published by Basic Books are available at special discounts for bulk purchases in the United States by corporations, institutions, and other organizations. For more information, please contact the Special Markets Department at Perseus Books, 2300 Chestnut Street, Suite 200, Philadelphia, PA 19103, or call (800) 810-4145, ext. 5000, or e-mail special.markets@perseusbooks.com.

Designed by Amy Quinn

Library of Congress Cataloging-in-Publication Data

Names: Cohen, Eliot A., author.
Title: The big stick : the limits of soft power and the necessity of military force / Eliot A. Cohen.
Description: New York : Basic Books, 2016. | Includes bibliographical references and index.
Identifiers: LCCN 2016040810| ISBN 9780465044726 (hardcover) | ISBN 9780465096572 (e-book)
Subjects: LCSH: United States--Military policy. | United States--Foreign relations--21st century. | United States--Military relations. | National security--United States. | United States--Armed Forces.
Classification: LCC UA23 .C584 2016 | DDC 355/.033573--dc23 LC record available at https://lccn.loc.gov/2016040810

10 9 8 7 6 5 4 3 2 1

To all who, in the service of the United States
of America, venture into harm's way

Contents

Introduction: "National Duties"

On September 3, 1901, Vice President Theodore Roosevelt addressed a large and approving crowd at the Minnesota State Fair on the topic "National Duties." It was a characteristically optimistic speech to an audience barely one generation removed from the pioneers of that region. After celebrating the energy and enterprise of the United States, discussing the qualities that made it great, and reviewing some questions of labor and corporate power, he turned to the outside world. "We may be certain of one thing: whether we wish it or not, we cannot avoid hereafter having duties to do in the face of other nations. All that we can do is to settle whether we shall perform these duties well or ill." Famously, he reminded his listeners of the proverb "Speak softly and carry a big stick—you will go far." His point was not, as some have supposed, a celebration of the bellicosity for which he was famous; rather, it was a sentiment that he expressed often and on other occasions. "Let us further make it evident that we use no words which we are not prepared to back up with deeds, and that while our speech is always moderate, we are ready and willing to make it good."[1]

Only four days later, an anarchist shot President William McKinley; and two weeks later, upon McKinley's death, Roosevelt took his place. Judging by his temper and colorful language, one might have expected an eruption of clashes with foreign nations. Not so. He presided over a period in which the United States asserted itself as one of the great powers in international politics, but without war. The unlikely winner of the Nobel Peace Prize, Roosevelt oversaw the settlement of the remaining disputes with Great Britain, the successful mediation of an end to the Russo-Japanese War, and the Open Door to China.

Roosevelt came in determined to renovate the American military. As assistant secretary of the navy, he had taken a keen interest in reforming that institution. As president, he supported such officers as William Sims, who overhauled the navy's antiquated approach to gunnery, and who later commanded American naval forces in Europe during World War I. Roosevelt pushed through the construction of a battleship fleet comparable in number, though not yet in quality, to that of Germany, and in his last year in office he sent a large chunk of it around the world, painted in festive white, to let the world know that the United States had arrived as a global power. "Boasting about what we have done does not impress foreign nations at all, except unfavorably," he later wrote, "but positive achievement does; and the two American achievements that really impressed foreign peoples during the first dozen years of this century were the digging of the Panama canal and the cruise of the battle fleet around the world."[2]

Roosevelt also helped transform the United States Army, a tough frontier constabulary of 27,000 men that nonetheless had proved barely capable of assembling and deploying an expeditionary force to Cuba during the Spanish-American War. During his presidency it acquired a general staff, institutions of higher military education, and the professional expertise that eventually enabled it to mobilize more than two million soldiers for the global war that erupted six years after Roosevelt left office. Military power was essential to Roosevelt's statecraft.

This is a book about "the big stick" more than a century after Roosevelt's speech, and after America's entrance as a peer into the realm of Great Power politics. It starts where Roosevelt also began, with the belief that military power is an essential support to American foreign policy. It is written, however, at a time when many Americans wonder whether the United States should continue to play a role that even he could not have envisaged—that of guarantor of world order, leader of an array of varied free states, a spokesman for, and in some cases defender of, the liberties of foreign peoples in remote lands.

While many Americans today accept that the United States should play that role in the world, a great many do not. In one 2014 poll, roughly half of those surveyed agreed that "the United States should mind its own business internationally and let other countries get along the best they can on their own," compared to one in five in 1964 and two in five in 1995 who took that position. To be sure, these numbers shift, and in particular cases (e.g., drone attacks on terrorists, or sending advisers in 2015 to aid in the fight against the Islamic State), solid majorities are in favor. Still, today more than ever, many Americans question the utility of "the big stick" as a tool of US foreign policy.[3]

This book addresses the issues that give rise to that skepticism. It asks what the role of armed force should be in American foreign policy, and explores the uses of military power as well as its limits. It addresses the component questions embedded in that larger topic: Why should the United States use military power at all, other than for self-defense as narrowly understood? What have been the lessons of the last decade and a half of war, much of it unsuccessful? Who are the main opponents that the United States will have to confront, either through the threatened or the actual use of force? What are the instruments of hard power, so-called, that the United States can and should wield, and what are the ways in which the nation should make the decisions to do so? This is a work of strategic analysis, not programmatics. While it is important to know something of how drones operate or what ordnance a cruiser can deliver, those are subordinate to the larger questions of in what ways force can, and cannot, serve policy.

Roosevelt faced a complicated world; ours is even more so. The United States faces four challenges that will require various kinds of military responses: the rise of China as a superpower comparable, if not equal, to itself; a collection of ever more violent, and metastasizing global Islamist movements; several powerful states, either nuclear armed or aspiring to nuclear status, that desire to transform the status quo; and the emergence of several ungoverned domains both real (outer space) and virtual (cyberspace) that require some kind of indirect control. These challenges overlap and interact with one another, but are logically and practically distinct—and that is even more of a problem for America's overworked political leaders and their military subordinates.

This is a book written at an unsettled time, after a period of prolonged war with a range of opponents in the Middle East and Asia, and at a time when the fundamentals of national power—ours and that of others—seem to be shifting. It is written at a moment when, in both major political parties in the United States, what can be fairly characterized as neo-isolationist factions are on the rise and have found articulate spokesmen. And it is written when many of the tools of armed power such as armored divisions or bombers may not always be the most relevant instruments of force, but others—cyberwarfare or space-based systems—have yet to demonstrate their potential.

My purpose is to offer an analysis of and an argument about the uses of hard power to all who care about America's place in the world. I will address seriously arguments whose implied recommendations I believe not merely to be wrong, but downright dangerous. My conclusions will probably meet disagreement from many Americans across the spectrum of belief and partisanship, and unsettle foreign readers who wish the United States would do less, as well as a smaller number who wish it would do more. In brief: the United States will need more and better military power in the future. Developing that sufficiency of force will be harder than in the past, and in particular, considerably more difficult than when Ronald Reagan took the defense budget from 4.5 percent of gross domestic product (GDP) in 1979 to 6 percent in 1986. Perhaps most troubling, the chances are growing that the United States will find itself using military power chronically, and at varying levels of intensity, throughout the early decades of the twenty-first century. This last is a prediction, not a desired outcome.[4]

The days of Theodore Roosevelt's boyish enthusiasm for American power are long gone; since his presidency, the United States has experienced a century of global power and responsibility, not all of it happy. The mood of ebullient optimism that Roosevelt radiated, even as he fretted about the ills of American society—from the power of concentrated wealth to the absorption of immigrants—is no longer familiar to us. Since the time of its twenty-sixth president, America has waged two world wars; four medium-size wars (Korea, Vietnam, and Gulf Wars I and II); a host of smaller interventions and limited uses of force; and a chronic campaign of targeted killing against terrorists, one group of which succeeded in landing a hard blow against the body politic in 2001. The century of preeminence has cost the United States dearly. In human terms, the cost has been some 626,000 dead and 1,180,000 wounded. Nor has the material cost been negligible. In Roosevelt's day, spending on defense amounted to roughly 1 percent of GDP; today it is at least 3 percent, and during some periods of the Cold War, it got as high as 10 percent. The military organizations over which a commander in chief presides have grown by an order of magnitude, and in some cases more. From 1908 to the present day, the Army has grown from 77,000 troops to 470,000; the Navy, from 42,000 to 326,000; the Marine Corps, from 9,000 to 183,000; and an entirely new service, the Air Force, today with 310,000, has emerged.[5]

This book has three parts. In the first, it asks whether that expense of blood and treasure was worth it. As well, it explores the arguments for scaling back American aims and the muscle behind them. These range from the highly optimistic contention that the world is either a more benign or more self-regulating place than US statesmen have been wont to claim, to the far darker view that even if the world is a bleak place, the United States is simply too incompetent to use force sensibly in it. This last proposition will be pursued further in a discussion of the lessons of the last fifteen years of war, which some read as conclusive evidence of the inability of the United States to use force prudently and effectively in the world as it is.

The book continues by exploring the American hand—the mix of human, technological, and economic resources that the United States can bring to bear on international security. It then examines separately the four main challenges to which military power is a necessary if partial component of the response—the rise of China; the long-term struggle with Islamist terrorist movements; the rivalry of hostile states, such as Russia, Iran, and North Korea; and the problem of ungoverned space. The concluding chapter of the book explores how the United States government should think about and use force: both the software, so to speak—the art of strategic decision making—and the hardware of military power.

This is not a historical work, but a view of American and world history shapes its arguments; it is not a work of reminiscence or apologetics, although it is written by someone who has, in several ways, been engaged in the making of policy, particularly since 2000; nor is it yet a piece of technical analysis, although it is grounded in the details of hardware and force structure that are indispensable to understanding military power. Rather, it is a study of one dimension of statecraft—hard power. In that respect it runs counter to several prevailing fashions, because hard power is itself rather unfashionable, and those who study it are somewhat suspect. Military historian Cyril Falls once ruefully noted the predicament of his profession, explaining that the study of military affairs no more breeds a desire for violence "than an ornithologist is likely to feed his children on gobbets of raw flesh, still warm, because he has become fascinated by the behavior of birds of prey."[6]

Someone writing a book about the uses as well as the limits of military power faces a similar challenge. The most beneficent form of military strength is that which is so overwhelming that it need not be used. Korea and Vietnam (and a host of lesser conflicts) notwithstanding, that was the case for the central conflict of the Cold War, when American military superiority over any rival, save the Soviet Union—and even, for much of the time, vis-à-vis the USSR as well—made possible a period of prosperity unparalleled in the history of humanity.

Today, as in the past, force remains the last argument of kings—or presidents. Readers who look askance on an author who, in some circumstances, advocates the employment as well as the preparation of force might wish to consider the way in which Barack Obama, the forty-fourth president of the United States, evolved during his time in power. He came to office on a platform of opposition to one war (Iraq), and announced his termination of another (Afghanistan), and near conclusion of a third (al-Qaeda). And yet he found himself reneging on his commitment to disengage from Afghanistan, launching an undeclared war in Libya, sending thousands of American troops into the deserts of Mesopotamia for the third war there in a generation, ordering bombing and commando raids in Syria, expanding by an order of magnitude the intensity and scope of a campaign of assassination of terrorists, launching regular deployments of military aircraft and armored units to Poland and the Baltic states, shifting American warships and planes to confront China, and ordering US Navy ships to sail very (some might say, provocatively) close to new Chinese island bases. These uncomfortable facts may reflect either Clio's (goddess of history) sense of irony or hard necessities worthy of contemplation. More likely, both.

CHAPTER ONE

WHY THE UNITED STATES?

Why indeed? Why should Americans take on a web of entangling alliances and responsibility for maintaining order, including through the use of force, in the world beyond their own borders? To most Americans from the middle through to the end of the twentieth century, the answers to this question seemed self-evident. To do otherwise would mean not only to acquiesce in civilization-shattering horrors, but to jeopardize their own prosperity and freedoms. This was the logic that led both Roosevelts to favor intervention in the world wars; it was the logic that led Americans, even many who were deeply reluctant to do so, to accept the burdens of world leadership after 1945.

Today, as those who carry with them personal memories of World War II disappear from our midst, the case is no longer self-evident. And even if it were, it would warrant a reexamination. If it is to be acted upon, a conviction that America's foreign policy requires commitments to deploy and use force overseas should reflect live belief, not dead dogma.

Let us begin with examining why at least two generations of Americans came to believe that theirs should be a global power; considering the arguments for retreating from, or at least ratcheting down that role; and then asking what the arguments are on the contrary for maintaining it.

On September 6, 1943, Harvard University hosted a special convocation to award an honorary degree to Winston Churchill, prime minister of Great Britain. He spoke first in Sanders Theatre, and then before an audience that included 6,000 undergraduates in uniform, and almost as many civilians in the open space between Widener Library and Memorial Church. The *Harvard Crimson* reporter thought he had heard Churchill offering some warnings about postwar isolationism in the United States. Actually, the British prime minister's speech had a larger meaning.

Churchill, recently returned from a difficult conference in Quebec at which the decisions for the invasion of Europe were forged, had a simple and pressing message. He began by noting that twice in his lifetime, the United States had had to send vast armies overseas.

> There was no use in saying "We don't want it; we won't have it; our forebears left Europe to avoid these quarrels; we have founded a new world which has no contact with the old." There was no use in that.

Why in Churchill's view did the Americans find themselves committed abroad?

> The price of greatness is responsibility . . . one cannot rise to be in many ways the leading community in the civilised world without being involved in its problems, without being convulsed by its agonies and inspired by its causes . . .

He then turned directly to his audience. "You cannot stop," he said.

> There is no halting-place at this point. We have now reached a stage in the journey where there can be no pause. We must go on. It must be world anarchy or world order.[1]

Churchill summoned the United States to not only engage in the world, but assume responsibility for setting the rules of international politics and maintaining order. It was no accident, moreover, that he addressed not only the middle-aged and elderly members of Congress, but the thousands of young men in uniform at a university that produced more than its share of America's leaders. Churchill made his appeal to America's youth, and he understood that although leadership might take many forms, military power would be chief among them.

The United States, as the half-American prime minister knew better than most, had never been truly isolated from the rest of the world. Every one of the great global wars between Britain and France from the end of the seventeenth century through the beginning of the nineteenth had, in one way or another, engaged the American colonies and then the infant United States. Two of those wars—the Seven Years' War and the American Revolution—started there. As a young and growing power, the United States employed force globally as most countries have—to protect its interests. During the early years of the republic it twice sent fleets to the Mediterranean to punish the piratical states of the North African littoral and protect its commerce. When Commodore Perry and his flotilla knocked on the doors of a closed Japan in 1853 and again in 1854, they did so in pursuit of American interests. Through the Monroe Doctrine, the United States gradually levered European powers out of Latin America, confronting even Great Britain during the Venezuelan crises of 1895 and 1902. And, of course, it employed military power to wrest much of the continent from Mexico in 1846, threatened to use more to evict French influence from that state after the Civil War, and at the end of the nineteenth century forcefully stripped Spain of its colonial possessions in the Caribbean and the Philippines. In the First World War it engaged in conflict at least in part because of attacks on its shipping, but also because of a conviction that a changed balance of power in Europe would be inimical to its interests.

But all these uses of force were, with the possible exception of the intervention in the European conflict in 1917, designed to promote American interests as narrowly understood. Until 1914 even Theodore Roosevelt, proponent of a navy on a par with the Royal Navy and a larger, modernized army, had not yet conceived of the United States as the guarantor of the international system—although at that point, alarmed at the likely consequences of German domination in Europe, he favored an early entry into the Great War. The isolationism of the 1930s, far from being consonant with the American tradition

in foreign policy, was more a historically anomalous twitch of withdrawal from international power politics in the wake of disillusionment with what was, until then, the second costliest war in American
history after the Civil War. The norm had been American strategic
engagement in the world but for limited interests. What was at stake
in Churchill's speech, however, and in the decisions of the immediate
postwar period, was something far more expansive and consequential.

The United States took up Churchill's challenge. In the wake of
the desolation of Europe and Asia resulting from World War II, the
rise of communism, a virulent ideology hostile to American principles,
and the fatal weakening of its strongest ally, Great Britain, the United
States was impelled to take on the duty that Churchill flung before
it—the accretion of massive military power not to defend merely
American prerogatives or interests, but rather to maintain global order. The United States government did not make that decision easily
or swiftly in the years immediately after World War II. But by the end
of the Korean War it had become clear that the United States would
remain a global military power, locked in permanent, peacetime alliances, and using its strength to sustain an order that it was painfully
rebuilding in the aftermath of the catastrophe of more than a decade
of interstate war. Even after Vietnam, despite some retrenchment (the
so-called Nixon Doctrine, which placed greater burdens on local allies
to defend themselves), the United States sustained its role as guarantor. Indeed, under President Jimmy Carter, it actually expanded
its military commitments in the increasingly important Persian Gulf.
Under Ronald Reagan it deepened its involvement in European security, rebuilding American forces that had been depleted during
the Vietnam War, and preparing to deploy advanced theater nuclear
weapons there as well.[2]

The American consensus behind playing the dominant role in the
world remained intact beyond the conclusion of the Cold War at the
end of the ninth decade of the twentieth century. For a time it appeared that the US commitment to using force to maintain a peaceful
global system would continue indefinitely. The United States won a
short, smashing, and astoundingly cheap war in 1991 against Iraqi
dictator Saddam Hussein, who had invaded the oil-rich emirate of

Kuwait. In the run-up to the war, President George H. W. Bush suggested the creation of a "new world order" maintained by the force of American arms as a possible objective. In its wake, he more triumphantly affirmed it.

> Now, we can see a new world coming into view. A world in which there is the very real prospect of a new world order. . . . The Gulf war put this new world to its first test. And my fellow Americans, we passed that test.[3]

In 1998, Madeleine Albright, the secretary of state of his Democratic successor, Bill Clinton, took a similar view proclaiming the United States "the indispensable nation." The Clinton administration waged two short, nearly bloodless (from the American point of view) wars in the Balkans in 1995 and 1999, and periodically administered punishment to the fractious Iraqi rump state still controlled by Saddam Hussein. All things considered, the military power required for world order was cheap, drawing as the United States could on the arsenals built in the 1980s under Ronald Reagan and even before. The cost of using this power was limited in blood and treasure—fewer than 150 battle deaths in the 1991 Gulf War, for example—its efficacy remarkable. Hard power, and ample quantities of it, in support of being the global sheriff seemed a good bargain.[4]

It no longer appeared so in the early years of the twenty-first century. Ten years to the day after President George H. W. Bush's first proclamation of a new world order, during his son's presidency, airplanes hijacked by al-Qaeda terrorists plowed into the Twin Towers in New York and the Pentagon in Washington, DC. In the aftermath of these attacks, the United States engaged in three grueling wars: in Afghanistan against the Taliban; in Iraq against the regime of Saddam Hussein; and then against a variety of Sunni and Shia guerrilla and terrorist movements, and globally, affiliates of and successors to al-Qaeda. This period saw, as well, the rise of China as a great power. Unlike the Soviet Union, China had a dynamic economy that might in time surpass even that of the United States in size, and which was building a military to match. American statesmen during this time contemplated problems—the Iranian and North Korean nuclear threats, in particular, but also a revanchist Russia's brandishing a nuclear arsenal while brutalizing several of its neighbors,· former states of the Soviet Union—that might only be contained or remedied with conflicts far bloodier than those in Yugoslavia in the 1990s or even in Iraq in 1991 and 2003. And although militant Islamic movements posed a widespread threat, including to the continental United States, American leaders and their society could see no coherent ideology comparable to Nazism or communism that could threaten American institutions or offer an alternative to the basic formula of liberal economics and democratic politics underpinned by religious tolerance and the rule of law.

In this context, then, the first-order question has reopened: why American military power? Or, rather, why American military power for any purpose other than self-defense and the pursuit of national interests as narrowly defined? Why should not the United States content itself with a nuclear arsenal to deter attack, an air force to protect its skies, a navy to protect its commerce, and a small army to defend its shores and serve as the nucleus for expansion should circumstances warrant it? This, after all, was the traditional American posture. One could argue that the United States should draw a line under the period 1940–2000. For two generations it had maintained a liberal world order by force of arms. Now that the two great totalitarian ideologies that threatened order were crushed, however, should it not henceforth bear arms only in its own defense, and in support of its own interests? Such a position is not isolationist per se—no one suggests that the United States should stop trading globally, withdraw from the United Nations, or unilaterally disarm. It is merely a return to pre-1914 traditions of American statecraft.

Such arguments have been made in recent years, in five distinct variants: the contention that the world is becoming a more peaceful place and hence not in need of policing; the assertion that the logic of power politics will maintain the peace in ways that it has not in the past; the suggestion that soft power can replace hard power; the proposition that the United States is simply incompetent at using hard power and would do better not to try; and the argument that more urgent domestic priorities require a period of inward focus rather than external activity. All deserve serious examination.

The first and most optimistic argument has it that—despite the headlines that so often highlight mayhem and massacre—the world is an increasingly peaceful place. This runs against the grain for students of military history, who naturally tend toward pessimism, taking a dark view of humanity's proclivity to use violence, and doubting its ability to learn from its mistakes. But perhaps they are wrong, ignoring hard data to the contrary.

Steven Pinker, a psychology professor at Harvard University, certainly believes so. In his book *The Better Angels of Our Nature: Why Violence Has Declined*, he argues that the use of violence has declined precipitously throughout human history, and that this decline reflects changes in society and indeed conceptions of what it is to be human that make the trend well-nigh irreversible. A variety of changes "allow a greater and greater proportion of humanity to live in peace and die of natural causes," he concludes.[5]

Pinker is unquestionably right in documenting the decline of violence in the very long sweep of human history. Whereas anthropologists in the early twentieth century liked to portray primitive men and women as generally peaceful, their less starry-eyed colleagues of today accept that tribal life was often extremely brutal and bloody. Even a cursory familiarity with the Middle Ages makes one understand that violent death was far more prevalent then than today, not just through crime, but as a matter of calculated policy. In the Bamiyan province of Afghanistan there stands on a picturesque hill a ruined city, Shahr-e Gholghola; it is known to the locals as the City of Silence (and alternatively, the City of Screams), because in 1221 Genghis Khan put its inhabitants to death in a three-day orgy of killing to avenge the death of his grandson. The conqueror Tamerlane left behind pyramids of freshly severed heads—over a bloody career, hundreds of thousands, if not millions of them—to make clear to all who stood in his path the penalty for resistance or rebellion. The Crusaders, their horses' fetlocks stained red with blood, rode into Jerusalem in 1099, making their way to the center of a city carpeted with the bodies of Muslim and Jewish defenders and their families.[6]

In many ways, violence has declined in most, if not quite all, societies—there are fewer homicides, and there is less frequent war. Indeed, despite what many believe, there is actually much less gun violence in the United States now than twenty years ago. The causes for this decline in violence within societies and among them are multiple, Pinker argues: the rise of states that can maintain law and order; changing norms with regard to the use of force to include a growing reverence for human life; the declining utility of force as a way of acquiring money, possessions, or other goods (to include, in the case of men, sexual favors) for both individuals and groups; and the rising utility of other means—chiefly economic acquisition—for achieving the same; the global spread of democratic norms; and the extension of rights beyond adult males to women, children, and even to animals.[7]

Pinker's argument is the most serious, extensive, and scholarly of many such. Many of the trends and much of the data that he presents are true and support his views, although the older the statistic the more questionable it often becomes. And over the long sweep of time, Pinker is correct. As he admits, the world wars of the twentieth century pose something of a challenge to optimists such as himself. But, he insists, "the enduring moral trend of the [twentieth] century was a violence-averse humanism that originated in the Enlightenment, became overshadowed by counter-Enlightenment ideologies wedded to agents of growing destructive power, and regained momentum in the wake of World War II." To be sure, some of his use of statistics is problematic, to include his inflation of earlier centuries' death statistics by including nonviolent deaths (the Indian famines of the nineteenth century, for example, and the wiping out of Native Americans by disease in the sixteenth through the nineteenth). Moreover, his focusing on the number of deaths as a proportion of total population size is calculated to support his argument by diminishing somewhat the absolute magnitude of slaughter during the twentieth century. He relies as well on quantitative studies of the numbers of wars per century that count a nasty border conflict in Latin America and World War I as one war each, a rule that by its nature misleads.[8]

But more to the heart of the problem, Pinker, like social theorist and Stanford researcher Francis Fukuyama in his earlier famous argument about the end of history, has to view the slaughter of the twentieth century—the world wars, not to mention the massacres committed by totalitarian regimes of left and right—as a kind of blip, explosions of violence that owed a great deal to the randomness of circumstances, the unfortunate coming together of particular events and particular leaders that do not, however, invalidate the general trend. As Pinker freely admits, there is something heartless about brushing aside the deaths of tens of millions in the world wars with reference to an overall benign trend. But leaving the question of callousness aside, the world wars nonetheless present three deeper problems with his argument.[9]

The first is that Pinker might just as easily have written his book in 1900, for the trends he describes were already well in place then. But he could not have in any way anticipated the mayhem that a child born in that year would then have witnessed by the time he was forty-five. Or, put another way, if the world's randomness is such that it can produce slaughter on such an epic scale, why should we today be any less fearful of it in today's world—a world with far better tools for inflicting mass death than those available in the early twentieth century? In any way you care to measure it, ours is a more complicated world than that of 1900—over two hundred independent states rather than mere dozens, for example. But more complicated systems are more prone to unforeseen and unforeseeable accidents than simple ones.[10]

A second problem is that by introducing randomness as an explanation, Pinker has created a proposition that cannot be logically disproven. If the twenty-first century turns out to be generally peaceful, Pinker could claim to be right; if, however, it includes a decade of war that takes a hundred million lives, he could set that down, too, to randomness and still be right. It is an enviable debating position, but not convincing. "Randomness" is a cop-out: our lives are filled with randomness, but that does not diminish human responsibility or our ability to react to unpredictable circumstances in ways that shape them. Big choices, to include the United States' decision not to intervene in the European conflict until 1917, or the British and French governments' decision to appease Hitler in the 1930s, had real consequences.

Third, interestingly, the one explanation that Pinker does not explore as a cause for the limiting or controlling of violence is statecraft, the application of political and military judgment to particular circumstances. Yet politicians must decide, and most of us believe, that choices have consequences as well as that skill in conceiving and conducting policy can—not always, but often—make the difference between war and peace, between a swiftly concluded victory or a prolonged and painful defeat. Pinker's is a social scientist's, not a historian's argument; it falls prey to the rationalist's fascination with structural causes, long-term trends, and impersonal forces. He is right that wars seem to have decreased in number, as has mayhem in general (though not in particular—see the Great Lakes region of Africa, the devastated countries of Syria and Iraq, the ruined lands of eastern Ukraine). But there is reason to believe that contingent events, and the deliberate action of one state above all—the United States—has had something to do with the relative peacefulness of the world after 1945, even as the action of Great Britain as the world's dominant maritime power had a similar effect after the final defeat of Napoleon in 1815. It follows that an American decision to stop acting that way could yield a far nastier twenty-first century than the one Pinker expects.

One may doubt that human beings are turning into a nicer lot, however, and still believe that the need for American power to maintain world order has diminished. Indeed, the second case against American predominance could be described as "pacific realism." It takes the hard-headed view that human beings and states are rational, self-interested, and amoral. In the world of contemporary social science, the term *realist* is used to describe political scientists who have a certain common understanding of international politics: that it is dominated by states, and that state behavior internationally can be understood in terms of either a drive for security, or a drive for power over other states; that the domestic constitution of states has little to do with their behavior abroad; and that responsible statecraft sees its duties overwhelmingly in terms of prudently furthering security, rather than advancing particular ideals.[11]

Despite what one might expect, some realists these days are a fairly cheerful lot, at least in terms of how they view world order. They believe that the United States may have been prudent to exert power abroad so as to beat back Nazi Germany and the Soviet Union. These states were mortal threats not because of their pernicious ideas, but because of their ambition to conquer and absorb other states, and particularly the productive heartland of Europe, one of the great engines of the global economy. The threat to global order created first by Germany and Japan, and then after World War II by the Soviet Union and its allies, was properly met by a United States that led a countervailing coalition. In time, being richer and more advanced, the United States and its allies prevailed.

In the realists' view, the world having resolved itself into a more familiar pattern of competing powers, the United States has far less need to meddle in matters abroad. The natural logic of the balance of power, to include the notion that "the enemy of my enemy is my friend," will naturally stabilize international politics: a rising China will be balanced by a coalition of its apprehensive neighbors, as will Iran or Russia in their respective regions. At the most, a gentle pressure on the scales from the United States acting as an "offshore balancer" will restore equipoise to international politics. A more assertive American foreign policy is not only unnecessary, but possibly dangerous. A typical product of this way of thinking is an article suitably titled "America Unhinged," by John Mearsheimer. In his view, the United States has never been more secure than it is today. And while declaring that he is not an isolationist, he sympathizes with that position: "If the case for isolationism was powerful before Pearl Harbor, it is even more compelling today." The chief threat to the United States that Mearsheimer detects is the misguided behavior of its interventionist foreign policy elites, hence the title of the article.[12]

Realists often argue, further, that nuclear weapons will have a profoundly dampening effect on conflict. Hydrogen bombs are the great equalizer of international politics. Their gradual spread should not be rejected but welcomed by politicians and publics, because they inhibit traditional forms of aggression. As one analogy famously has it, international relations becomes like a room crowded with individuals severely affected by arthritis—no jostling or shoving, because it will hurt the aggressor as much as the victim. The more states that have nuclear weapons, the less the need for American intervention abroad. Since states, no matter what their forms of government, are deeply rational, they will deter one another from the most gross forms of violence that have, in the past, preceded all-out war.

Finally, the realists argue, a change in the nature of economics has diminished the utility of force. In the bad old days, conquest meant the acquisition of material resources—slaves, coal mines, and agricultural land. But in a world in which one of the most prosperous societies, Singapore, exists on a tiny, sandy, hot, and humid island devoid of just about any usable material asset, what is the point? In a world in which value is created by information technology and higher forms of organization, in which labor is increasingly creative, and raw materials a readily available commodity, what is the point of seizing territory?

The realists' argument begins with the advantage of a semantic preemptive strike: if those who hold these views are "realists," after all, those who hold contrary points of view are, by definition, unrealistic. Their contentions have, moreover, the great attraction of simplicity, allowing students of international affairs to overlook the messiness of day-to-day politics and the ambiguities of culture and contingent events. But they are problematic as well. They disregard the role of personalities and regime type; they also put little weight on the importance of nonstate actors, and even less on ideology.

The most fundamental principle of contemporary realism is that all states are alike, that they have interests, and will use power to protect and further those interests. But common sense and even a slight knowledge of history suggests that such judgments are true only up to a point. Hitler was not Bismarck with bad manners: his aims, his methods, his tolerance of risk, and his willingness to kill put him in a different place. Indeed, he benefited from the inability of his English and French counterparts in the 1930s to comprehend the scale on which he planned on playing a role in the world, or his intentions to enslave and kill. In more recent times, any Iraqi government would likely have viewed Kuwait as a problem for insisting on repayment of war debts run up during the war with Iran, and quite possibly as an illegitimate state that should logically be under Baghdad's rule. In

1990, however, it took a Saddam Hussein to seize it by force, and wager his country's welfare on a war with the United States to retain it.

Contemporary realists have trouble taking substate or transstate actors seriously. Like Stalin, they ask how many divisions the pope has, and sneer accordingly—yet in the end, Pope John Paul II was probably more lethal to the Soviet Union than the Bundeswehr. Al-Qaeda and other radical Islamist movements are often dismissed by realists as epiphenomenal, unimportant to what really matters in the scope of human affairs. When such movements take a state, or blow a giant hole in Manhattan, sweeping away thousands of lives, realists have to resort to the explanation that such events, while unfortunate, are, again, minor ones on the margins of the great dance of states. It is true, as they often point out, that many more Americans, Frenchmen, and Israelis die in car accidents than in terrorist attacks, but they fail to capture the larger political consequences of motivated as opposed to random violence.

Realists are unrealistic in their failure to appreciate the intangibles, to include the power of faith and ideology. For the realist, in fact, the great ideological revolutions of the last three centuries—from the American Revolution to the French, Russian, Chinese, and Iranian Revolutions—were similarly superficial events in a political world in which the real game is the game of states, not the great struggles over political order and the very meaning of justice. In their view, the Ayatollah Khomeini and his successors in Iran must be understood as nationalists in turbans, not as religious revolutionaries. Coolly detached secularists themselves, the realists find it difficult to take seriously talk of caliphates or hidden imams. But as the people of Syria and Iraq have discovered to their sorrow, and as many others have learned before them, passionate belief can trump interest as understood by those for whom faith has no fire.

Such a flattening and limiting of one's understanding of human nature has strategic consequences. It leads, eventually, to a prediction of a kind of automaticity in human behavior, in which states push and shove, but in ways similar to the algorithms of swarms of simple robots. If politics really worked that way, statesmanship would not exist, and equilibrium would be enforced by a system, not by politicians making decisions. In fact, the realists would have no reason to argue for a given policy rather than merely proceed with their scientific analyses. Sooner rather than later, reality would expose their opponents' misconceptions. Of course, politics does not behave that way.

John Mearsheimer and Stephen Walt's *The Israel Lobby* is a useful if extreme case of academic realism baffled and unaccountably angered by a policy that it cannot predict—in this case, America's steadfast friendship with Israel over a period of half a century or more. Since Mearsheimer and Walt's conceptual framework excludes commonality of values, shared history and traditions, and simple affection as motivations for foreign policy, they resort to what is, in essence, a conspiracy theory, in which a semicovert organization has successfully manipulated a great power for decades, causing it to act contrary to its best interests, and in a manner that their own theories could not anticipate. Revealingly, just as the Middle East exploded in a set of upheavals that had nothing to do with Israel, they attributed to the Israeli-Arab conflict a centrality that had long passed, if it had ever existed to begin with.[13]

Realism not as a theory but as a frame of thought does offer insights. There is a crude logic of balancing and bandwagoning, although the room for variation is often greater than realists might think. States often have concrete interests in material things—access to air and sea ports, supplies of energy, and above all an irreducible core of security in their borders and their possessions. There is indeed a certain logic in allying with an unsavory state against a deeply hostile one, even at the risk of some injury to one's principles. And perhaps most important, states retain vast reserves of wealth and power that are not available to other kinds of organizations or movements. Even there, however, the realists may overlook in some measure the web of restraint international agreements and globalized trade and communication cast over states. Arguably, there is an erosion of sovereignty as such institutions as the International Criminal Court or the World Trade Organization exercise authority independently of states. Indeed, one of the greatest challenges faced by American strategists is that they live in a world both of states and nonstate actors, of traditional interest-based policy and behavior and ideologically driven conduct, of autonomous countries and international covenants and understandings that constrain them.

In the internal battles of the academy, the realists are themselves balanced, so to speak, by a school that argues against their narrow definitions not only of the national interest, but of the tools to protect and advance it. Realists, by and large, are not pacifists: they believe in tangible hard power. But in 1990, as the Cold War ended, Harvard professor Joseph Nye made the case that "soft power" could supplement, and in some cases replace, military force. Nye called upon his readers "not to abandon the traditional concern for the military balance of power, but to accept its limitations and to supplement it with insights about interdependence." More extreme advocates of soft power, however, saw both a decline in the efficacy of military force, and the possibility of replacing it with nonviolent means. They represent the third challenge to the post-1945 American foreign policy consensus.[14]

Advocates of soft power, defined in part as "the ability of a country to structure a situation so that other countries develop preferences or define their interests in ways consistent with its own," believe that the growing interdependence of states through trade, communication, and movement of peoples gives the United States in particular the ability to exercise influence without needing to use muscle. Nye did not dismiss the importance of military power, and indeed has come increasingly to value it as the international scene has become more difficult. Others, however, hoped that soft would supplant hard power as the prime tool of American policy. The positive dimensions of American soft power—the appeal of American culture, the spread of English, the strength of its educational and financial systems, for example—would allow the United States to draw potentially hostile states and movements into its orbit. The negative forms of soft power—sanctions, embargoes, the marshaling of the public opinion—would provide nonviolent but effective means of coercion. Where military power is morally unattractive and unpredictable because it relies on violence, soft power may take longer, but is more potent and enduring.[15]

The advocates of soft power, who believed in both the national interest as well as in the centrality of maintaining the global order of the postwar period, had a point. The magnetism of the United States has real political consequences. Take, for example, America's shifting relationship with India. Understood in realist terms, an alignment with India is an ideal way of balancing the power of China in Asia. Soft power advocates would agree, but argue that behind the common interests of the two countries lie some measure of fellow feeling in the world's two largest democracies, and an extensive Indian diaspora that has come to play an ever larger role in American society and politics. Indian entrepreneurs in Silicon Valley and Indian students in American universities contribute to a steadily developing relationship that is independent of the interaction of diplomats. Prudent statecraft should cultivate those relationships as much as, or more than, arms deals and joint military exercises.[16]

Yet if soft power has its effects, it also has its limits. English, for example, is indeed now the global lingua franca, but that does not guarantee American influence. In the eighteenth century, English aristocrats, and especially military commanders, were often fluent in French, at the time the language of culture and diplomacy. That did not prevent them from waging a century of relentless war against France, driving it first to financial collapse and then to revolution. In the late nineteenth and early twentieth centuries, the language of science in the United States was German, but the United States fought two wars to humble, and then eliminate, German power. American universities are attractive places to study, but Khalid Sheikh Mohammed, the mastermind of 9/11, did not conceive a deep affection for the United States during his time at North Carolina Agricultural and Technical State University (bachelor of science, 1986).

Power is the ability to get people to do things that they would not otherwise do. It implies purposiveness—the ability to make things happen. Much of what is termed soft power is not controllable; that is, it cannot be directed with precision—and indeed, sometimes it cannot be directed at all. This turns out to be true even of sanctions.[17]

The developed world's long isolation of and sanctions on first Rhodesia and then South Africa helped bring down the white supremacist regimes of both countries in 1979 and 1994. In the early twenty-first century, creative American officials developed ways of exerting increasing pressure on hostile countries by curtailing and in some cases severing their links with the international financial system. Yet the twenty-first century saw as well the limits of sanctions. Arguably, they brought the Islamic Republic of Iran to the negotiating table concerning its nuclear program, although one may just as plausibly claim that some of the credit goes to the demonstration of American military power in Iraq in 2003. Still, squeezed by both UN sanctions and American unilateral measures, Iranian oil exports fell from 2.5 billion barrels a day to 1.1 billion from 2011 to 2013; its economy grew less than it otherwise would have and inflation soared. Sanctions undoubtedly played some role, although so, too, did sheer mismanagement. In the end, however, the Iranian nuclear program continued to expand, going from fewer than 6,000 early model IR-1 centrifuges installed at its Natanz plant in 2008, to more than 15,000 only seven years later, in addition to more than a thousand IR-2 centrifuges added to the inventory. This occurred even as steadily mounting sanctions helped reduce Iran's growth rate below zero and increase its inflation rate to nearly 30 percent.[18]

In a similar vein, when Russian covert operators and special forces overthrew Ukrainian rule in Crimea and then ignited a war in eastern Ukraine in 2014, the West clapped sanctions on businessmen and officials close to Prime Minister Vladimir Putin; a second round of sanctions in July 2014 helped drive down the value of the ruble by roughly 40 percent against the dollar and downgrade Russia's international credit. But the Russians continued to press their advantages in eastern Ukraine. Again, tumbling oil prices and economic mismanagement deserve some of the credit, but sanctions may have made matters marginally worse. Even so, in 2015, Russia began a major new geopolitical adventure by engaging in the Syrian civil war with air power, advisers, and special forces against the wishes of the United States, whose soft power was neither a constraint nor a deterrent.[19]

The largest problem with sanctions as a tool of policy is that it assumes that leaders care deeply about the state of their country's economy, or that they can be touched personally by restrictions imposed on (for example) its banking system. But they may not care and may not be affected. No country on earth has suffered more under such sanctions as miserable, impoverished North Korea, which continues to flout numerous UN Security Council resolutions by developing nuclear weapons, as well as the missiles to deliver them. In another case, the limits of coercive soft power were conceded by the Obama administration at the end of 2014 when it lifted a half-century-old trade embargo on Cuba, arguing that the sanctions had yielded nothing. With enough will, callousness, and if necessary, brutality, leaders can carry their countries through the most rigorous sanctions imaginable.

Moreover, no tool of power, to include sanctions, is free from costs. These may be contractual costs, which for a long time made the French loath to suspend their sale of two amphibious warships to Russia in 2014. They may be reputational costs, as the United States suffered when it continued to impose trade restrictions on Saddam Hussein's Iraq in the period between the first and second wars with that country in 1991 and 2003, causing America to come under increasing criticism for contributing to the suffering of the Iraqi people. They may include financial loss to one's own side, either through retaliation (say, a Russia that suspends the shipment of titanium to Boeing) or forgone trade. Since few sanction regimes are airtight, for a certain premium, a regime under pressure can usually find a way of getting what it needs.

In the early twenty-first century, the United States pioneered new kinds of sanctions directed against nations' or movements' ability to use the international financial system. But the effectiveness of restraints on banking (particularly secondary sanctions against banks or commercial firms that do business with a sanctioned entity) has a half-life. Other countries—including the world's second largest economy, China—have large incentives to counter America's use of financial sanctions, in particular, either by creating alternative banking and financial transfer systems, or by retaliating in ways that will be painful for American business. Sanctions are like any other weapon. No matter how innovative and devastating at first, in a competitive world sooner or later opponents will devise counters to them. In a world of rising powers that dislike the United States' ability to apply economic coercion unilaterally there is every incentive in the system to do so.[20]

Soft power is not necessarily gentle. It may deprive a country of medical supplies, clean water, and electricity; of necessity, its weight tends to fall more on populations at large than on elites who can insulate themselves through theft, bribery, or confiscation. Soft power is not easily dialed up and down: once abandoned, sanctions can be almost impossible to restore, for political reasons. Moreover, soft power also engenders conflict. The appeal of American democratic manners, of rights for women and religious minorities and popular culture, particularly through its entertainment industry, engenders as much hostility and animus as it does attraction. If our culture were not so tempting, so many jihadis would not hate us, on the one hand, even as foreign dissidents build papier-mâché copies of the Statue of Liberty for their protests, on the other.

Most assuredly, nonviolent forms of power have their place in any country's statecraft. One can argue that the United States erred in the early twenty-first century in failing to develop the kinds of campaigns of propaganda and subversion against radical Islam that were an important part of its arsenal in the twentieth-century struggle with communism. And in conjunction with hard power—warships enforcing a blockade, for example—such policy instruments as embargoes and isolation from international financial transactions can have a powerful effect. But soft power on its own has limited effects, and second- and third-order consequences that American leaders cannot control and may even regret.

One might think, *pace* the optimists, that the world is a dangerous place; one might disagree with the realists who believe that an assertive foreign policy would only disrupt a well-functioning balance of power; one might even concede that soft power cannot substitute for hard power, and yet conclude that the United States simply cannot effectively lead the international system and maintain a free and open international order. The fourth argument against American maintenance of global order with military power rests therefore not on a view that the world needs less policing, and not on the substitution of gentler means for force, but on America's irreducible strategic incompetence.

Gulliver's Troubles is a classic study of American foreign policy written in the 1960s by Stanley Hoffmann, Henry Kissinger's counterpart and rival in the Harvard Government Department. American political leaders often feel themselves to be, like Gulliver, giants tied down by the numerous, persistent, and unreasonable inhabitants of Lilliput. At least in Jonathan Swift's tale, Gulliver was naive, but not a fool. A steady stream of commentary since Vietnam, however, has argued that the United States is simply unable to use force successfully, and would be better off not to try.[21]

The next chapter, on the lessons of fifteen years of war, will examine these arguments more closely at least as they apply to the recent past. But those who believe in American incompetence go back further than that. They contend that the United States has failed in every major war since at least Vietnam if not Korea; that the pathologies of its bureaucracies prevent it from making intelligent use of the vast military power that it has commanded; that American culture itself is part of the problem, for it suffocates in its self-absorption any possibility of understanding the societies into which Americans plunge. There are even darker strains of this critique, perhaps more often heard abroad than at home, to the effect that the United States is more generally a destructive force when it ventures beyond its borders. But even the more benign view, captured in novels such as Graham Greene's *The Ugly American* and John Updike's *The Coup*, is that the American desire to do good in the world almost inevitably leads to disasters bred of good intentions, ignorance, and a fatally short attention span.[22]

All of these arguments have some truth to them. But then again, it is difficult to find other nations that have garnered more success in the world in their uses of force. The Soviet Union, run out of Afghanistan, in a conflict that ended up leading to the convulsion that destroyed not only the Soviet empire, but the USSR itself? The former European imperial powers, humiliated repeatedly by their former colonial possessions? China, whose military swagger and conceit has given birth to a coalition of its neighbors fearful of its rise and plunging into an embrace with the United States despite, in at least one case, a long and bitter war fought with it (Vietnam) and decades of cool suspicion and antagonism (India)? The Gulliverists, as one may call them, neglect the ways in which failure and incompetence are more the norm in international politics than success and skill—even as they also overlook the perils of inaction, which can be as great as those of action.

Nor is it right to reduce all of America's uses of force abroad to simple tales of failure. At the lower end of the spectrum of violence, the nation's persistent commitment to Colombia, for example, has helped that country escape the coils of a long-standing and brutal insurrection. At the higher levels, US intervention in Yugoslavia twice prevented mass murder, or at least curtailed it. Even the larger interventions in Vietnam, Iraq, and Afghanistan have yielded more complex outcomes than are often acknowledged. The 1991 Gulf War reversed an invasion that nearly overthrew the order of the Persian Gulf; the 2003 war removed a dictator whose ambitions, to include those aimed at acquiring nuclear weapons, had not diminished. Fifty years before, the Korean War ensured that at least one half of that peninsula had the opportunity for freedom and prosperity. Even the Vietnam War achieved important objectives in Southeast Asia, in the view of Lee Kuan Yew, the founding prime minister of Singapore. He argued forcefully that the Vietnam War "bought time for the rest of Southeast Asia." Recalling 1965, the year of Singapore's traumatic independence, he recalled armed communist insurgencies throughout southeast Asia, to include his own city-state. A decade later, the Southeast Asian states

> were in better shape to stand up to the communists. Had there been
> no U.S. intervention, the will of these countries to resist them would
> have melted and Southeast Asia would most likely have gone com-
> munist. The prosperous emerging market economies of ASEAN
> [Association of Southeast Asian Nations] were nurtured during the
> Vietnam War years.[23]

As for Afghanistan and Iraq, the story is not yet fully written, nor will it be for decades.

The use of force is always fraught. But so, too, is passivity; it is also a choice. In 2012–2016, the Western states refused to intervene in a substantial way in the Syrian civil war, which then metastasized into a much larger Middle Eastern conflict. As of this writing, one result of holding back has been the flourishing there of radical Islamist movements, including the so-called Islamic State, which has acted as a magnet for tens of thousands of foreign fighters, whom it has trained, hardened in battle, and many of whom are returning to the lands of their birth. The rise of the Islamic State has been accompanied by the mass slaughter of the Syrian war, the collapse of the Syrian and much of the neighboring Iraqi state, and the movement of millions as refugees.

Finally, akin to the argument of incompetence is that for "nation building at home," as President Barack Obama put it in his State of the Union speech on January 24, 2012. It is the view that global military power and engagement is too expensive, and that the domestic needs of the United States are too great, for the United States to sustain a global role, which may be fruitless or unnecessary in any case. This is, in many ways, the weakest of all arguments against global policy engagement backed by armed force. The United States spends today slightly over 3 percent of its GDP on defense. During the Cold War, it spent from 6 to 10 percent, and as recently as 1993, it spent over 4 percent. The pressure on the American budget today and going forward is not from discretionary spending on infrastructure but from nondiscretionary spending on entitlements, which have skyrocketed. Even the Iraq and Afghan wars, expensive as they were, were far from breaking the bank, with defense spending during these wars never breaking 6 percent, which was close to the Cold War minimum.[24]

The deeper fallacy with this argument is that it supposes a tension between war and domestic development that history does not bear out. During America's greatest conflict, the Civil War, the US government commenced such massive projects as the transcontinental railroad, passed the Homestead and Morrill Acts that provided for the orderly settlement of the west, and launched the National Banking Acts that helped establish the modern American banking system. A result of the Second World War was that the United States made some of its greatest investments in human capital through the GI Bill, which opened university educations to millions of veterans. It was during Vietnam that the epic Civil Rights Acts were passed and desegregation on a large scale begun; Great Society programs, such as Medicare and Medicaid, launched; the Wilderness and Clean Air acts passed; and the National Endowments for the Arts and for the Humanities created. This is not to suggest that one should go to war to develop a country; the point, rather, is that the growth and even the use of military power are in no ways incompatible with development at home.

These five schools—the "better angels of our nature," academic realism, soft power as a substitute for hard, American incompetence, and nation-building at home—all fail, at least in part and sometimes altogether, to make a persuasive case against American global engagement backed by military force. That still, however, does not add up to an adequate argument *for* America's global engagement backed by armed force. To do that requires both a discussion of why it is necessary and how it might be done. The second part of the argument will be discussed in later chapters, but the case for global engagement must begin with the realization of how unrepresentative our times have been.

Those in the developed world born after World War II have lived through a relatively peaceful half-century, roughly from 1950 to 2000. Despite wars in Korea (1950s), Vietnam (1960s), Afghanistan (1980s), the Balkans (1990s), the Great Lakes region of Africa (early 2000s), the Middle East (chronically), and elsewhere, the developed states aligned either with the United States or the Soviet Union did not experience the horrors of general war, along the lines of the two world wars. To a large extent this was because the might of the superpowers with their vast arsenals, their capacity for mutual destruction using nuclear weapons, and their essentially optimistic views of their own futures (each expecting to win the long-term competition) froze conflict. Even so, on several occasions the superpowers lurched closer to the brink than could ever be comfortable, only to pull back before it was too late. Statesmanship played a role: but so, too, did luck.

If, as Francis Fukuyama seems to believe, the big wars of the twentieth century were mere blips on a path to universally accepted norms of governance, one has to entertain the possibility that sustained peace, or at least the absence of massive war, was a blip, too. There are precedents for "peace blips" in history, to include the century-long western European peace of 1815–1914 that was marred only by localized and relatively brief if bloody conflicts resolved by military success and a negotiated peace such as the Crimean War and wars of German unification. There is no necessary reason that large-scale war should remain off the table, particularly if something were to occur that changes in a dramatic fashion attitudes to the use of force.

To assume that nuclear weapons, or some overwhelming logic of international politics, make statesmen cautious, is to assume that human beings are not capable of tremendous error, which is almost to assume that they are not human. Yet we see error all around us: a Mikhail Gorbachev who blew up the Soviet Union while thinking he would save it; a Saddam Hussein who twice, disastrously for him, chose war with the United States. The cognitive psychologists teach us that human beings tend to underrate randomness and overrate their own competence at many things, including anticipating the future. And this is, if anything, more true of politicians than anyone else, which is one of the reasons that British parliamentarian Enoch Powell acidly remarked, "all political careers end in failure."[25]

To take only one example: suppose a nuclear weapon is used in anger. It could happen—in a conflict in which Pakistan, for example, feels itself at a mortal threat from India, or Israel from Iran, or even the United States from North Korea. It could happen if Russia were to think that its limited conventional strength was jeopardized by a robust Western response to its aggressive behavior in Ukraine. A world after a nuclear weapon has been used in anger will likely be very different from the world of today: we may imagine it, but we cannot know its visceral reality. In such a world, having witnessed the massive and instantaneous devastation that only nuclear weapons can cause, everyone's arsenal, including our own, will be on a hair trigger because the penalties of inaction will seem so much greater than those of action. We have seen a lesser version of this before. The notion of mass-casualty terrorism had been amply discussed by academics and within the US government before the multiple attacks of September 11. But the shock of the events themselves transformed American attitudes toward the use of force, toward civil liberties, and even toward the use of assassination and torture against enemies, in ways that few could have fully anticipated.

Despite the contentions of the "better angels of our nature" school, the world remains a dangerous place, one in which formerly peaceful countries—such as Syria, Afghanistan, Ukraine, and others—have been consumed by horrific violence. But perhaps the United States can follow the strategy of the rich in 1970s New York as described by Tom Wolfe in *The Bonfire of the Vanities*: "insulate, insulate, insulate." As readers of that novel know, the hero, having thought that he had protected himself from the vagaries of urban life by living in a protected apartment in New York, having a high-paying job, and keeping his expensive car in a secure garage, found that insulation does not work.[26]

So, too, with the United States. The United States cannot insulate itself from world disorder for many reasons, and not least because, in some measure, it is necessarily a cause of it. American beliefs about political equality, rights (to include rights of women), religious freedom, and civil liberties, including the right to property, are a menace in many places, often without America's knowing or wishing it. Lincoln got at the heart of the issue in the Gettysburg Address when he insisted that the Civil War was a test whether "*any* nation so conceived and so dedicated" could survive. By its very existence—by its freedoms of speech, religion, and property, by its prosperity, by the global reach of its culture and economy—the United States is a magnet for some, and a source of infection for others. Wealthy Chinese and Russians flee to the United States, but not the other way around, because they know that there their wealth will not be confiscated, they themselves will not be imprisoned, by government fiat without real process of law. Americans probably do not wish to change that fact; but they could not, even if they did, without becoming something different than what they are.

The United States cannot impose liberties of speech, property, and civil society on the rest of the world by force. At the same time, however, neither can it hope to flourish in a world increasingly hostile to those values. Globalization means that corruption and coercion will come to us, as dictatorial regimes of various types resort to whatever means they wish, including bribery and intimidation, to buy or force the silence or compliance of individual Americans, companies, news organizations, or nongovernmental organizations. More insidiously, they may be tempted to play along with those who are quite happy to use state power for economic or national gain. American companies and universities are already prepared to curry favor with China's Communist Party or Arab monarchies in return for lucrative contracts. American academic associations have noticed with alarm that on many overseas campuses of American universities in authoritarian states, a "lack of respect for freedom of speech permeates the entire enterprise." Apple is reported to have deleted from its Chinese online marketplace apps that relate to the Dalai Lama, and Facebook has censored some foreign dissidents on US social media. No less troubling are other forms of corruption, to include the hiring of Chinese "princelings," the payment of kickbacks, and other forms of indirect bribery. In a globalized world, corruption does not stay abroad: in various and subtle ways, it leaches back into the United States. On the one hand, while American predominance, including military predominance, cannot prevent these threats to the integrity of its own society, it helps the United States set international rules of the road that protect itself no less than it does other countries.[27]

And on the other hand, a conflict-torn world will drag the United States into its quarrels. This is perhaps the greatest lesson of the Obama administration, which came into office desiring, in all sincerity, to end America's wars—and instead found itself waging them in the places it had most desired to leave. A disordered world in which, say, a China could assert its claims of sovereignty over the South China Sea as its territorial waters will probably be a world that sees the nuclearization of much of Asia and the possibility of large-scale conflict there. A Europe destabilized by massive flows of refugees from a chaotic Middle East and Africa will be no effective partner to the United States, and will itself generate more instability as its component states turn to a morose and often illiberal nationalism.

There is no more enduring cry from those who wish the United States to take a restrained view of its role in the world than John Quincy Adams's famous July 4, 1821, declaration that America "goes not abroad in search of monsters to destroy." In this view Adams wisely believed that America's only concerns for freedom were domestic; that its policy abroad must be guided by interest, not ideals; that the nation should recognize the uniqueness of its own institutions and refrain from projecting their modes and values abroad.

This is a misreading of Adams's speech. His note of restraint was counterbalanced by his insistence that the United States must always speak on behalf of freedom, and that "wherever the standard of freedom and independence has been or shall be unfurled, there will her heart, her benedictions and her prayers be." Adams believed, moreover, that American values were not merely universal but destined to triumph. The Declaration of Independence, he insisted, "stands, and must forever stand alone, a beacon on the summit of the mountain, to which all the inhabitants of the earth may turn their eyes for a genial and saving light, till time shall be lost in eternity, and this globe itself dissolve, nor leave a wreck behind." The Adams of the July 4, 1821, oration had, in an earlier incarnation as the chief negotiator of peace with Great Britain after the War of 1812, been relentless in his insistence that the United States would extend from coast to coast, and insistent that the Indian nations standing in the path of the onslaught of migrants moving west would be overwhelmed—and could claim no protection from the king of Great Britain. He was also the author of the Monroe Doctrine, aimed at gradually evicting European influence from Latin America (with the menace of force in the background). Adams's view that the United States should not seek to spread its values by force was balanced by a robust insistence on those values, belief that their triumph was inevitable, and a willingness to use power to secure America's rise.[28]

The contradictions of John Quincy Adams are echoed in virtually every period and under every president. Few presidents have articulated American foreign policy in as idealistic terms as Woodrow Wilson—and few were as hard-bitten as he in ordering American soldiers and Marines into troublesome neighboring countries. The same might be said of other great American idealists as presidents, to include Franklin Delano Roosevelt and Ronald Reagan, who cut deals with unsavory characters to further American interests. Conversely, even a president inclined to realpolitik, such as Richard Nixon, found himself taking stands in support of beleaguered democratic allies (Israel in 1973, most notably). So, too, with Barack Obama, who came to office promising and believing in a modest American foreign policy, and found himself waging war on humanitarian as well as pragmatic grounds.

The challenge for American foreign policy is to reconcile the claims of American interests and American values on a global stage. Most presidents find ways to do so, which are invariably, and necessarily, unsatisfying to their doctrinaire critics at home, and to wary observers abroad. The United States, even in the early twenty-first century, thus finds itself as it has since colonial times, engaged globally; it does so, as it has since independence, motivated by both values and interests; and it continues in many of the same ways that it has since 1945, resorting to force to maintain its interests, support its values, and uphold global order. It is difficult to imagine that these patterns will change dramatically in our lifetime.[29]

The current world order, as we shall see in the following chapters, faces four challenges: from a rising China that seeks to impose its will on its weaker neighbors; from adherents to several fanatical strains of Islam that are at war with us and many others; from states that in a variety of ways seek to dominate their regions and are willing to use force to do so; and from the expansion of several realms of ungoverned space, both physical and intangible, that can be both the homes of disruptive forces and the sources of conflict. American armed force, used wisely by American statecraft, cannot eliminate these challenges, but it can manage, contain, and reduce them. In its absence, our children and grandchildren will see a far more disordered world, characterized by the unrestrained use of force, humanitarian catastrophe, and pressures on free institutions not only abroad, but at home. The American stake in global order is enormous—and if it does not take the lead in maintaining it, its own prosperity and freedoms will suffer as well. A weakened British Empire and largely enslaved Europe could turn to the United States in 1943 when Churchill made his speech at Harvard. The United States has no alternative United States to its west, no single country or collection of countries that can relieve it of its burdens.

The arguments discussed were bruited about at the very end of the twentieth century, and sometimes before that. The doubt about

America's role in the world reflected to some extent a natural slackening of international purpose after the Cold War. But there is another dimension, too, which requires more extended consideration: disillusionment after fifteen years of chronic war after the terrorist attacks of 9/11. If there has been a general loss of confidence in America's strategic acumen abroad, and confidence in its national security policy at home, it is because of how the United States has fought wars in Afghanistan and Iraq, and against radical Islamists globally. The ambiguous record of two very different administrations, those of George W. Bush and Barack Obama, hang over all discussions of the uses of American power. To that record we now turn.

CHAPTER TWO

FIFTEEN YEARS OF WAR

Without coming to terms with America's recent strategic past, it is impossible to think clearly about its strategic future. Since 2001 the United States has been visibly, and self-consciously, at war. It has fought al-Qaeda and similar jihadist groups, particularly the Islamic State, throughout the Middle East and beyond, waging a campaign of assassination by drone strike in South Asia and Yemen, in particular. It invaded Afghanistan in 2001, and after overthrowing the Taliban regime there, engaged in a protracted counterinsurgency campaign against its reconstituted enemy. It invaded Iraq in 2003, crushed the regime of Saddam Hussein, suppressed the residual forces aligned with the dictator, and then waged another set of complex campaigns against both Sunni jihadists and Iranian-sponsored Shia militias. In 2014 it found itself engaged in its third Iraq war in a quarter-century as it fought, albeit on a smaller scale, with the Islamic State, a transformed outgrowth of al-Qaeda in Iraq that controlled large parts of Syria as well. And there were other smaller, but important uses of force as well, such as participation in the overthrow of Libyan dictator Muammar Gaddafi in 2011.

This chapter takes as its premise that these wars should be examined together and not, as is often the case, only as distinct conflicts. Psychologically and practically they are in many ways interconnected, and not only because they have occurred simultaneously. This chapter also rests on the assumption that there can be no sound consideration of future American strategy without asking of these wars what went right and what went wrong, and what their lingering effects will be. It will ask whether Iraq was a mistake, how the handling of prisoners affected America's war effort, and what were the consequences of bureaucratic routines and standard operating procedures for success or failure. It will explore the ways in which Presidents Bush and Obama resembled each other more than admirers of either might like to admit, and discuss the enduring civil-military tensions to which the wars have given birth.

The American ripostes to 9/11 began with smashing campaigns—each lasting no more than a few weeks—that shattered the Taliban and Hussein regimes but quickly became wars without discernible fronts, in which progress was obscure. Each entailed great domestic and international controversy. That these wars are each still suffused with partisan animus makes it more rather than less urgent to come to terms with them. While none of these conflicts has caused the domestic disruption that Vietnam did in the late 1960s and early 1970s—largely though not entirely because of the end of the military draft—collectively they have caused deep divides about the purposes and effectiveness of American military power.

Vietnam did that as well, for a time: the Nixon, Ford, Carter, and Reagan administrations initially held back from using military power, although they realized, in different ways, the need to restore the global military balance with the Soviet Union. Under President George H. W. Bush the United States was willing to go to war over the invasion of Kuwait in 1990, but it did so with a strong belief that it knew the lessons of Vietnam—make wars short, violent, conventional, and end cleanly. Apparently it did so, although the aftermath of the 1991 Iraq war was a semipermanent deployment of forces in the heart of the Persian Gulf and continued, indeed escalating military action against a still-defiant Iraq through the 1990s. Both the Bush and Clinton administrations used force in Somalia, Bosnia, Kosovo, and Haiti, among other places, although always with the shadow of Vietnam still lying over them. The debate about the 2001 Afghan and 2003 Iraq wars evoked Vietnam metaphors as when, less than a month after American forces arrived in Afghanistan, a *New York Times* journalist wrote an article titled "A Military Quagmire: Afghanistan as Vietnam." If the aftermath of Vietnam lasted at least twenty years, it may be expected that the aftermath of these wars, which are continuing, will last at least as long. And they may well have effects as profound as Vietnam on American strategic style, on how the American military fights its wars, and on how political leaders think about the use of force to further American interests.[1]

The new era of American wars began in a manner, and on a scale, reminiscent of the Japanese surprise attack at Pearl Harbor some sixty years earlier. On September 11, 2001, hijackers hurled two airliners into the Twin Towers in Manhattan, tore a gaping hole in the Pentagon with a third, and might have crashed a fourth jet into the Capitol had it not been for a heroic effort by the passengers of the doomed United Airlines Flight 93 to wrest control of it from the hijackers. Nearly 3,000 people died, but the sheer fact of death on that scale was not what gave these events their enduring power.

This was, for most Americans (if not all experts), a bolt from the blue, a sudden explosion of violence for which nothing had prepared them. There had been previous terrorist plots and attacks on the United States perpetrated by radical Islamists, including one on the World Trade Center itself in 1993, but nothing remotely on this scale. The effect on senior government officials was more wrenching yet. They had the intelligence briefs, and they understood as a theoretical possibility that something like this could occur; it had been the stuff of numerous studies and simulations. But a gulf separates what one can imagine and what one experiences. It was one thing to participate in a war game that contemplated thousands of deaths; it was another thing to stare into a vast, smoking pit scooped out of Lower Manhattan. The weight of officials' responsibilities compounded the visceral impact of the blows received by the country they had sworn to protect. As Secretary of State Condoleezza Rice (then the national security adviser) repeatedly said: "If you were in the White House on that day, as I was, every day since has been September twelfth. And your great fear is that it may be September tenth." Members of the Bush administration, like their successors in the Obama administration, now scanned with heightened anxiety the daily "threat matrix" that reported ongoing plots, including those potentially involving chemical or biological weapons. Their attitudes toward political risk, toward what forms of the use of force were acceptable, changed permanently. Senior members of the Bush administration, very much including the new president himself, who came to office dismissive of peacekeeping and nation-building, found themselves committed to not one but two vast projects of nation-building in Afghanistan and Iraq. Similarly, the Obama administration, withering in its condemnation of the bellicosity of its predecessor, vastly expanded a global campaign of targeted killing without precedent in the history of any great power, which by 2015 had eliminated something on the order of 3,000 suspected terrorists.[2]

The three wars that followed 9/11 were linked in a number of ways. Al-Qaeda had used Afghanistan as a refuge from which to plan the 9/11 attacks, hence the assault on the Taliban regime that had sheltered it. When it became clear that al-Qaeda had recovered in Pakistan's turbulent North-West Frontier Province, a second, and increasingly global, front opened up against the organization. Over time, new offshoots of al-Qaeda (e.g., its Yemeni branch, al-Qaeda in the Arabian Peninsula) became the targets of a campaign of raids and air strikes. Initially, some American leaders suspected a connection between the Iraqi regime and the movement led by Osama bin Laden—a set of relationships that indeed existed, but were probably not critical to the attacks on the United States.[3]

The most controversial of these wars, the invasion of Iraq in 2003, was linked to 9/11 in other ways. The government of George W. Bush was decidedly more inclined to act preemptively against Iraq after the terrorist attacks. Taking seriously intelligence that suggested that the Saddam Hussein regime was reconstituting its weapons of mass destruction programs, after 9/11 the Bush administration was more unwilling to accept risk than it might otherwise have been. Nor was it alone in that. Testifying before a committee inquiring into the origins and conduct of the Iraq war, former British prime minister Tony Blair said,

> I would fairly describe our policy up to September 11 as doing our best, hoping for the best, but with a different calculus of risk

assessment; in other words, up to September 11, we thought he [Saddam] was a risk but we thought it was worth trying to contain it. The crucial thing after September 11 is that the calculus of risk changed.[4]

And to some extent, behind the intent to overthrow the Saddam Hussein regime was a desire not so much to remake the Arab world altogether, but to inflict a blow that would shock it. While historians—indeed, the participants themselves—may dispute how important this consideration was in the launching of America's second Iraq war in 2003, it was surely there. "The transformation would have an impact beyond Iraq's borders," President George W. Bush recalled as he reflected on his decision to finish off the regime of Saddam Hussein. By eliminating Saddam's decaying and brutal regime, American leaders hoped first and foremost to eliminate a threat that they believed had connections with al-Qaeda and that posed a continuing threat to the stability of the Middle East. But looking beyond this, they also saw an opportunity to open what had traditionally been one of the Arab world's most advanced and secular societies to a different, and more liberal, future.[5]

Therefore, the roots of these conflicts lay more deeply in the past than contemporaries, and particularly critics of these wars, often believed, as we shall see in Chapter 5. The inspiration for bin Laden and other jihadis came in part from Sayyid Qutb, an Egyptian Islamist put to death by Gamal Abdel Nasser in 1966, who in his turn looked to minority, but authentic, streams of Islamic thought going much further back than that. Similarly, the Iraq campaign of 2003 was much more than the reaction of Western decision-makers to the events of 2001. At the very least, it emerged from the unsustainable status quo after the 1991 Gulf War. That conflict, followed by repeated bouts of bombing and Western intervention in Iraq to protect the Kurdish minority in the north and the Shia majority in the south through the use of no-fly zones, had resulted in a protracted standoff. The sanctions pushed through the United Nations by the United States (starting with UN Security Council Resolution 661, passed in August 1990) contributed to a collapse of Iraq's per capita gross domestic product (GDP) of roughly 85 percent from 1980 levels, and to unemployment rates of 50 percent. While claims of skyrocketing infant mortality rates as a result of sanctions were later disproved, they were believed and played a large role in mobilizing Arab and to some extent broader Muslim public opinion against the United States. Bin Laden took full advantage of this, declaring in 1996, "More than 600,000 Iraqi children have died due to lack of food and medicine and as a result of the unjustifiable aggression (sanction) imposed on Iraq and its nation. The children of Iraq are our children. You, the USA, together with the Saudi regime are responsible for the shedding of the blood of these innocent children." Furthermore, by 2000 the UN inspections of the Hussein regime's nuclear program had been suspended, though restored partially at the end of 2002 under the pressure of UN Security Council Resolution 1441 (a "final opportunity") and the threat of imminent invasion. Even then, the Iraqi government continued to block and stonewall inspectors in a variety of ways. The extensive economic sanctions against the regime were eroding as Saddam Hussein played the United States and its allies off against Russia and third parties. Even absent 9/11, therefore, an American government would have faced a fork in the road, leading either to conflict with or accommodation of an Iraq that, having escaped both inspections and sanctions, was ready—with its ample oil reserves—to begin rebuilding its strength in the Arab world.[6]

A confrontation of some sort with Iraq was probably inevitable. Indeed, one audacious Canadian political scientist has argued that had Al Gore, rather than George W. Bush, won the election of 2000, the United States would have invaded Iraq. This may go too far: one can imagine a United States that in 2003 took the lead in tightening the screws on the Saddam Hussein regime but did not invade Iraq—particularly if the intelligence had revealed what we now know, but policymakers at the time did not: that Saddam's weapons of mass destruction programs lay dormant. Absent the belief that the Hussein regime was seeking to restore its nuclear and biological weapons programs, it is difficult to see how the Bush administration could have secured the permissive UN resolutions, congressional support, and coalition participation in the war that it did. One may reasonably doubt that it would even have tried.[7]

Iraq was a war of choice, although perhaps somewhat less choice than is often assumed. The war against al-Qaeda, after 9/11, most assuredly was not. Once having committed itself to wiping out al-Qaeda's base in Afghanistan, it was but a short step to defeating the Taliban government that sheltered al-Qaeda and drew strength from it. Having defeated the Taliban, it is difficult to imagine how the United States could then have withdrawn from a chaotic Afghanistan, repeating what was generally conceded to be a mistake in the wake of the anti-Soviet insurgency there in the 1980s. Having chased the core al-Qaeda leadership out of Afghanistan, it was bound to pursue it over the border and beyond; and as al-Qaeda in turn attempted to spread beyond South Asia, the United States was bound to pursue it there as well. And so America found itself engaged in multiple wars, none of them entirely of its own will.

At a time when each of these conflicts, in different ways, have disappointed those who have launched and conducted them, it is important to begin by remembering the ways in which they succeeded. The al-Qaeda attack of 9/11 has been the only mass terrorism attack on the US homeland to kill hundreds or thousands of Americans. Although there were numerous plots and some much smaller attacks thereafter (e.g., the Fort Hood shootings in 2009, the bombing of the Boston Marathon in 2013, the attack on a military recruiting station in Chattanooga in 2015, the San Bernardino massacre in 2015, the Orlando massacre in 2016), al-Qaeda and other jihadi organizations have never again been able to strike the homeland with anything like the force of 9/11. The extended campaign of apprehension and assassination subsequently waged against these movements may be debated, but undoubtedly, combined with improved security at the borders and monitoring by federal and local police, it has contained that threat.

In both Iraq and Afghanistan the immediate goal of overthrowing two dangerous regimes was achieved within weeks of the launch of operations. In Afghanistan, the United States and its allies established a reasonably stable government, as well as conducting a series of freely contested elections. In Iraq, too, over a prolonged and painful period a workable government was built, although the fragile consensus that kept Iraqis together began to erode with the American withdrawal from that country in 2011—a withdrawal that more than a few officials (including two ambassadors, both vastly experienced in the Arab world, and neither of them Iraq hawks before 2003—Ryan Crocker and James Jeffrey—believed was premature. In both cases, the United States military and intelligence agencies, together with local forces and foreign allies, were able to beat down multiple insurgencies, including those of al-Qaeda and Taliban fighters, remnants of the Saddam regime, Shia militias, and new groups that were offshoots of al-Qaeda. At least as of 2008–2009, Iraq seemed to be on a fragile trajectory to success, albeit with the need for sustained American support. As Emma Sky, a British development official who had opposed the war but became a key, if critical, civilian adviser to American commanders put it, "there was nothing inevitable about the way the story unfolded."[8]

These three wars were costly, but in terms of treasure, less than is often assumed. The Costs of War project at Brown University, which at best is antipathetic to the rationales and purposes of these wars, estimated a total cost as of 2015 of $4.4 trillion, a sum that uses a broad definition of war costs including future obligations to veterans. This is a very large sum—although it should be noted that as of 2015 the American GDP was over $18 trillion, and the costs were spread over fifteen years and indeed beyond.[9]

During the fifteen years of war, American defense spending did not break a threshold of 6 percent of GDP. By comparison, the United States spent 10 percent or more of GDP on defense in the early Cold War, and around 8 percent during the 1980s—both periods of remarkable prosperity. The economic crisis of 2008 and thereafter had nothing to do with the wars in Iraq and Afghanistan. America's economic ills, such as they are, have much more to do with fundamentals of government policy and educational achievement than defense spending. Societies that routinely spend substantial percentages of GDP on defense—for example, Singapore (over 3 percent, but historically more) and Israel (over 6 percent) come to mind—have also been able to sustain high growth rates and successful economies.

These wars strained but did not exhaust the American military. All of the services, but the Army and Marine Corps above all, endured repeated deployments. Inevitably, the heaviest burden fell on the two land services, although the Navy and the Air Force played large direct (i.e., combat) and indirect roles (e.g., through staffing headquarters, Provincial Reconstruction Teams, and prisoner camps). Remarkably, the United States did not expand its military to any great extent to fight these wars: an active duty force of 1.36 million in 2000 peaked at 1.55 million in 2006, the period of maximum stress in Iraq. Unusually, given its history in Vietnam, where few reservists and Guardsmen were called up (fewer than 25,000) and even fewer deployed overseas, the United States mobilized large numbers of these citizen-soldiers for duty either in Iraq and Afghanistan, or to backfill active duty units going there themselves. Between September 2001 and November 30, 2007, over a quarter of a million National Guard personnel were deployed to Iraq and Afghanistan. Indeed, by 2005 so-called weekend warriors (including the various reserves and National Guards) constituted around 40 percent of total US military personnel in Iraq.[10]

Active-duty Army units were rotated through Iraq and Afghanistan on a one-year-on, one-year-off basis—and indeed, during the surge in Iraq some units served over a year in the combat zone. The price for these deployments was undoubtedly a higher incidence of mental disorders than usual, including suicides. Although historically the suicide death rates in the US Army have been well below the civilian rate, the rate began climbing in the early 2000s, and by 2008, it slightly exceeded the demographically matched civilian rate (20.2 suicide deaths per 100,000 vs. 19.2).[11]

Moreover, for a time during these conflicts, recruitment standards were lowered somewhat, to include allowing in some recruits from the lowest mental category (Category IV) and giving increased numbers of waivers to recruits with criminal records. However, the actual numbers of the latter involved were small—249 felony waivers in the Army in 2006, for example, and 511 in 2007. Helped by generous compensation (and, it must be confessed, the economic recession of the end of the first decade of the twenty-first century), the armed forces sustained their numerical strength, and by the middle of the second decade had recovered their poise. Particularly for the services most directly affected, the Army and the Marine Corps, it is important to remember that rapid turnover in the enlisted ranks (roughly half of all Marines leave after their first four-year tour) means that in remarkably short time, front-line personnel are fresh. Given that retention rates for officers and senior enlisted personnel have held up, what remains is a cadre of veteran noncommissioned officers, specialists, and officers.[12]

The catchphrases *battle-hardened* and *battle-weary* capture two of the effects of combat. The former may apply more to the career service personnel who have decided to stay in. Today, the United States military has one of the world's most experienced forces in land combat; and its higher leaders, as well, have passed through the challenges of command at senior levels. This is an intangible strength, but an important one. However, the costs of war has probably contributed to the underfunding of conventional military power not directly related to the conflicts—high-end air power, naval, and space forces in particular.

There is, finally, the human cost of war. As of early 2015, it was estimated that some 6,800 personnel had been killed in war zones, and another 52,000 wounded in action—this is quite apart from psychological trauma, which is harder to measure. Each loss, each serious wound, is a tragedy for the individual and the families concerned. The very high wound rates—well above historical norms, which have been much more like three wounded for every soldier killed in combat—reflect dramatic improvements in protective equipment, but even more so in combat medical care, particularly during the so-called golden hour following injury, when rapid first aid and evacuation can save a life. Many surviving soldiers would have perished in earlier wars, to include Vietnam, but they often did so at the price of extreme mutilation and disability.[13]

These losses can be compared with those in Korea and Vietnam. In the former, the United States lost over 36,000 dead and 103,000 wounded, and in the latter 58,000 dead and 153,000 wounded. As costly as the wars of the post-9/11 period have surely been, they have inflicted substantially fewer losses on a larger American population

(152 million in 1950, 194 million in 1965, 320 million in 2015) than have the previous conflicts. Like Vietnam, the post-9/11 wars were controversial, though not to the same extent, and not accompanied, as that war was, by social upheaval and occasionally violent domestic conflict. Nothing post-9/11 is comparable to the disruption of the armed forces through the ravages of drugs and racial conflict following Vietnam. Unlike Korea, veterans of recent wars have not been forgotten by a society generally ignorant of their sacrifice; unlike Vietnam, they were not treated with contempt by those who had opposed the war—just the reverse in most cases. Therefore, without understating the sacrifices made by servicemen and women and their families, the judgment must be made that the United States has come through these conflicts at considerably lower cost in life, treasure, and social conflict than was the case in Vietnam.[14]

How well did the armed forces perform the duties they were assigned? "Every war," wrote Carl von Clausewitz in his classic work *On War*, "is rich in unique episodes. Each is an uncharted sea, full of reefs." War tests the ability of military organizations to adapt to new circumstances and to innovate. The American military that went into the post-9/11 wars had under its belt a substantial conventional success in 1991 in the war with Iraq, several smaller engagements in the Balkans and against Iraq in the succeeding decade, and peacekeeping and humanitarian interventions, as well as some modest counterterrorism operations in the Middle East and Southwest Asia. However, it was unprepared, intellectually and organizationally, for the extended campaigns of counterinsurgency that it subsequently faced. Its counterinsurgency manuals in 2003 were those of Vietnam, and a decade of belief that such messy entanglements would be avoided in the future left it complacent, and worse, intellectually unprepared for the challenges that it soon faced.[15]

In some respects, the US military's adaptation to contemporary counterinsurgency against sophisticated opponents in both Iraq and Afghanistan was successful. Some old lessons—the absolute centrality of developing local forces who can replace our own on the front line—were painfully relearned, many of them codified in a new counterinsurgency manual (FM3–24) published in 2006. Some lessons were borrowed: to the extent that what occurred in Baghdad in 2006–2007 was a consequence of intersectarian hostility, it could be met by a remedy concocted by the British in Northern Ireland in the 1970s and 1980s—walls separating neighborhoods, with connections controlled by checkpoints. Some old skills had to be developed again, such as working closely with local irregular movements, as in the successful Anbar Awakening in Iraq. After several false starts in which Sunni tribes turned on al-Qaeda movements but were beaten down because of lack of prompt and effective American support, the United States was able to support a local movement in Anbar province that, for a time, nearly obliterated al-Qaeda in western Iraq.[16]

In some cases, the return to lessons of the past was painfully slow. It was not until 2007 that the United States finally managed to make its detainee operations in Iraq adequate in terms of facilities, guards, and no less important, a coherent doctrine for this dimension of counterinsurgency. From the point of propaganda, however, the United States had already suffered a substantial defeat because of the incompetence of the early commander, Brigadier General Janis Karpinski, and the 800th Military Police Brigade in managing the thousands of prisoners who had come their way. One particularly disgraceful set of episodes occurred in which Iraqi prisoners were abused at the Abu Ghraib prison outside Baghdad. Any organization's real as opposed to stated priorities are revealed by where it assigns its best and its worst personnel. As the outlandish and shameful behavior of the inept and in some cases abusive guards at Abu Ghraib demonstrated, until then handling detainees had been a matter of little consequence to military commanders.[17]

And yet, one of the outstanding lessons of previous counterinsurgency and counterterrorist campaigns should have been the centrality of detainee operations. In conventional combat, on the one hand, prisoners of war are taken, interrogated, and quickly passed back to holding areas or prisoner-of-war camps; they are, for regular forces, usually a burden and a nuisance, of some but usually minor intelligence value. In irregular warfare, on the other hand, they can be not only an invaluable source of information about enemy organizations, but an opportunity to turn insurgents on behalf of the government. This was nothing new: in Vietnam the United States had run the successful Chieu Hoi and Phung Hoang programs, which brought both defectors and valuable intelligence to the fight against the Vietcong. Israeli successes in containing terror attacks has rested heavily on human intelligence gathered by interrogation and detainee operations. By the time American forces in Afghanistan and Iraq grasped the centrality of these operations, in most cases it was too late: prisons were being handed over to local authorities, with the result that prisoners were often mistreated, turned loose, or sprung in a series of prison breaks, such as the attacks that freed 1,200 Taliban in 2008 and another 500 in 2011 from Afghanistan's huge Sarposa prison in Kandahar, or the 2013 break into Iraq's Abu Ghraib prison that freed hundreds of al-Qaeda prisoners.

A similar case can be made about the detention operations conducted against al-Qaeda operatives internationally. The use of so-called enhanced interrogation techniques—that is, lesser forms of torture, such as waterboarding—probably yielded useful information. Leon Panetta, who served President Obama as director of central intelligence and then as secretary of defense after Obama had banned these techniques, and thus had no stake in previous decisions, probably had the soundest judgment:

> At bottom, we know we got important, even critical intelligence from individuals subjected to these enhanced interrogation techniques. What we can't know—what we'll never know—is whether those were the only ways to elicit that information. . . . It is foolish to maintain that those interrogations did not achieve anything, but it is also callous to pretend that we did not sacrifice idealism in return for those leads.[18]

The intelligence obtained, whatever its value, came at the expense of tremendous political and propaganda damage to the United States. It reflected in part the Central Intelligence Agency's lack of experience, as of 2001, in coping with prisoners to interrogate. Again, by the time these deficiencies in technique were remedied, the political damage had been done. In the ensuing debate about waterboarding, the shrillness of the argument about its morality, legality, and efficacy in eliciting information has suppressed a more coldblooded analysis of its strategic consequences.

The building of Afghan and Iraqi armed forces to take on the burden of the fight against their local enemies was a somewhat happier story, although here, too, the common declaration that this was America's "exit strategy" from both countries did not always reflect itself in action. Initially, the US occupying forces disbanded the Iraqi military (or, as some in charge later claimed, allowed it to disband itself). They had, however, no decent plan for reconstructing something in its place, and certainly not an army and police competent to handle the postinvasion insurgencies and civil conflict that broke out. "No serious plans for indigenous forces had been prepared for either Afghanistan or Iraq," writes retired Marine colonel T. X. Hammes. As he then notes, the actual numbers and quality of officers and noncommissioned officers assigned to the task of training and coaching Afghan and Iraqi forces did not match the supposed priority of this mission until late in both conflicts. The test of war showed that the Iraqi military was more fragile than had been believed: a force that most American commanders thought was in pretty good shape in 2009 crumbled in 2014, once intimate American involvement had lapsed, and corruption and sectarian favoritism returned. By 2015 the Afghan army, after seeming to perform considerably better than its Iraqi counterpart, was failing under the strain of renewed attacks by the Taliban. In both cases, the United States eventually created large indigenous forces that became accustomed to American "enablers"— intelligence gathering, logistical support to keep vehicles and aircraft running and troops in the field well supplied, and urgent medical care for casualties. These were effective—but usually only so long as the Americans were present in force to guarantee such support, as well as to supervise officers who, left to their own devices, might revert to traditional practices of garnishing their soldiers' wages and leading from the rear, or not at all. The proof lay in the Obama administration's reluctant decisions to increase force levels in Iraq and maintain them in Afghanistan in 2016, with resulting improvements in Iraqi and Afghan military performance.[19]

In three areas at least, the United States military either took advantage of innovations that had appeared elsewhere and took them to a completely different scale, or came up with new approaches altogether. The first of these was the extraordinary man-hunting operation led by General Stanley McChrystal in Iraq, which used elite special operations forces to capture or kill key enemy operatives. The key to their success, however, was not merely the ability to apprehend key operatives (more important and more useful than killing them), but to swiftly exploit the papers, thumb drives, laptops, cell phones, and the like found in one location, and to immediately act on the basis of such information to pounce on a secondary target. The upshot of this was a sustained, national campaign, first in Iraq and then in Afghanistan, against such organizations as al-Qaeda in Iraq, which disabled their key leaders.[20]

A second innovation, chiefly deployed in the war against al-Qaeda and similar movements, was the use of unmanned aerial vehicles (UAVs) to attack leaders of terrorist organizations. The use of exceptional but perishable intelligence to coordinate the killing of a particular enemy commander was not new, per se—in 1943, US Army Air Forces fighter planes, cued by radio intercepts, ambushed the commander in chief of Japanese naval forces in the Pacific, Admiral Isoroku Yamamoto. But the first decade of the twenty-first century saw this concept used on a vast scale in a campaign of routine assassination, particularly in South Asia and Yemen, of al-Qaeda and other operatives. The innovation consisted as well in the use of UAVs that had the advantages of persistence (they can linger on station for hours, unlike a fast-moving jet aircraft, and do so unseen if not always unheard) and the subtler advantage of being less politically provocative than a manned aircraft. Many South Asians, for example, resented the protracted campaign of UAV strikes in their countries, but less so than they would have if manned F-15E Strike Eagles had come screaming across the border.

Behind the targeted killing campaign was a third set of advances that cannot be easily discussed in an unclassified format: advances in signals intelligence, the interception and interpretation not only of communications (phone calls) but virtually any electronic emanation. Traditionally, it had been assumed that the key to counterinsurgency was human intelligence, and in many ways, so it was and remains. But in the era of ubiquitous cell phones, e-mail accounts, and social media, the interception and interpretation of electronic information offers tremendous advantages to technologically sophisticated countries. And it is fair to say that America exploited those advantages to the maximum. Moreover, when the organizations that the United States targeted took extraordinary measures to protect their leaders from technical intelligence gathering, the result was to hamper their ability to coordinate activities and respond to changing circumstances. Couriers do not move as quickly as e-mails.[21]

These were large operational innovations. There were also institutional innovations that had more mixed success. The United States military was grossly unprepared for the mission of military governance in Iraq, a task that it had executed rather well in Germany and Japan after World War II. Although the Department of Defense had won a bureaucratic tussle with the Department of State for the control of postwar Iraq, it did not have the organizations ready to administer the defeated state. Instead, an improvised organization, the Office of Reconstruction and Humanitarian Assistance (ORHA), was created in late January 2003—barely a couple of months before the war began. With fewer than two hundred people under a recently retired lieutenant general, Jay Garner, it was hastily assembled and thrown into the theater. Despite Garner's best efforts, it was subsequently disbanded in mid-April and replaced with the Coalition Provisional Authority (CPA) headed by a retired ambassador, Paul "Jerry" Bremer. The fiasco of ORHA showed that the United States government, including the departments in Washington and Central Command under General Tommy Franks, had collectively failed utterly in preparing for the governance of Iraq in the wake of the overthrow of the Hussein regime. CPA did better (given ORHA's scanty resources and preparation, that is not surprising), but its leadership found itself in constant tension with the military authorities on the ground under Lieutenant General Ricardo Sanchez.

Military and civilian leaders concluded that it would not be enough to restore order in Iraq and Afghanistan, but that there would be a need for economic and political development work. The chief innovation here was the Provincial Reconstruction Teams (PRTs) that were created in Afghanistan a year after the overthrow of the Taliban in 2002, adopted in Iraq starting in 2005, and then re-exported to Afghanistan. The PRTs brought together a variety of experts from different agencies, usually although not always under State Department leadership, to implement development projects in support of counterinsurgency. Their success varied widely, often depending on the personal relationship between the PRT leader and the local American brigade commander, and on their skills in dealing with local officials, sheikhs or other tribal leaders, notables, and clerics. The PRTs' long-term success depended more crucially yet on the relationship between development and garnering support for the host government.[22]

This was a more fraught problem. In some cases, the PRTs came dangerously close to supplanting local governments. With money to spend, they and not local officials became the source of influence. Moreover, many development projects—water purification plants and the like—proved unsustainable after sources of Western funding dried up. And, in general, large-scale Western intervention often distorted local economies and power structures by draining off educated locals into relatively high-paying jobs, such as interpreting for American forces, and away from the local governments and social services.

Some kind of aid had to accompany counterinsurgency, often in the form of basic works projects designed to keep young men employed and doing something productive rather than planting roadside bombs in return for cash. At the higher level, it certainly made sense to help train government officials and enable the Afghan and Iraqi governments to find their feet after decades of internal turmoil. But a very large question mark hovers over the entire aid enterprise in both wars. The debate between those in favor of soft counterinsurgency (emphasizing "hearts and minds" and winning the affection or gratitude of the local population) and hard counterinsurgency (emphasizing capturing or killing insurgents and isolating them from the population) remains open, with the preponderance of evidence supporting the latter. Counterinsurgents may lose even if the local population likes them more than they do the insurgents, so long as the latter are sufficiently ruthless in exerting pressure on unprotected civilians.[23]

These irregular wars were the first large conflicts of their kind fought following the reforms of the late 1980s that centralized military advice to the president under the chairman of the Joint Chiefs of Staff. It was not always an entirely successful project. The Bush administration eventually created, and its successor, the Obama administration retained, a position of deputy national security adviser (misnamed "the war czar") to coordinate strategy and policy implementation in these conflicts, echoing the Vietnam-era appointment of Robert Komer to a similar position during the Johnson administration. Particularly in the case of Lieutenant General Douglas Lute, the most successful of these deputy national security advisers, the result was inevitably tension with the JCS chairman, who resented what he conceived to be an alternative stream of military advice, and occasionally of military command, going directly to the field. Technology, however, pushed in this direction. The advent of the routine secure video teleconference meant that a president could communicate directly, easily, and routinely with his commander in the field, as did President Bush, and to a lesser extent, President Obama. The irregular nature of these wars, their troublesome consequences for regional politics, and a counterinsurgency strategy that rested heavily on development aid meant that interagency coordination at the White House became particularly important. Routine travel by White House officials to the theaters of war—unprecedented even in Vietnam—compounded the sense of some in the military had that the center of gravity for war direction had moved decisively to the White House, including on matters well below large-scale strategic decision making.[24]

Collaborative effort on the ground was indispensable. In some cases—most famously, the combination of General David Petraeus and Ambassador Ryan Crocker in Iraq, and earlier, Lieutenant General David Barno and Ambassador Zalmay Khalilzad in Afghanistan—colocated military and State Department leadership in Baghdad and Kabul was tremendously successful. In other cases (most notoriously the dysfunctional relationship between Lieutenant General Ricardo

Sanchez and Ambassador Paul Bremer in Iraq, but that was not the only one), the civilian and military sides of the US government in country either did their best to ignore each other or actively feuded. As in all wars, leading personalities made a very large difference in how organizations collaborated or failed to do so, and in the relationship with the host governments.

By and large, the US military adapted—though sometimes too late—to the challenges of the wars of the early twenty-first century. Some of those successes required innovation; others, merely the recovery of older institutional knowledge about the conduct of counterinsurgency. But unfortunately, its failures were just as notable, and more consequential. They had deeper roots, and will be harder to rectify in the future. They must be confronted because, no matter what the intentions of current policymakers, or the wishes of today's voters, the United States may encounter them again.

The first of these was a failure to understand the societies in which the United States was conducting its wars. American leaders in two administrations struggled to find the words to describe the phenomenon of global jihad as anything other than a caricature of purposeless malevolence. Similarly, American leaders made fundamental misjudgments about both Afghanistan and Iraq. The initial operation in Afghanistan had a "light footprint": it was a bravura performance, from a technical point of view, using as it did only a few hundred special forces and CIA operatives to bring air power to bear on the Taliban regime. It was all that could be mounted on very short notice. But it also rested on an unexamined assumption about the Afghan people: that they would ferociously resent any substantial Western presence on their territory. This notion, buttressed by facile references to the annihilation of a British army in Afghanistan in 1842 (the incompetence of the British far more than the ferocity of the Afghans explains the catastrophe) was false. Almost fifteen years after the initial dispatch of American forces to Afghanistan, the presence of Western forces there was far less an irritant to the population than the corruption and incompetence of their own government. Still, this poor reading of history caused the United States to fail to immediately deploy American light infantry—paratroops or units, such as the Tenth

Mountain Division—to capture or wipe out the fleeing al-Qaeda in the fall of 2001. Bin Laden and his subordinates were subsequently rousted from Afghanistan in 2001 and 2002 through a prolonged and incomplete campaign waged by proxy forces, but they were not trapped or annihilated, which is what a larger force of thousands of American light infantry sent in October 2001 could have done.[25]

In Iraq, American occupying forces expected to find a society that had the human capital of the 1960s and 1970s, when Iraq was one of the better educated, largely secular societies of the Middle East, with effective bureaucracies. Instead, they found chaos, and a society in which tribes had resumed their previous importance as governmental institutions had been weakened; they found too a society in which sectarian divisions and influences, particularly among the Shia communities, were far more potent than they had expected. This should not have been a surprise: if all other authority structures collapse, religious organization is what remains.[26]

In neither case did these misjudgments rest on complete fantasy. Rather, they arose from a failure to realize what decades of totalitarian misrule and protracted war had done to these societies. A core mistake was misunderstanding the way in which an increasingly desperate Saddam Hussein in Iraq had Islamized its regime so as to retain control, particularly of the Sunni Arab population. In the case of Afghanistan, the decades of civil war and years of Taliban misrule had left a society so wretched and fearful that it welcomed a Western presence in a way that it would not have done a century before. In the case of Iraq, it meant that the United States and its allies had far less to work with in reconstructing the Iraqi state than it had understood. In both cases, the Western forces had to start nearly from scratch in the painful work of understanding what became known as the human terrain—the complex web of tribal, clan, and personal relationships that governed politics in countries whose state structures had collapsed, leaving more primal forms of relationship to replace them.

The United States did not foresee that it would be forced by circumstances to take the lead in rebuilding the fundamental institutions of governance in both countries. In both cases, partly through inattention, partly through a foolish belief in the utility of United Nations bureaucrats as the designers of national governments, it connived at the construction of state institutions that ended up being ruinous for their countries. In Afghanistan, a decentralized country if ever there was one, the United States helped bring into line the various warlords (who subsequently resumed their enterprises in different guises), but then built a system in which resources and nominal power were concentrated at the center. Centrally appointed governors and the politics of Kabul dominated the life of people in regions remote from the capital and mistrustful of President Hamid Karzai's relatives and cronies. In Iraq, an electoral system based on proportional representation reinforced sectarian divisions rather than smoothing them over. In neither case was the US military prepared to exercise the governmental functions that it had in the aftermath of World War II.

American intelligence in these wars was good, as it ever was, in counting up pieces of equipment, identifying command structures, and monitoring the flow of enemy forces. But it, and even more so, its consumers at the top of government, were unable or in some cases unwilling to identify whom they were fighting. For two critical years, American policymakers referred to those who were attacking US troops in Iraq as "bitter enders" or "former regime elements," when what was beginning was, in fact, a complex insurgency combined with a sectarian civil war. In Afghanistan, the use of the term "Taliban" covered a range of opponents, some of whom could be pried away from elements controlled by the Quetta Shura (which directed much of the Taliban's activity) and the Haqqani network (one of the most formidable anti-American groups, also based in Pakistan) and others who could not. In public statements and in private discussions, the debate often resembled earlier accounts of the Vietnam War, in which the enemy was simply a hazy and undefined Other, neither understood nor studied, a kind of force to be smashed or contained, but never comprehended. It was fitting that only in 2015 did American intelligence learn of the death of their chief Taliban foe, Mullah Omar, a good two years after his demise in a Karachi hospital.

Even worse was the unwillingness to admit some hard truths about other powers. Pakistan and Iran both waged proxy war against the United States, the former supporting the Haqqani network, which operated in Afghanistan against American forces; the latter, funded, trained, and directed Shia militias in Iraq. Both provided sanctuary and intelligence to those attacking American forces. Iran, in particular, provided lethal expertise in the form of roadside bombs, of which the most dangerous types—explosively formed projectiles, or EFPs— were manufactured in that country. Iran may have been indirectly responsible for five hundred American deaths in Iraq and Afghanistan, and perhaps more. Neither Pakistan nor Iran ever felt serious pressure from US leaders, and certainly neither experienced the lash of US military power, even indirectly. It was a stunning strategic concession by the United States.[27]

Both the Bush and the Obama administrations at different stages convinced themselves prematurely of their successes. Bush famously was photographed with a "mission accomplished" banner shortly after the invasion of Iraq, although in private he had a more cautious view. The Obama administration, particularly after the spectacular raid that killed bin Laden in 2011, insisted that al-Qaeda was on the verge of strategic defeat, and that the long war against radical Islam was ending. "Today, the core of al Qaeda in Afghanistan and Pakistan is on the path to defeat," the president declared in a speech at the National Defense University in 2013. He echoed, somewhat more cautiously, the speech given by his then counterterrorism adviser, later head of the CIA, John Brennan, who insisted in 2011 that "al-Qa'ida and its ilk have been left on the sidelines, watching history pass them by . . . we have put al-Qa'ida on a path to defeat." Brennan claimed that before he was killed in 2011 Osama bin Laden was "isolated from the world" and realized that he was "losing the larger battle for hearts and minds." The collection of translated materials from bin Laden's Abbottabad lair in Pakistan, available online from West Point's Combating Terrorism Center, tells a different story—as does the US Department of Justice's 2015 use of some of these communications in the trial of Abid Naseer, a Pakistani national who was accused of plotting to carry out a bomb attack in Manchester, England. The United States government found itself unprepared when a wave of al-Qaeda-inspired riots and attacks hit American embassies in the Middle East in 2012, and similarly surprised when a little-known Islamist movement, the Islamic State, did better than al-Qaeda, seizing large swaths of Iraq and Syria in 2014.[28]

"Know your enemy and know yourself, and in a hundred battles you will not be defeated," wrote the ancient Chinese strategic thinker Sun Tzu. Iraq, Afghanistan, and the conflict with al-Qaeda showed that the United States often misunderstood its enemies. It did little better in understanding itself. Neither the Bush nor the Obama administration adequately prepared the American people for what it had to anticipate would be long wars. Neither made an effort to mobilize public opinion in the traditional way—with speeches, symbolic sacrifices on the home front (taxes or bonds), mobilization of domestic resources, and the popularization of military achievements on the battlefield. Plenty of attention was paid to the few dramatic successes, particularly the initial invasions of Afghanistan and Iraq, and the killing of bin Laden, but after that these three wars became the forgotten wars, waged by a tiny fraction of the population, largely ignored by the rest of it until things seemed to be going quite badly. Remarkably, the American people nonetheless gave at least passive approval to these wars, supporting the Iraq conflict for at least three years after the initial invasion in 2003, and more robust if declining backing for the Afghanistan war through 2014.[29]

Nor did the United States manage at all well its mobilization for war. The most appalling evidence of that was the failure to deploy suitable wheeled armored vehicles for most Marines and soldiers until 2007. Until that time the Humvee—an unarmored modernized version of the jeep—was the utility transport of choice. Soldiers slapped sheets of armor onto a vehicle that was never meant to carry such weight. It was a poor substitute for vehicles available on the international market, such as the Australian Bushmaster with its V-shaped hull to deflect the blast of mines and its organic armor to protect soldiers inside. It took four years from the initial invasion of Iraq, and thousands of deaths and wounds, for an outraged US secretary of defense to order the rapid, mass production of the Mine-Resistant Ambush Protected (MRAP) vehicle, with a corresponding fall in American casualties.

More broadly, the war with al-Qaeda and various Afghan and
Iraqi movements evoked only limited, and far from systematic, mobilization of American talent for the tasks of reconstruction, governance,
or development. The armed forces did create useful programs that
brought American police officers, many of them retired, into the field
to advise intelligence officers on matters like forensics. This Law Enforcement Professionals program, begun in 2006 as an initiative of the
Joint Improvised Explosive Device Defeat Organization (JIEDDO),
is generally regarded as a success. Less so were the Army's Human
Terrain Teams, also launched in 2006 to provide the US military with
deep local knowledge of clan and tribal structures by bringing in civilians with academic expertise, particularly in the field of anthropology.
The success of that program was at best mixed, and after being dogged
by problems of mismanagement and poor hiring practices, the Human Terrain Teams were abolished in 2014.[30]

Against these partial successes, there were no equivalents of the
civil affairs officers directly commissioned into the Army, nor lateral
recruitment of foreign area experts into the intelligence community
as during World War II. There was no adroit ramping up of a massive and ingenious campaign of political and psychological warfare
against radical Islam, as occurred against the Soviet Union during the
early stages of the Cold War. And even the expansion of the armed
forces themselves, from roughly 1,365,000 on active duty in 2001
to 1,546,000 five years later—a growth of less than 15 percent—was
slow and painful. To be sure, new organizations were created, but for
the most part peacetime routines persisted.

In 1972 Robert Komer, the former deputy national security adviser for Vietnam, who had gone on to direct the most successful
counterinsurgency program there, wrote a depressing study of that
conflict. Drawing on both experience and reflection, he concluded
that the biggest obstacle to success in Vietnam was the American government's own entrenched routines, habits, and attitudes. Perhaps the
most dispiriting reading of the early twenty-first century was that very
same work, *Bureaucracy Does Its Thing*. As more than one bitter veteran of the post-9/11 wars noted, much of it could be taken verbatim
and applied to their struggles.[31]

For the Iraq war, the United States successfully built a coalition of willing international partners, some more able than others. Even the best were not always effective—the British occupation of Basra, in particular, turned into a grave embarrassment—but at least they operated under American supervision with some resulting unity of effort. In the shadow war against al-Qaeda, the United States made use of a vast array of working partnerships with intelligence agencies around the world. It did not, however, attempt to build a public consensus for a common approach to handling the detainees whom it picked up on various battlefields, who were certainly not normal prisoners of war, but could not be handled by normal criminal processes, either. The result was friction over the detention facility in Guantánamo, Cuba, that persisted for years.

In Afghanistan, however, where perhaps its chances of success had been greatest, the United States made its greatest organizational error: turning to the North Atlantic Treaty Organization (NATO) to provide the coalitional command and control structure for what was incorrectly anticipated to be a peacekeeping mission. It was a failure, inadvertently anticipated by a headline in the *Guardian* newspaper in August 2003: "NATO Takes Control of Afghanistan Peace Mission." NATO was not really in control, and Afghanistan was anything but a peace mission. The result of bringing NATO into a conflict for which it was neither designed nor competent was a fractured chain of command, in which some American forces operated well outside a NATO framework, and in which an American commander nominally reported to a German general sitting in Brunssum, Holland. The so-called caveats—each country's elaborate prohibitions on the use of its forces except for narrowly defined purposes, or with the explicit prior approval of governments—hampered commanders seeking to maneuver and apply forces on a fluid battlefield. The dividing up of national responsibilities similarly got in the way of a unified effort: having the Germans in charge of training Afghan police, for example, was a recipe for failure. Afghanistan needed not a German-style police force with its exquisite sensitivities to civil liberties and gender equality, among other things, but a national, paramilitary gendarmerie, probably closer to the Colombian national police force (which is under Ministry of Defense control for a reason).[32]

As wartime presidents both George W. Bush and Barack Obama had their strengths and weaknesses. Bush did not exercise much supervision over his high command until the crisis of 2006; he then rose to the challenge by replacing military leadership in Iraq and, against the advice of most of his stateside general officers, ordering a reinforced effort in Iraq with five additional maneuver brigades. The Obama administration came in mistrustful of the high command, and frequently in conflict with it. Civil-military conflict erupted visibly during both administrations—in the public resignation of the director of operations on the Joint Staff, Lieutenant General Greg Newbold, in the open spat between the civilian leadership and Chief of Staff of the Army Eric Shinseki before the invasion of Iraq, and the public denunciation of the Obama administration by Lieutenant General Michael Flynn of the Defense Intelligence Agency (fired). The two administrations dismissed three four-star commanders: Admiral Fox Fallon in 2008, and Generals David McKiernan in 2009 and Stanley McChrystal in 2010.[33]

More insidious, if less visible, was the continuing tension between the military and its civilian leadership. The former often refused to recognize their own failures (e.g., a ruinous policy of rotating higher headquarters staffs through Afghanistan and Iraq every year, thereby impeding continuity of command), but believed that their civilian superiors had failed to set them up for success. The civilians, for their part, alternatively claimed that the military had misled them with happy talk, or attempted to box them in to making their preferred decisions. This rupture in civil-military confidence is not the least damaging of the dangerous legacies of the wars of the early twenty-first century.

———

These wars are not over, but one can begin to discern some of their long-term effects. It is trite and incorrect to say that generals refight the last war. It is more accurate to say that the efforts to wage war, and the scars they inflict, last, leaving their mark on individuals and institutions alike. Historians will explore those consequences from a more distant and tolerant point of view than contemporaries; the latter, however, have no choice but to draw conclusions for the immediate future.

Each of the three wars—against al-Qaeda, the Afghan Taliban, and in Iraq—were initially popular. They received congressional support as well as endorsement from a broad political spectrum among politicians and intellectuals alike, albeit with varying degrees of enthusiasm. In the House of Representatives almost two fifths of Democrats voted in favor of the Iraq war, as did nearly three fifths of Democrats in the Senate. A prominent roster of liberal politicians (including Senators Hillary Clinton, Tom Daschle, Charles Schumer, and Dianne Feinstein) supported the war. In this they reflected the views of a majority of registered Democrats (54 percent) and Independents (64 percent) at the time. The war also received support (albeit with an array of qualifications and reservations) from prominent liberal intellectuals, such as Tom Friedman, Christopher Hitchens, Paul Berman, George Packer, Fareed Zakaria, David Remnick, and Jonathan Chait.[34]

A decade later, only the war against Islamist radicals retained popular support. By June 2014, for example, more than half of the American population regretted intervention in Iraq, and the numbers were barely even on Afghanistan. Indeed, the supposed folly of the Iraq war had become a rallying cry on both left (much, though not all of which, had always opposed it) and right. At a debate among Republican candidates for president in December 2015, Donald Trump, the GOP's leading (if utterly unconventional) candidate, said of Iraq:

What do we have now? We have nothing. We've spent $3 trillion and probably much more—I have no idea what we've spent. Thousands and thousands of lives, we have nothing.

A conservative *New York Times* columnist declared that that was the "only line in two hours of debating that made me want to stand up and applaud."[35]

The election of an antiwar president, Barack Obama, in 2008 both reflected and reinforced the judgment that Iraq had been a terrible error. He had vigorously opposed the Iraq war in 2002, and made his determination to wind down all three wars a central theme of his presidential rhetoric. And so he did: American forces in Iraq went from 68,000 in 2003 to a high of 190,000 by 2009, falling to 300 by 2014. The force in Afghanistan went from 2,500 in 2001 up to 98,000 by 2011, with a fall to 14,500 by 2015. After an initial increase in a campaign of targeted killing of al-Qaeda leaders, the Obama administration ratcheted that back as well, going down, for example, from 122 drone strikes in Pakistan in 2010 to 22 four years later.[36]

It is unclear how much of this retrenchment reflected "war weariness" and how much was a deliberate choice by an administration convinced that it had to chart a very different course than its predecessor. Certainly, American attitudes, for the time, had become more ambivalent about what role the United States should play internationally. In the wake of the 9/11 attacks, American internationalism was strong, with a two-to-one margin (61 to 32 percent) favoring taking a more active role in the world. In 2014, however, while slightly more than half of those interviewed said the world's problems would be worse without American involvement, two fifths of those queried said that United States involvement in international problems made matters worse. One has to assume that views of Iraq played a large role in this shift.[37]

The military that these wars have left behind is a mixture of strengths and weaknesses. As new recruits came in and current soldiers left the force, the phenomenon of war weariness, such as it was, ebbed. What was left behind were armed forces that, in the Army and Marine Corps in particular (but not exclusively), had tremendous combat experience. Yet combat experience is only part of what the US military brought back from these wars. The vast logistical hubs constructed overseas, working with numerous and varied allies in difficult circumstances, putting together real rather than hypothetical campaign plans, were invaluable experiences. The American armed forces came out of fifteen years of war knowing in their gut, which is different than a theoretical understanding, that immediate successes could be illusory, and that failing campaigns could be turned around.

At the same time, however, and despite the large authorizations for ongoing expenses in these wars, the United States forewent large-scale modernization of its forces during them. This was particularly true for the kinds of forces needed to balance China, Russia, and lesser states, which, as we shall see in later chapters, continued to build up arsenals and modernize their forces. A protracted struggle over the national budget between Congress and the White House during the Obama administration further cramped military modernization spending. As a result, as the second presidency of the twenty-first century came to an end, the relative military strength of the United States looked less than it had been at the end of the twentieth.

The controversies surrounding these wars, and in particular, the Iraq war, will swirl into the old age of those who launched and conducted them. The partisan acrimony, and the regret many Americans feel at having wasted blood and treasure in the Middle East, makes it difficult to judge them accurately. Two of the wars—against al-Qaeda and the Taliban regime in Afghanistan—were unavoidable. As for Iraq, no one can know what the Middle East would have looked like absent the 2003 war—whether Saddam Hussein would have resumed a quest for biological and nuclear weapons, whether the upheavals in the Arab world would have taken the course they did. It is also entirely conceivable that Saddam's regime could have collapsed in a different way, perhaps in the context of another war with an Iran eager to repay old scores.[38]

Still, the Iraq war was a mistake. The publicly articulated premise of an active and dangerous Iraqi weapons of massive destruction program was false; the credibility of the United States government took a severe blow from that alone. The war strained alliance relationships in many ways—with France, for example, which opposed the war, and no less, in some ways, with Great Britain, which supported and participated in it. The British population turned even more fiercely against the conflict and the government of Prime Minister Tony Blair that had launched it. As corrosive as the war was for American civil-military relations, it was far worse in the United Kingdom, whose overstretched army faltered in both Iraq and Afghanistan, losing domestic support, American trust, and perhaps even some self-respect as it did so. This weakening of what had been America's most important global partner was a cost of the war that counted for little with the American public perhaps, but was enormously consequential.[39]

The conduct of the war in Afghanistan went better in some ways, but as of 2015 the successes achieved there seemed fragile, as President Obama reluctantly agreed to a continuing combat role for American forces into the last year of his term in office. Endemic corruption, a resilient enemy based in neighboring Pakistan, and the country's fragile politics meant that success, if it came in Afghanistan at all, would take years and most likely decades. Whether Americans would have the patience to stick it out was unclear.

Even the morally unambiguous war against al-Qaeda brought its share of woes. The waterboarding of prisoners undoubtedly did damage to America's good name, whether or not it yielded actionable intelligence. The protracted targeted killing campaign in South Asia excited its share of animus against the United States, even if it went on with the tacit consent of some governments. And its very successes, which were real, may have lulled the US government in 2011 and 2012 to thinking that it had Islamist terror on the run, when it was about to break forth in new, and possibly more virulent, forms.

These dismal conclusions must be balanced by an awareness of the real successes as well. By bringing down Saddam Hussein the United States eliminated one of the most brutal regimes in the Middle East. By overthrowing the Taliban it made possible a better life for millions of Afghans, particularly young women, millions of whom finally gained access to education no matter how rudimentary. And by conducting more than a decade of relentless attacks on Islamist terrorists the United States may have saved the world an even worse set of attacks by movements that, as we shall see in a later chapter, are deeply rooted and unlikely to disappear any time soon.

Wars must be judged by what they helped avoid as well as by what they produced. Those who direct them should be judged by what they knew and could have known, as well as what the underlying facts actually were. Once a war has been launched, even in error, one must judge how well or poorly it was waged, because it is possible to recover from a misconceived conflict. On all of these points, the wars of 2001 to the present offer a mixed and unsettling record.

Historians will almost surely frame these wars differently than contemporaries have, looking back more deeply into their roots in the

1970s and 1980s rather than with the foreshortened perspective of the day. They will see more contingency, and more of a mixed record, and almost certainly more complicated pictures of both presidents who directed them and the subordinates who waged them. For now, the best one can conclude is that the United States came out of this period with a tougher military but a more ambivalent political culture; a wiser sense of its own limits, perhaps, but possibly less resolution; a continued, if subdued, sense of its own uniqueness as a great power; and a desire to accommodate rather than confront rivals; but increasingly, an awareness that new challenges were rising and that in one way or another, force would be needed to meet them.

It is essential to reflect on these fifteen years of war. It will be equally important not to be overwhelmed by these experiences, or to read too much into them. To draw conclusions exclusively from them would be to misunderstand America's strategic challenges, and the strengths that America can bring to bear on them. The threat posed by the enemies of the early twenty-first century is but one of multiple problems facing American leaders. Before examining in detail what those problems are, however, one more step remains: to review the American hand—the collection of resources, aptitudes, and capabilities relevant to hard power that the United States brings to its foreign policy.

CHAPTER THREE

THE AMERICAN HAND

The bottom line here is simple: despite all the disappointments and losses of recent years, America is immensely strong, across many dimensions of power. Yes, others have used these fifteen years to take advantage of the nation's preoccupation. Yes, the United States has bungled some of its recent operations—but it has been immensely successful in others. Yes, other powers are on the rise, and its relative edge is diminishing. But its armed forces are large, competent, and the inheritors of two generations of global military endeavor. Behind America's hard power lies a productive economy, a well-established if raucous political order, encouraging demographics, and networks of relationships abroad unmatched by any competitor real or prospective. No other country, or collection of countries, has a better hand to play in international politics.

That said, the game to which it brings this hand is changing: in some areas the United States' military edge is eroding or endangered and needs to be restored or refashioned. To change the metaphor: American hard power is healthy in some ways, but exhibits signs of sclerosis in others. Its dominance remains, but has diminished as a result of its competitors' efforts, the age of its arsenal, and the obsolescence of some of the concepts that inform it. This is all the more worrisome given the rise of challenges that are at once disparate and pressing, which we will discuss in later chapters. Still, with good judgment the United States can generate adequate military power to

Defense Expenditures, 1988–2015						
Year	United States ($)	Soviet/ Russian ($)	China ($)	US % World	Russia % World	China % World
1988	591	530	14	36	32	1
1995	436	36	24	38	3	2
2000	417	33	39	35	3	3
2005	615	49	78	41	3	5
2015	595	91	214	34	5	12

SOURCE: expenditures (rounded) in billions of 2015 US$. Source: "SIPRI Military Expenditure Database," Stockholm International Peace Research Institute, 2016. www.sipri.org /research/armaments/milex/milex_database. Accessed June 3, 2016.

enable it to sustain global leadership, albeit with less of a margin for error than in the past.

One must begin with overall defense spending, the first and crudest measure of military power. It is one in which America's relative position has seemingly diminished only slightly since the end of the Cold War.

The United States still outspends its rivals by a large margin—perhaps three times as much as China and more than six times as much as Russia, by some counts. As of 2015 American defense spending was only a couple of points less, as a percent of global military spending than it was in 1988, the last year of the Cold War. Meanwhile, instead of facing one superpower rival that very nearly spends as much as it does, it now faces two major opponents, China and Russia, which collectively spend perhaps one half what it does.[1]

These numbers, however, do not fully capture the dimensions of competing powers' military buildups in the last fifteen years, or underlying weaknesses in the American position. One set of issues has to do with concealed or manipulated statistics (particularly in the case of China), accounting conventions (e.g., whether veterans' pensions or research and development are counted in the budgets), and widely different standards of pay and living conditions (e.g., American barracks versus their Russian equivalents). The top line of the US defense budget, for example, includes high personnel costs, which have been something like a steady 30 percent of the total budget even as the active-duty force shrank from 2.2 million in the mid-1980s to fewer than 1.5 million today, making growing costs per service member one of the fastest growing segments of the budget. In a similar vein, continuing expenditures on combat operations often come at the expense of the acquisition of new weapons. Nor do the crude numbers account for differences in logistical costs. The United States has to deploy forces at vast distances from its homeland, whereas China and Russia project power chiefly around their periphery.[2]

Moreover, the geopolitical circumstances are very different than in the past. China's defense buildup draws on a strong and growing economy, not—as in the case of the Soviet Union in 1988—a stagnating one. By contrast, the defense spending of some American allies has receded. For example, despite the expansion of NATO to include the old Warsaw Pact states (including the former East Germany and Poland), total non-US NATO expenditure is actually less in absolute terms than it was in the late 1980s. Furthermore, these top-line numbers do not take into account the calculations of American resolve that foreign leaders make when considering US threats and promises; they do not capture the ability of small but disciplined powers to inflict damage disproportionate to their economic might; they do not measure resilience. Nor do they measure experience, strategic or tactical skill, and adaptability. Perhaps most important of all, these measures do not take into account whether a state's military expenditure is growing or remaining steady, or the edge that can be gained by having the latest and best technology in the field. The spectacular growth of Chinese military spending is particularly worrisome for what it augurs in the future. Russia's military spending, despite the limits of Russia's economy, is in its own (if lesser) way no less impressive.[3]

What has the American defense budget purchased? Today, the US military consists of some 1.4 million men and women on active duty plus approximately 855,000 reservists. Broadly speaking, the nation has at its disposal three kinds of hard power: nuclear, conventional, and unconventional. In each of these realms of hard power it retains some organizations and even technology that are rooted in the World War II and early Cold War experience. There is nothing surprising

US Nuclear Forces				
Year	Total Warheads (# of Deployed)	ICBMs (# of Deployed Warheads)	SSBNs (# of Deployed Warheads)	Bombers (Primary Authorized Aircraft)
1988	23,077 (14,795)	1,000+ (2,593)	34 (5,312)	349
2000	10,577 (6,200)	550 (2,104)	18 (3,456)	72
2005	10,350 (4,896)	510 (1,700)	14 (2,016)	72
2010	9,600 (2,468)	450 (450)	14 (1,152)	60
2015	7,260 (2,080)	450 (450)	14 (1,100)	60
New START	(1,550+)	454 (400)	14 (1,090)	60+

Source: ICBM—land-based, nuclear-armed intercontinental ballistic missile. SSBN—nuclear-armed ballistic missile carrying submarines. Data derived from Amy F. Woolf, "U.S. Strategic Nuclear Forces: Background, Developments, and Issues." Congressional Research Service, November 3, 2015, available at fas.org; National Resources Defense Council estimates various years available at nrdc.org; and the annual data of the Bulletin of the Atomic Scientists available at thebulletin.org. The question of bomber data is rendered complex by a number of factors, including how one counts the B-1 and B-52 bombers by type. In any event, the point here is the rough magnitude of the force.

or necessarily wrong about that, but it can be an obstacle to necessary change. And in each area, new challenges are increasing.

The United States retains more than enough nuclear weapons to obliterate any opponent. But those weapons reside on old bombers, or inside old land-based missiles, whose designs date back a half-century or more, in some cases. Behind its offensive capabilities is a large infrastructure of laboratories and command-and-control facilities—all neglected throughout most of the last several decades. In the nuclear realm, however, the greatest strategic change in the last thirty years has been a bipartisan acceptance of active defense—the ability to shoot down incoming missiles—as a necessary component of the force structure. In the 1970s and 1980s such a view was anathema in many circles. The elaborate logic of nuclear deterrence evolved during the late Cold War depended on mutually assured destruction, on the notion that both the United States and the Soviet Union could obliterate each other at will. Therefore, any kind of defenses were deemed dangerously provocative. Technology, thinking, and most important, geopolitics have changed that. Active defenses now rest on the US Navy's Aegis-class cruisers and destroyers and on land-based interceptors, chiefly in Alaska. The interception of ballistic missiles has been proven to work, despite the scorn of an earlier generation of scientists who, in their thousands, once pledged never to accept money going to Reagan's Strategic Defense Initiative, a program they denounced somewhat contradictorily as being at once impossible and wicked. As time has passed, the practicality of missile defense has been demonstrated on a small scale in war in both the Middle East and Persian Gulf, and this has softened doctrinaire opposition to such technologies. In fact, active defense has becoming increasingly important against the rising threat from such regimes as North Korea's.[4]

Missile defense, however, consumes a small part of the defense budget—$8 billion, less than 2 percent. Moreover, the United States has insisted that it is not attempting to defend against the large Russian and Chinese nuclear arsenals that could swamp these defenses in any case. Further, beyond defenses, America has paid little attention of late to its nuclear deterrent, beyond the work needed to maintain a decaying nuclear infrastructure, particularly compared with other powers.[5]

Other countries have been more aggressive. Russia, for example, has embarked on an ambitious modernization program, intending to introduce forty or more advanced long-range missiles a year, plus new submarines and aircraft platforms for launching them. By and large, arms control agreements with Moscow constrain the acquisition of more warheads, not more sophisticated platforms for delivering them. Pakistan, North Korea, and Iran have all expanded their nuclear programs over the last twenty years, with Pakistan's being the most successful, expanding its stockpile to between 110 and 130 warheads in 2015, with a projected arsenal size twice as large by 2025—and these to be delivered by half a dozen different types of ballistic missiles, with others (and two cruise missile systems) under development. Iran is constrained through the terms of its 2015 agreement with Western powers, Russia, and China, but only for a period of a decade or so, during which it can conduct further research and development, including for the missiles essential to deliver atomic weapons. France has modernized its nuclear arsenal. The size of the Chinese arsenal remains shrouded in more mystery than that of any other great power, although even the least alarmist authority, the *Bulletin of the Atomic*

Scientists, concedes that it "is the only one of the five original nuclear weapon states that is quantitatively increasing its nuclear arsenal" even as it modernizes that arsenal, shifting from liquid- to solid-fueled missiles, fixed to road mobile launchers, and adding ballistic missile firing submarines. Less sanguine experts, such as Phillip Karber of Georgetown University, believe that a much more ambitious program is in the works.[6]

A curious coalition of political figures who hoped for a world in which nuclear weapons could be abolished; defense intellectuals who thought that such weapons had little strategic value; and the military, which disliked the problems associated with securing nuclear weapons and thinking about their use, contributed to the steady erosion of America's capital and intellectual nuclear infrastructure. While the physical plant and warheads are gradually being refurbished (although not renewed or improved) as a result of an $85 billion commitment by the White House to secure passage of an arms control treaty with Russia, the thinking part remains stagnant. Nuclear strategy remains an arcane and deeply unpopular topic. This is even more pronounced in the area of tactical nuclear weapons, where the United States, which had built a powerful arsenal in Europe and elsewhere, essentially has gotten out of the business of developing new generations of weapons—unlike its rivals.[7]

The Cold War was the first nuclear age, characterized by the overwhelming dominance of two nuclear-armed superpowers that eventually came to regulate their competition through elaborate, bilateral arms-control treaties and a general norm against nuclear proliferation. However, we now live in a second nuclear age, in which circumstances have altered dramatically: as Yale professor Paul Bracken puts it, "Atomic weapons have returned for a second act. This isn't a welcome message, and yet it's one that we ignore at our peril." Russia still remains a nuclear superpower, but China has risen sharply—and most worrisomely, opaquely. To be sure, information about the Russian nuclear arsenal was never complete, even during the Cold War. It was a shock when the Intermediate Nuclear Forces Treaty of 1987 showed that the West had underestimated the numbers of weapons in the Soviet arsenal by anywhere from 20 to 50 percent, in some cases. Under the treaty the Russians destroyed just under 1,850 missiles; in its official report in 1987, however, the Pentagon had estimated they had just over 1,450—400 fewer. It was a second shock to learn thirty years later that Russia was violating that treaty, and had been doing so for at least six years. But China's nuclear arsenal is even more hidden, much of it in a vast array of tunnels rather than silos. Estimates of the total number of Chinese warheads range anywhere from the low hundreds to five hundred to, in some cases, over one thousand.[8]

And then there are the other nuclear powers: some friendly (the United Kingdom, France, and India, for example, all probably having sizable arsenals numbering in the hundreds of warheads), and others much less so. North Korea may have as many as several dozen warheads, and it is reliably believed that before long, it will have intercontinental ballistic missiles as well—no great surprise, given that the technology needed is a half-century old. Pakistan's nuclear program probably includes tactical warheads as well as much larger, city-destroying warheads. Iran's nuclear weapons aspirations have never been in doubt: the question is only whether it intends to acquire such weapons despite its agreement with the great powers in 2015.[9]

In the new nuclear age, it is not only the city-shattering weapons of the Cold War (warheads with yields of 50 or 100 kilotons or more) that matter, but less powerful weapons as well. Russia, though quite happy to sign an arms control agreement with the Obama administration in 2010, was adamant in its insistence that tactical nuclear weapons, with yields of only a few kilotons or less, be off the table. This is not surprising, given that Russia counts on its arsenal of thousands of these weapons to deter Chinese adventurism in the sparsely populated Russian Far East. Nuclear weapons with tailored effects, such as those designed to generate an electromagnetic pulse that would disrupt electronics, are now available to a number of countries. Thus, the great explosive power of nuclear weapons can be used in ways that may not cause enormous physical destruction, or lasting radiation, but that would be powerfully disruptive.

Nuclear weapons have not been used in anger since 1945. But they could be. If that ever happens, all of the taboos, restraints, and certainties that we have taken for granted since Nagasaki and Hiroshima will disappear. Just as mass terrorism was understood intellectually, but not viscerally, in the years before 9/11, so, too, we can today imagine a state's using a nuclear weapon. But if it happens in reality, the emotional and psychological consequences will be very different than what we might now conceive. In a world that has witnessed the use of nuclear weapons, an American president will find him- or herself thinking seriously about the requirements of conventional or even nuclear preemption—a purpose taken off the books early in the Cold War, and not really revisited since. A redesigned and modernized nuclear arsenal and the strategic concepts to accompany it are therefore one requirement of the new nuclear era.[10]

The largest element of American military power is its vast conventional forces—an Army with 2,300 tanks (and a Marine Corps with 450 more); a Navy with more than fifty attack submarines (SSNs), ten aircraft carriers (CVNs), and over eighty cruisers and destroyers; and an Air Force with over a thousand fighter-bombers and more than a hundred long-range bombers, including twenty of the stealthy B-2s. Substantial though these numbers are, however, they reflect a force that has been declining in size.

This force has repeatedly won conventional victories in the last twenty-five years. In two wars with Iraq—a much flimsier opponent than assumed at the time—American ground and air forces delivered crushing successes in weeks. Against similar kinds of opponents—say, in a war with North Korea, in which US forces would be reinforcing

US Navy Ships							
Year	CVs	Cruisers	Destroyers	Frigates	Large Amphibs	Attack Submarines	Total Surface Combat/ Active Ships
1988	14	32	69	107	58	101	217/583
2000	12	27	54	35	41	56	128/318
2005	12	23	46	30	37	54	111/282
2010	11	22	59	29	33	53	123/288
2015	10	22	62	0	30	54	99/271

Note: All ship counts are as of September 30 of their respective reporting year. Data is from "U.S. Ship Force Levels 1886–present," Naval History and Heritage Command, January 13, 2016, available at history.navy.mil. "Surface" refers to "surface combatants."

US Air Force

Year	Long-Range Bombers	Fighters	Heavy Transports	End Strength/ *Including Reserves*
1988	423	3,241	907	603,600/*846,900*
2000	208	2,361	668	353,600/*533,900*
2005	205	2,496	852	379,500/*562,700*
2010	154	2,158	756	334,342/*508,522*
2015	155	1,570	635	327,600/*503,400*

Note: Fighters include all aircraft capable of serving as fighters, even if currently designated in a fighter-ground attack role; heavy transports are defined here as aircraft capable of carrying a 20+ ton cargo (i.e., C-130 and larger).

US Army

Year	End Strength/ *Including Reserves*	Tanks*	Attack Helicopters
1988	776,400/*839,600*	15,600	1,496
2000	471,700/*199,900*	7,900	1,308
2005	502,000/*1,178,150*	7,620	1,477
2010	662,232/*1,109,435*	5,850	1,035
2015	539,450/*1,079,200*	2,338*	741

*Around 3,500 additional *Abrams* main battle tanks are in storage.

US Marine Corps

Year	End Strength/ *Including Reserves*	Tanks	Attack Helicopters
1988	198,200/*286,400*	716	72
2000	169,800/*265,060*	403	188
2005	175,350/*279,642*	403	148
2010	204,261/*313,861*	403	145
2015	191,150/*230,150*	447	151

the large South Korean military—the outcome would likely be similar, if considerably costlier. But these relatively easy victories against a second-rate opponent have been, in some measure, deceiving. The test of American forces against the far more determined, disciplined, and skillful North Vietnamese in the 1960s should stand as a caution against excessive optimism about using conventional power. A naval contest against China, for example, would be a different problem altogether—besides which, the United States has not fought a major battle at sea since the end of World War II.

Our understanding of conventional warfare remains shaped to a remarkable degree by the Second World War, a conflict which is just now passing from living memory, but whose stories are retold in best-selling histories; movies, such as *Saving Private Ryan*; and hit television series, such as *Band of Brothers*. Those images, however, are dangerously obsolete. A modern tank is nothing like the reliable Sherman of the Normandy battles, of which some 50,000 were produced in the space of five years. The American M-1 Abrams tank was designed in the 1970s, and only 10,000 were built (2,000 for foreign militaries). Unlike the Sherman, which was obsolete by the end of World War II, the M-1 has lasted for a third of a century, being continually upgraded and improved. Most important, the M-1, like most of the vehicles and even individuals in American land forces, is part of a larger networked force. The electronics of the M-1 were built on the back of the avionics for an F-16 fighter plane, which says something about its sophistication. But even that system now reflects outdated technologies from the 1970s and 1980s.

Sheer mass no longer counts the way it did during World War II. The first Gulf War made that clear when a US armored battalion of fifty-four tanks could easily overmatch a much larger Iraqi force armed with Soviet-built T-72s. This proposition was put to the test at the Battle of 73 Easting in February 26–27, 1991, when US forces, with half as many tanks as their Iraqi opponents, lost one man killed and one infantry fighting vehicle to enemy fire, while their Iraqi opponents suffered hundreds of dead and more than eighty tanks and infantry fighting vehicles destroyed. The outcome was overdetermined, reflecting superior American training, leadership, and manpower, to be sure, but also superior armor, communications, sensors, and tank guns. Air and ground forces are now equipped overwhelmingly with extraordinarily accurate systems, including both guided weapons and sighting and aiming systems (for tank guns, for example) that amount to the same thing for "dumb" projectiles. The image of fighter planes' dogfighting with lethal aerial acrobatics is similarly out of date; what matters far more now is an integrated suite of sensors that can detect enemy aircraft and fire guided missiles from ranges that may well be beyond sight.[11]

Modern air power has extended the depth of modern battlefields. During World War II, at least after 1942, the United States could assume that it had rear areas for supply dumps, motor pools, and headquarters subject to nothing more than harassing attacks by the lone enemy fighter plane. The proliferation of reasonably accurate surface-to-surface missiles has changed that, and probably forever. While active defenses can stop some long-range missiles, they will not get all of them. The US military's routine assumption of secure rear areas no longer holds. In all likelihood, the days of air supremacy, except in counterinsurgency campaigns, such as in Afghanistan and Iraq, and not even necessarily there, are gone.

The face of conventional warfare has changed. In the event of a clash between forces comparable in number, skill, and resolve, mass casualties are always possible. Information suffuses the modern conventional battlefield at orders of magnitude beyond those of any previous era—be it in the tracking not just of individual vehicles but also individual soldiers, real-time video and other forms of imagery, coordination of targeting information, just-in-time logistics, and much more. Weapons of precision now pervade the battlefield, including in the hands of guerrillas, and air and space are now available to all combatants in the form of satellite-aided navigation systems (e.g., GPS), or commercially available overhead imagery. Finally, unmanned systems, from bomb disposal robots, to snake-like machines that can enter underground tunnels, to lingering drones that can observe for days and deliver missiles from an invisible distance, are all part of the modern battlespace. On a reduced scale, they, too, are available to guerrilla and terrorist bands.

Thus, we live in a misleadingly familiar world. The same platforms—aircraft carriers, tanks, jet planes, artillery pieces—are all there, and bear the obvious imprint of their World War II ancestors. The M-1 Abrams tank, after all, was named after the general who first made his mark as a lieutenant colonel rolling with Patton's Third Army in France. The rank structures have not changed all that much, and neither have unit names, such as *battalion* and *brigade*. Underneath all this seeming continuity, however, are radical changes, the full nature of which will not become apparent unless and until there is a large war.

In a pioneering study of the British Army in World War I, the historian Timothy Travers noted that the British expeditionary force commander Sir Douglas Haig was neither stupid nor incurious. However, "he had learnt, and clung to, an ideal of war that formed a paradigm of what 'normal' war should be." In the same way that military thinkers before 1914 could only dimly imagine what a full-blown conflict would look like, today's civilian and military leaders are probably equally limited in foresight. Many of World War I's leaders thought about operational art in the terms of the wars of the previous century, the wars of German unification and the American Civil War, if not indeed the Napoleonic wars. They modified, but did not jettison, those ideas on the basis of the experience of conflicts against weak states or movements. Similarly, tomorrow's civilian and military leaders may find themselves trapped in obsolete thinking derived from the Cold War, the great contest of the mid-twentieth century, modified by the unrepresentative experience of waging wars against a crippled state like Iraq in the 1990s and early 2000s.[12]

In those wars, the United States military, having quickly disposed of a conventional enemy, had to shift quickly to irregular warfare. Unconventional war has coexisted with conventional warfare from the beginning. Assassins, raiders, and guerrillas were useful adjuncts to ancient armies, and the Roman legions learned the hard way about insurgency in forests and deserts. The War of American Independence was fought as what contemporary military theorists now call "hybrid warfare," in which, for example, Indians used irregular methods to support more or less regular American and British forces.

Modern unconventional warfare, however, matured during World War II and in its aftermath. In addition to the insurgent groups that (often with state support) successfully fought against the occupying forces of Germany and Japan, the combatants, and in particular the Allies, made effective use of it against the Axis powers. Commandos raided the coasts of occupied France, Russian partisans attacked German supply lines and gathered intelligence, Office of Strategic Service's Jedburgh teams coordinated the French resistance, Britain's Special Air Service plausibly claimed to have destroyed more German aircraft on the ground in North Africa than the Royal Air Force shot down in the air. New organizations, such as the British Special Operations Executive, existed for no other purpose than to orchestrate irregular warfare behind enemy lines.

During the Cold War, unconventional warfare mushroomed, both in the form of state support to insurgent groups and in the creation of Western and Eastern special units—the US Army Special Forces, US Navy SEALs, Soviet Spetsnaz, and many more—that could conduct independent missions. In the case of the United States, the Special Forces, or Green Berets, were created initially to organize guerrilla bands behind Soviet lines, but their mission (as is inevitable with such units) expanded over time. Special operations forces have always offered politicians a seemingly precise, seemingly covert, and even deniable tool of military statecraft.[13]

As the Cold War headed into its final decade, the special operators grew in numbers, and their organizations became less shadowy phantoms and more like separate services, with their own civilian and military bureaucracies. In the United States this became even truer after the creation of the Special Operations Command (SOCOM) in 1987, and with the gradual public emergence of the elite Joint Special Operations Command (JSOC), created years earlier. As communications and intelligence-gathering technologies improved, the special operators became increasingly effective. And after the end of the Cold War, a further expansion of special operations forces occurred, both to engage in the hunting down and arrest or killing of terrorist or insurgent leaders, and to train and support the local forces operating against them. In 2001 a few special operators riding on horseback with anti-Taliban insurgents in Afghanistan were able to bring down devastating air strikes because they knew precisely where they were and where the enemy was (thanks to satellite navigation and laser designation), and because they could communicate reliably and safely with headquarters and aircraft overhead. The US Army Special Forces had been created in the 1950s to train indigenous forces to fight either insurgents or, in some cases, regular forces. They numbered in the hundreds, initially, and by the end of the 1950s a few thousand. Today, the Special Forces mission has grown enormously, and the SOCOM comprises over 60,000 soldiers, sailors, Marines, and airmen. At that number it is slightly larger than the entire Australian military.[14]

Special operations forces have always been a temptation to the politicians whom they serve. This is particularly true today, for an America that is averse to substantial military engagements overseas and to large-scale, protracted warfare. The deployment of these shadow warriors promises, at first glance, precise effects, limited exposure, and minimal publicity. But the history of special operations forces suggests their dangers as well. Composed of men (very few women, at least thus far) of exceptional talents and training, they are easily misused, being assigned missions that belong more properly to large conventional forces—as happened to the British Commandos and US Army Rangers on occasions in World War II. Moreover, they are singularly vulnerable to just a little bit of bad luck—as, for example, in the failure of the mission to rescue American hostages in Iran in 1980, and in the 1993 "Blackhawk Down" mission in Somalia.

What special operators—and in particular, the elite commandos who constitute their cutting edge—can actually accomplish is necessarily limited in scope. They may be able to scoop up terrorist leaders and ransack their computers and file cabinets, but it is difficult to translate that into an enduring strategic effect. The lure to apprehensive Western politicians of a "light footprint," in which they only have to send in special operators and provide covering air power, was seen in Libya in 2011, when a victory on the ground—not particularly rapid—translated into chaos in the aftermath, in the absence of a more substantial force to consolidate and control the liberated country.

Indeed, the initial operation in Afghanistan in 2001 that toppled the Taliban would have been considerably enhanced had several thousand regular light infantrymen been dispatched to trap fleeing al-Qaeda forces. Dazzling tactical accomplishments can, and often do, mislead politicians and publics about the true strategic situation, and imply, if not promise, far more than they can be reasonably expected to deliver. And although covert or unconventional operations in support of local fighters can succeed, as they did in Afghanistan against Soviet forces in the 1980s, they can also fail miserably, as was the case with aid to Syrian rebels in 2012–2014. As of July 2015, an ambitious training program for Syrian rebels conducted by the Department of Defense had yielded precisely 54 graduates out of an original 1,200 who had been willing to join it.[15]

American nuclear, conventional, and unconventional forces have one tremendous advantage over any prospective opponent: an extraordinary global logistical infrastructure. China deploys forces abroad in the hundreds, chiefly in support of peacekeeping operations. It has facilities overseas, but as of this writing no bases comparable to Diego Garcia in the Indian Ocean and Yokosuka in Japan, or advanced headquarters in Stuttgart, Germany. This is, however, beginning to change as China develops a base in Djibouti and an array of island facilities in the South China Sea. Russia's forces abroad are chiefly stationed in the "near abroad"—the semi-independent successor states of the former Soviet Union, such as Georgia, Moldova, and Ukraine—with the exception of a growing base in Syria. It has nothing abroad remotely like the 50,000 American service personnel stationed in Japan. The United States has almost six hundred bases of various sizes and functions abroad, in over forty countries, as well as over a hundred more in some of its far-flung territories, including Samoa, Guam, and Wake Island.[16]

One of the competences that accompany this web of bases is the ability to build up forces around the world as needed. Americans take for granted having deployed a force of half a million service personnel to the Persian Gulf in less than six months after Saddam Hussein's invasion of Iraq in 1990, and the US military's ability to take down the government of remote Afghanistan in less than two months following the attacks of 9/11. They similarly are unsurprised when the United States can keep armies of 150,000 or more well fed, healthy, and fit in the punishing climate of the Tigris and Euphrates river basins for years on end. Americans see nothing unusual in the sustained presence of US fleets off the shores of China and Iran. By historical standards, however, these are all remarkable achievements. Despite the occasional feat of staging a large noncombatant evacuation operation, or deploying a few ships or airplanes around the world, neither Russia nor China—yet—can deploy such large forces overseas in operational environments for such an extended period of time.

America's system for developing and acquiring new weapons is a less happy story. To be sure, with its vast research and development budget—some $70 billion, or roughly 12 percent of the total defense budget—it has the ability to advance military technology in a way that no other country has thus far. But in recent years, actual acquisition has been a different story. The American acquisition system is notoriously cumbersome, and in some cases disastrously so. The top US long-range stealth fighter, the F-22 Raptor, emerged out of requirements formulated in the early 1980s. A final design was approved in 1991, the jet first flew in 1997, and it was introduced into service in 2005. Thus, an airplane designed primarily for combat in Europe in the Cold War became operational in an utterly different geopolitical environment. But at least the F-22 showed up. Other large, expensive programs—the Army's Comanche attack helicopter and the Crusader artillery system, and the Navy's Zumwalt-class destroyers—were either aborted or canceled when they had yielded up only a few pieces of equipment. The F-35 joint strike fighter will be procured, but at terrific cost to the aircraft budget: in 2015 something like a quarter of the USAF budget went to F-35 procurement, yielding a total of only twenty-eight aircraft.[17]

In a number of cases, acquisition has not matched strategic challenges. After decades of facing no surface naval threat to speak of, in 2015 the United States Navy found itself equipped with a ship-to-ship missile, the Harpoon, which had been first designed in the early 1970s (although upgraded considerably since then). The current version is roughly half the range of its Russian and Chinese counterparts, has a smaller warhead, and is slower (subsonic). In the mid-2010s the Navy belatedly realized that a naval fight with China would mean that its surface combatants might have to engage an enemy directly rather than rely on carrier air power to sink enemy ships. And even that carrier air power had in some important respects been crimped by the Navy's reliance on the relatively short-range F-35 fighter, with a roughly 700-mile combat radius compared to the 1,100-mile reach of the old A-6E carrier-based bomber. Until the Navy's new missile programs produce weapons that enter service, however, it will still be fighting with less powerful tools than those in the hands of China and Russia.[18]

Even in some very standard kinds of systems, US military technology is not, despite what Americans would like to think, always best in class—the Russian Kornet antitank missile, for example, easily matches the American Javelin and is a somewhat newer system. Moreover, the overall technological edge of the United States is continuously jeopardized by the extremely aggressive and apparently successful efforts at espionage by Russia, China, and other countries. The larger point is simply that the technological superiority that Americans take for granted should not be. Americans have been at a technological disadvantage before (for example, when in 1942 the Japanese had better torpedoes and the Germans had better infantry firearms), and they are equally at risk of being so today.[19]

The measures of military power discussed thus far do not adequately capture one of the most important dimensions of it: the ability to generate more when it is needed. The United States Army was, both absolutely and relatively, one of the smaller ones in the world in 1940; within five short years, however, it was one of the largest, best equipped, and most effective. All of the services exploded in size during World War II, introducing and deploying new technologies, building vast forces, introducing new concepts of operations and novel organizations in four short years. It is unlikely that such a marvel could be reproduced today, in part because of the nature of military technology then and now, but also because of the enormous expansion of America's defense bureaucracies.[20]

The American defense system today, powerful as it is, reflects an enormous amount of inertia. It is a victim of its own success in World

War II, the Cold War, and the immediate post–Cold War period. The creativity of the architects of victory in 1940–1945 resulted in part from necessity: they did not have the luxury of adopting orderly procedures and methodical measures. The challenge for US leaders in the years ahead is to recover something like that creativity while hampered, perversely, by the legacy of their predecessors' successes. One hopes that they will be able to do so without another kind of spur to creativity—the kind provided by the spectacle of Panzer divisions rolling into Paris, or waves of attacking Japanese aircraft sending four battleships to the bottom of Pearl Harbor.

The obstacles to such flexibility today are numerous: the absence of an overwhelming threat, the existence of rules and laws (governing everything from hiring to environmental impact; testing to accountability of funds) that slow everything down; and overall, a vast bureaucracy that does what bureaucracies do—monitor, report, and implement slowly. The quality of high command is also an issue. The military leaders of World War II were the products of a deeply established system, but were willing to throw away prewar processes and rules in a ruthless quest for military effectiveness. It is not clear whether their successors, emerging from a much larger and more established system, would do the same.

The final dimension of military power is its high-level organization and the quality of its directing intelligence. In 1890 Spenser Wilkinson, a British journalist turned professor of military history, published a book entitled *The Brain of an Army* that described the German general staff. His fundamental point—one that British reformers made with limited effect during the next two decades—was that German military superiority depended not just on the size of its army and the quality of its technology, but also on how its general staff thought about the next war, mobilized and controlled the forces at its disposal, and co-ordinated military operations. That point applies today as well. If it is necessary to consider the flesh and sinew of a military organization—its weapons, organizations, and manpower—it is equally important to consider the quality of the guiding intelligence behind them.[21]

The Pentagon building is the product of World War II. Then a model of size, simplicity of organization, and rapidity of construction—the ground was broken in September 1941, before the United States was at war, and the building was dedicated less than eighteen months later, in January 1943—it has become today more of a code word for vast bureaucracy, powerful but lumbering. Even the internal layout of corridors and offices, once so simple that even a second lieutenant could figure it out within minutes, has become so byzantine that visitors need escorts not only for security reasons, but simply to find their way around.[22]

The basic organizational structures of the American armed forces resemble that of their national headquarters. The US Army, Air Force, Navy, and Marine Corps are all evolved from, but in many respects are still like, their World War II predecessors. This is inevitable to some degree: the requirements of the physical environments of land, air, and sea mandate separate services with distinctive organizational cultures. When the Canadian military boldly experimented in 1968 with creating a single, unified service with a common forest green uniform, it discovered that it did not work. Today, the Royal Canadian Navy, Air Force, and Army are back, wearing familiar uniforms that are as distinctive as those of the US services.

The global command system of the United States, with the Joint Chiefs of Staff headed by a chairman at the center, and regional commands of enormous size and scope, are similarly evolved from the World War II fiefdoms of a MacArthur, a Nimitz, and an Eisenhower. And at the very bottom too, the institutions have changed less than one might think. Not only are the lineages preserved (ship names, such as *Wasp*, dating back to the founding of the US Navy; Army Ranger School for infantrymen, harking back to woodland warfare in the 1750s), but many of the basic experiences, such as basic training, and the cultures (the dominance of pilots over other air force specialties), seem very like those of the past.[23]

Here, too, however, changes have occurred underneath the surface of continuity. There has been a steady decline of the chiefs of the individual services as military advisers to the president, resulting in the rise of the chairman of the Joint Chiefs of Staff as the principal adviser to the president and of the theater commanders. Ever since the invention of the telegraph and its first use for the purposes of high-level command in the Civil War, the steady improvement of information technology has increased the amount of central control over military operations. The possibility of routine video teleconferencing, in particular, makes it easy for Washington military and political authorities to consult routinely (although not necessarily privately) with military commanders in the field.

At the same time, attitudes toward the use of force by the services have changed. A presumption in favor of joint rather than single service operations is now the norm, and casualty sensitivity on the part of military leaders is constant (Joint Chiefs of Staff chairman General Martin Dempsey kept a box on his desk containing the names of servicemen and women who had died during his tenure in office). Perhaps most important of all, the distinction between war and peace, in terms of the rhythms of military life, has eroded. American forces today are constantly operational—doing something somewhere, forward deployed, training, and exercising—when not actually engaged in combat. A supremely busy military, increasingly isolated from the public it serves, located on fewer and fewer mega-bases scattered around rural areas of the United States, supported by its own industrial base of defense contractors for everything from mess halls to satellite maintenance, is in some respects its own world. Such introversion, busyness, and self-containment work against high-quality strategic thought.[24]

Congressional and executive branch attention follows the money, and the Pentagon's money goes to people and things—military salaries and benefits (about a quarter of the budget in direct costs), operations and maintenance (over 40 percent), and procurement, research, and development (30 percent).With very few and honorable exceptions, the intellectual infrastructure of hard power, and in particular its thinking part, gets very little money—some hundreds of million dollars, if that, are spent on an array of staff and war colleges for midlevel and senior officers, plus some in-house military think tanks. As a result, the thinking part, and in particular the educational system, gets less attention.[25]

The American military remains tactically competent (although it has not been challenged in several domains, particularly at sea and in space, for a very long time and in some cases ever). It can pull off large operations, such as the invasion of Iraq in 2003, and massive relief operations, such as those following the Indian Ocean tsunami in 2004 and the Japanese tsunami in 2011. But strategic thinking about the nature of war, and how to align military means with political ends, is a very different matter. There, arguably, it has done poorly. There are few major uniformed strategic thinkers. Writing about the nature of contemporary war is largely a civilian enterprise; and although the United States has designated strategists in its uniformed ranks, they are not always used as such.

This seems odd at first sight, because the nation has a large collection of military colleges and research institutes, staffed by large numbers of academics as well as military officers. By normal academic standards, these are well-funded institutions, even if senior faculty are underpaid by comparison with counterparts in top-notch civilian institutions. The war colleges' problems are subtler. Begin with their students: no one applies for entry to these institutions, and almost no one is denied entry because of a poor academic record. Once in, it is virtually impossible to flunk out. Rather, these are schools for a large chunk of the officer corps on their way to further rank— although it is widely known that being selected for attendance is more important than actually performing well once in. Attendance reflects not an interest in furthering knowledge, but a necessary tick mark in a career—and to some extent, a welcome break from an intense operational career. Noticeably, the numbers of war college students has actually grown as the United States military has shrunk. In the civilian world, educational institutions understand that if they take a larger percentage of their applicant pool, the chances are that they are lowering standards and that the educational experience in the classroom is declining. In the military world, however, it is assumed that if educating fifty colonels is good, educating a hundred is better, and two hundred is better yet.[26]

At the top of the war colleges, which educate senior officers at the rank of commander or lieutenant colonel and above, sit two- or three-star officers as presidents or commandants. They are not necessarily chosen for any academic expertise, pedagogical talent, or interest in the educational enterprise. For them it is a good but usually terminal job. No university could possibly thrive with that kind of turnover or lack of scholarly credentials at the top. Like all academic institutions, moreover, the war colleges suffer from the growth of an administrative class at the expense of faculty, a mushrooming of deans and provosts and underlings. No less problematic is the difficulty military bureaucracies have in understanding a good academic's need to devote a considerable amount of time to research as well as teaching.

The American military has some centers of intellectual excellence—the Office of the Secretary of Defense's Office of Net Assessment, for example; the Army's Combat Studies Institute; the Navy's China Maritime Security Institute; and the Air Force's internal think tank, Checkmate—but by and large it does not produce its own intellectual capital. Civilian academic institutions and think tanks cannot pick up all of the slack. Military studies are unpopular at most universities, and usually confined to small numbers of overworked faculty at the exceptions. Quasi-public contractors, such as RAND and the Center for Naval Analyses, do some very interesting work and exhibit some intellectual independence, but in the end are beholden to the bureaucracies that pay their bills. Think tanks, such as Brookings and the American Enterprise Institute, are usually public organizations that do not do classified research, and besides they often have a mandate to do short-term work heavily tilted to op-eds, testimony before Congress, and short-form writing. In any case, there is a need for professional officers with both operational experience and intellectual training as well as access to classified material and recent operational experience, to contribute to high-order thought about the nature of war.

"So long as no acceptable theory, no intelligent analysis of the conduct of war exists, routine methods will tend to take over even at the highest levels." This statement of Clausewitz applies today as it did two centuries ago. There are a number of reasons that the wars in Iraq and Afghanistan went as poorly as they did, including some that resulted exclusively from how the civilian leadership decided to use military power. But in at least some respects, the services and Joint Staff allowed routine methods to take over, as we have seen in the previous chapter. Strategic thought is an intellectual discipline, and the best of the war college curricula recognize that, compelling officers to read deeply in history and military thought. A true theory of war (as Clausewitz put it), recognizes those elements of war that are lasting and in some measure universal, as well as the very specific circumstances of any given conflict. Therein lies the purpose of strategic education. In an era of growing strategic complexity and uncertainty, repairing and rebuilding this, the least heeded part of the defense infrastructure, is one of the more important tasks faced by the American military.[27]

The American military hand, therefore, is strong but mixed. Its combination of quality and quantity remain unique, although relatively speaking, others are catching up, as we shall see in following chapters. It has great experience of low-intensity war, but has not experienced intense conventional conflict with a military peer in generations. Although its experience of operating large forces at sea over prolonged distances is unique, the nation has not fought a major naval opponent since 1944, and never an enemy in space. Nor has it encountered a first-class air defense system backed by an equally capable air force since Vietnam. The relative geographical isolation of the United States is a source of strength in some respects, but a source of weakness in others: it has to get to the fight, and countries that are mainly bent on dominating their neighborhoods have an intrinsic logistical as well as cultural advantage.

In its upper reaches, the American military is a meritocratic and technocratic elite. It is not always strategically shrewd, but its senior leaders have risen to the top through a rigorous winnowing. We take for granted that it is neither corrupt nor heavily politicized, but that is no small advantage. The comparison with senior Chinese generals who have been stripped of their positions and prosecuted for personal corruption (e.g., two former vice chairmen of the all-important Central Military Commission, Xu Caihou and Guo Boxiong) is striking.

Military power is ultimately a reflection of the society and polity that produce it, which means that we have to ask, what are the deeper qualities of the United States that provide the basis for military strength? Of all the elements of national power, none is more fundamental than demography. In the past, demography was chiefly of concern for what it said about the pool of available manpower for military service: such countries as France in the early twentieth century obsessed about the number of young males available for service in the mass conscript armies of the day. This matters much less in the age of career armies that are far smaller in proportion to population than in the past. To be sure, around the world conscription-driven militaries can, in theory, deploy vast forces, both absolutely and relative to population. Officially, upon complete mobilization, tiny Singapore (population 5.5 million) has nearly 400,000 service personnel; and only slightly larger is Israel (population 7.8 million), with more than 600,000. Both societies, in other words, have well over 7 percent of their population trained and either on active duty or in reserve. The United States, by way of comparison, has considerably less than one percent of its population on active or reserve status.[28]

The numbers do matter. War remains a young person's business, at least at the sharp end. A limited pool of young people will be fit enough, sufficiently well educated, and motivated to operate a modern high-technology military. In the United States, the military has to recruit something under a quarter of a million men and women each year to keep its armed forces at full strength. Most of those are high school graduates who are not going directly to college—a small part of a pool of potential recruits further limited by the fact that two thirds or more of potential applicants cannot meet the military's fitness standards. To attract fit and qualified individuals, and then to retain them, the military competes with the private sector, and as a result spends vast sums on salary, benefits, and the indirect costs (attractive accommodations, for example, or retirement benefits for reservists) of an all-volunteer force.[29]

Still, the real significance of demographics is what it augurs for a country's long-term vitality. An aging population, in which every year fewer workers support more retired individuals, will face inexorable pressures to cut discretionary spending—of which defense is almost always the largest element—to provide for entitlements in the form of pensions and medical care. Herein lies the fundamental crisis of the modern welfare state, constructed in Europe and to a lesser extent the United States during and after World War II, and expanded throughout the world thereafter. Entitlements that seemed affordable during the postwar demographic boom, at a time of shorter life expectancies than today and less technologically advanced medical care, become far harder to sustain when there is no longer a bulge of youthful workers, when nonagenarians are far more common (720,000 in 1980 in the United States, 1.9 million in 2010, headed to 3 million in 2050, even as the population aged 65 to 89 is expected to double), and when medical care is capable of more and more exotic, successful, and expensive efforts to keep people alive.[30]

There are the more subtle consequences of demography as well. Young people are turbulent: the student revolts of the late 1960s occurred not only in reaction to the Vietnam War but to the swamping of universities with a tidal wave of eighteen- to twenty-two-year-olds. Younger people are also, by and large, more creative; older people, generally more cautious. Declining populations will have family structures unprecedented in human history. In many countries, societies are emerging with large numbers of individuals who will have no aunts or uncles, no brothers or sisters, no cousins. The long-term consequences of such a departure from the human past are unknown. It might make societies at once more atomized and more risk averse, as individuals lose the socialization of extended families, and any individual sent to war becomes, from a genetic point of view, irreplaceable.[31]

Broadly speaking, then, military power is more likely to emanate from societies that are at the least demographically balanced, with birth rates of 2.1 per female (the generally accepted number to maintain population size). In this respect, the United States still looks the most promising of any major power. The American replacement rate is only slightly above 2 percent, but that is much higher than that of any of its competitors (2.01 percent, for example, to China's 1.55 percent). In addition, the United States can absorb large immigrant populations. The upshot is simple: by 2050 America may have, on the whole, the lowest median age of any great power save India. China will be aging swiftly, meaning that within the next thirty or forty years, it will have fewer than one worker for every pensioner.

Taken together, the results mean that the United States, which has a population of 322 million today, is expected to add 30 million more inhabitants in the next fifteen years, and a further 35 million in twenty years, for a projected population of 389 million by 2050. The populations of two of its chief rivals, Russia and China, will decline slightly (in China's case) or steeply (in Russia's), while aging faster. Put differently, as its major rivals stagnate, the United States will grow itself by the size of Great Britain (or eight Switzerlands) in the space of a generation.[32]

America's demographic strengths contribute to its economic power as well. In the last forty years eminent scholars have argued that the American economy would be displaced first by Japan, then by Europe, and now by China. Ezra Vogel's 1979 book, *Japan as Number One*, made that argument about a Japan that would displace the United States; Charles Kupchan made a comparable argument about Europe in 2004 (to include the claim that the introduction of a single currency was "an unqualified success"). That the first two arguments were proven ludicrously wrong—both Japan and Europe, rather than becoming number one, slipped into long-term stagnation—does not necessarily mean that the third is. But it should make us wonder.[33]

Economically, the United States is not in absolute decline—not by a long shot. America's gross domestic product (GDP) is roughly four times what it was fifty years ago; per capita GDP has grown during the same period by roughly 2.5 times. But it may be in relative decline, that is, losing strength compared with potential opponents, and particularly with a China whose economy continues to grow, although less and less rapidly.[34]

The United States in 1960 accounted for around 30 percent of global GDP; today, it accounts for around 22 percent, a statistic that reflects a slight decline. China has risen from less than 1 percent to 9 percent—a phenomenal rise, to be sure, but far from one that has eclipsed the United States. China's dramatic rise is the story of the last several decades. It is a rise that is slowing as that country gradually assumes middle-income status, and as structural considerations—a model of growth driven by exports, state-owned enterprises whose access to financing is not necessarily driven by economic rationality, excessive and murky borrowing throughout the public and private sectors, and the heavy hand of the Communist Party—kick in.[35]

Military power in the last several centuries has rested, in part, on manufacturing ability. Few countries today are completely self-reliant in terms of major pieces of military equipment; none, probably, are independent of a global supply chain. But manufacturing ability, in various domains, reflects as well a country's level of technological sophistication in handling weapons, including advanced weapon systems. Here, too, the United States has lost some ground, its share of world manufacturing in billions of constant dollars having fallen from 22 percent in 1980 to just over 17 percent today; and although China's manufacturing (24 percent of global total) has surpassed that of the United States, much of that is in areas in which the United States has no need or desire to participate. Conversely, new manufacturing technologies (including 3-D printing) seem likely to bring manufacturing back to America's shores.[36]

The hydrocarbon revolution that is on the verge of making the United States a net exporter of energy is a further advantage, at multiple levels. By making energy cheap, it gives the America a competitive advantage in manufacturing. By freeing the United States (although not its allies) from dependence on Persian Gulf oil, it makes America more difficult to blackmail. This does not mean that Washington can or should disregard a chaotic Persian Gulf—the stability of the global economy depends on a reliable supply of energy, and at the end of the day, that means oil from that part of the world. But it does give the United States more room to maneuver.

Economic strength depends on creativity and innovation, and on the flexibility and depth of financial markets. In these respects as well, the United States is not badly off, filing a slightly higher percentage of the world's patent applications today than it did in 1990; and although Chinese applications have skyrocketed, it is unclear how many of these reflect real innovation. The American financial position is similarly strong, with US asset managers holding 45 percent of the global total of long-term conventional assets, and managing more than half of total global pension assets. As for the intellectual capital on which growth rests, there is nothing anywhere like the hotbed of ideas and capital that is Silicon Valley, or the sprawling infrastructure of American universities and research institutes. By one common Chinese ranking of world universities, 16 of the top 20, 52 of the top 100, and 146 of the top 500 are American. By comparison, China manages none of the top 20 or 100, and only 44 of the top 500. Russia, with only 2 in the top 500, lags behind Finland and Belgium, among others.[37]

None of this makes a case for complacency about the US lead; none of it diminishes the undeniable fact that America's relative economic position in the world has declined, and may very well continue to do so. None of it counteracts the basic fact of a system that has proven unable to adjust its entitlement spending to make it possible to invest large sums in military power and domestic infrastructure. It is, rather, to say that the United States remains the world's most powerful, diverse, and in many ways promising economy, and that it has, and will continue to have, the financial and human resources to remain the world's leading military power.

Modern military power depends on scientific and technological competence. Here, too, the United States remains relatively well off, with several caveats. Its base of military-relevant technology has been, for decades now, the subject of constant and on the whole successful theft by other countries, most notably Russia and China. More worrying, however, is that many militarily relevant technologies are no longer, as they once were, proprietary or difficult to imitate. There is nothing remarkable about designing a nuclear weapon, for example: the technology is over seventy years old. Militarily useful unmanned aerial vehicles, once a prerogative of the most advanced societies, are sold to hobbyists and all kinds of companies in the hundreds of thousands. The tools of cyberwarfare are available, for those who wish to find them, on the Internet.[38]

The most advanced technologies (think: for example, submarine construction, or extremely accurate long-range missiles) are the province of relatively few countries. But recent decades have seen an expansion in the market for both technologists and the technologies themselves, such that even nonstate actors can acquire state-of-the-art antitank weapons, man-portable antiaircraft missiles, and the like.

The ability of a nonstate actor, Hezbollah, to nearly destroy the Israeli warship *Hanit* in 2006 by using a Chinese antiship missile, was revealing. The advantage for the United States resides—and will as far as can be projected—in some leading-edge capabilities, and even more so, in its ability to integrate the many dimensions of military power on a large scale.

Economic preeminence does not guarantee military superiority. It does not necessarily translate into adequate or intelligent spending; it does not prevent foolish projects or inept execution of sound ones. And inferior opponents who have the advantage of geographical location, determination, and selected technologies can win battles and even, for months on end, major campaigns. Ultimately, they may be defeated or overwhelmed, but in the interim they can do far more damage than the raw numbers would suggest.

The case of Japan in 1942 is a good illustration. Despite having a population more than half the size of the United States, its economy was less than a sixth the size of that of its main enemy. Even in this, the first full year of hostilities, it was outproduced five to one in aircraft, ten to one in warships, and twenty to one in finished steel. In 1943 and 1944, the Japanese fell even further behind the United States in these measures, and could not compete in all kinds of technologies, from the mundane (bulldozers, jeeps, antimalarial drugs) to the very sophisticated (proximity fuzes that blew up shells when they were close to an airplane rather than when they hit it). But with a qualitative edge in a few key areas—such as torpedoes and highly maneuverable if vulnerable fighter planes, some solid basic industrial abilities (ship construction), and fighting spirit—for a year Japan rampaged across Asia and the Pacific, dealing humiliating defeats to the United States, Great Britain, and their allies. With sound planning (for example, promptly fortifying the islands they had seized, promptly mobilizing industry, and using submarines to attack American lines of communication), Japan might have done more.[39]

═══════════

The US economy, therefore, can sustain American global military power; however, economics represents chiefly the tangible elements of power. Social cohesion and political ability reflect intangibles: the ability to endure loss, the willingness to mobilize national resources, the ability to persevere, having a system able to make decisions—these are elements of militarily relevant national power, too. It is a long-standing argument—and one not entirely without a respectable pedigree—that democracies in general, and the United States in particular, have less of these qualities than authoritarian regimes. But this is not true. Again, some basic data are revealing.[40]

After a period of wishing to disengage from the world, by 2014 more than half of Americans believed that the United States was not doing enough to solve the world's problems, two thirds arguing that the world has been getting more dangerous. Such numbers may ebb and flow over time, but one basic observation about American opinion remains: that a majority of Americans (who generally have a high view of their own country, two thirds of them describing themselves as unambiguously patriotic) believe that their country should play a large and active role in the world, including in maintaining international security. While the wars of the early twenty-first century increased American ambivalence about global engagement, the bedrock of opinion supporting an active foreign and military policy remains. By 2016, the predominant critique was of a foreign policy that was insufficiently tough. Republican presidential candidate Donald Trump advocated a foreign policy tinged with both isolationism and belligerence, a promise to make allies pay up while promising to make America ever more militarily powerful, representing a coherent, but not likely the majority view of the American people.[41]

In recent years Americans have been pessimistic about their country's immediate prospects. But by and large, they do not flee abroad to guarantee that their children will have a safer and more prosperous future with Chinese, Russian, or even, for that matter, German or Swedish citizenship. According to one poll, by contrast, nearly half of Chinese millionaires plan to emigrate, while a fifth say that they are not sure—"the highest rate of planned millionaire flight in the world" according to one reporter. With all the partisanship that afflicts American politics in the early twenty-first century, as it has throughout most of its history, Americans remain remarkably committed to the idea that their system is the best in the world, and the one that they would most prefer to live under. The US military is a stunningly popular institution, with three quarters of Americans declaring that members of the armed forces contribute a lot to the nation's well-being—more than teachers, doctors, and scientists.[42]

American strengths go deeper yet. The United States remains a nation of immigrants; it has the ability to absorb foreigners in a way no other country can. This in turn provides other, multiple strengths. Since immigrants tend to be young or at least of working age, they improve the demographic posture of the country. Immigrants create a large pool of bi- or multicultural individuals who can bridge the divide with other societies—a tremendous boon for intelligence agencies and the military. And despite the political turmoil over illegal immigration in the early 2000s, the fact of being a nation of immigrants contributes to the sense of optimism that has long been a distinguishing American characteristic.

Nor is the American political system a negligible asset. The Constitution of the United States has extraordinary legitimacy. Whereas even a country as well established as Great Britain can come breathtakingly close to breakup (as it did in 2014 with the referendum on Scottish independence), that is an outcome unimaginable in the United States. A strong presidential system has its problems, but it offers, as Alexander Hamilton put it more than two centuries ago, the opportunity for "energy in the executive," which is indispensable for diplomacy as well as the use of force. Although the denizens of the bureaucracy often complain about the "interagency process"—the grind of coordination among different organizations within the executive branch—the truth is that even its most ardent critics have trouble coming up with an example of another country that does it better. In recent years, in fact, other countries, including well-established powers, have attempted to imitate it: Britain creating a National Security Council in 2010, China and Japan doing so in 2013. If the US National Security Council process is broken, the question that requires an answer is why other countries, including our most important rival, seek to imitate it.[43]

One final critical element of national strength that underlies military power is a country's coalition portfolio. This goes beyond numbers, including as it does such intangible elements of strength as the ability to integrate allied forces into ongoing operations, skill at managing relationships in multinational headquarters, sensitivity to allied needs, and even linguistic abilities. In all these less tangible respects of coalitional strength, the United States is nonpareil. Since 1941 it has, in one form or another, presided over a coalition of the leading democratic states in the world. It has built one permanent multinational alliance, NATO, and has deepened its relationships with allied or friendly states around the world on a bilateral basis. American officers and officials take it for granted that when they visit the Pentagon or a US military headquarters in the field, they will encounter individuals in foreign uniforms working alongside their American counterparts, and generally, in mutually respectful harmony. While the occasional friction over, on the one hand, over-bearing American influence, or on the other, "caveats" (restrictions on the use of foreign forces imposed by their governments) occur, such sentiments pale in significance compared to the habit of cooperation. America's allies often find their superpower partner irritating, but no other country in the world has the experience, the capabilities, and the mere routine tact to make an alliance function effectively. That is why there are very few militaries in the world, and none of those allied to the United States, that are not eager to work as closely as possible with it.

The American alliance network spans the globe. It includes the most advanced economies and some of the most formidable militaries in the world. Considered as a portfolio, however, the weight of certain assets has decreased, while others have risen. In 1988, for example, the big three European powers—France, Germany, and Great Britain—accounted collectively for 12.5 percent of global defense spending. By 2014 they accounted for barely 9.5 percent. At the same time, Japan's spending, once below that of the main European powers, had passed all of them but France, and was continuing to grow as a share of global defense spending.[44]

Perhaps America's most important relationship from 1940 on-ward has been the one with Great Britain. During World War II the two countries formed combined headquarters to the most senior levels—the Combined Chiefs of Staff were headquartered in Washington, DC, and senior US leaders felt so strongly about their British counterpart, Field Marshal Sir John Dill, that at their request he was buried in Arlington National Cemetery following his untimely death in 1944. Astonishingly, during the war the two countries merged their most sensitive weapons project (the atom bomb) and most of their intelligence establishments, creating a partnership that has lasted until the present day.

Britain's long retreat from empire, and the erosion of its own domestic consensus for a vigorous role abroad, however, have reduced its military to a remnant of its former self. It retains a modest nuclear deterrent of four missile submarines, although one increasingly in jeopardy from budget cutters. As recently as 2000, for example, the Royal Navy, the leading service in the United Kingdom that once dominated the oceans, had three aircraft carriers and thirty-one major surface combatants. Today it has no aircraft carriers (two are being built, albeit without enough aircraft to equip even one) and only nineteen principal surface combatants. The steep decline of British military power is not merely absolute: it is relative as well. To continue the comparison, the Japanese navy, with two helicopter carriers, forty-five surface combatants and eighteen attack submarines (to six nuclear attack submarines for the Royal Navy) is a much more formidable force. In fact, the Australian military is not that much smaller than that of Great Britain by many measures, despite having a population and an economy about a third the size of the former mother country. The deep cultural and historical ties between the United States and Great Britain, and the latter's prominent (although generally unhappy) participation in the Afghanistan and Iraq wars, have masked the precipitous decline in British military power. It is true that as a matter of habit American political leaders will instinctively hop the plane to London, or at least pick up the phone to call there. There is, however, less and less reason to do so.[45]

Meanwhile, other parts of the American coalitional portfolio have grown in weight. In 1985, no one could have considered India as a country whose strategic interests aligned with those of the United States. Just the reverse: India, though nominally neutral in the Cold War, tilted for a large part of it to the Soviet Union, which provided the bulk of its weaponry. A generation later, the situation is different: the Indian and American militaries conduct joint exercises; the United States sells New Delhi advanced weapons, such as Apache attack helicopters; and most important, both countries recognize a common interest in balancing the rise of an assertive China that New Delhi believes threatens its maritime and even its land frontiers. India and the United States are not allies in anything like the NATO sense and will not be so. Increasingly, however, they are strategic partners, particularly vis-à-vis Beijing.

Smaller American allies have grown in military power and competence. This is true not only of traditional Anglophone nations, such as Australia and Canada, but also of smaller states in the Persian Gulf, particularly the United Arab Emirates. Israel, once a mere client of the United States, is now a medium-size power, with an air force and army larger than that of Germany (440 combat-capable aircraft vs. 237, and 500 main battle tanks vs. 410). Under the pressure of war, a number of American partners have substantially improved their capabilities. Colombia, for example, a country wracked by civil war and in the midst of a crisis in the 1980s and 1990s that threatened the very existence of constitutional government there, has acquired one of the most proficient and battle-tested armies in Latin America. And even an old enemy, Vietnam, has, cautiously and quietly, opened up a path to cooperation with the United States.

The United States in the early twenty-first century remains the world's dominant military power. Its armed forces are large, experienced, well equipped, and well led and trained. It has behind it the best demographics of any developed country, a huge and powerful economy, and a far stronger political system than that of Russia or China—the controls on freedom to criticize the government in those countries testify to that. But it also faces a host of challenges. Its technological edge is slipping, aspects of its higher defense organization have stultified, and its concepts of war may be inadequate. More to the point, it faces an array of actual and potential opponents of a different kind than it faced in the twentieth century, operating under different conditions and with different purposes than did the Soviet Union and its allies during the Cold War. These opponents are diverse, sophisticated, and dispersed: they require different types of forces to match them, and different ways of thinking about military operations to defeat or thwart. It is to those challenges we now turn, beginning with the largest of them: China.

CHAPTER FOUR

CHINA

The first security challenge to the United States that requires a hard power response is not the Islamic State and kindred jihadi movements, which, although they are murderous and have vast ambitions, are highly unlikely to transform the international order in the long run. It is not Russia, although it is one of only two nations that could wipe out the United States with thermonuclear weapons. Russia is a threat to countries on its periphery and a disruptive force globally, but its economic resources and demographic profile doom it to long-term decline. No, America's greatest challenge is China: to balance and prevent it from establishing hegemony over its neighbors and attempting to reshape an international order in its image.

The emergence of China into the center of the global economy and world politics is the most important international phenomenon of the twenty-first century. Given its size, the energy and entrepreneurial spirit of its people, and the depth and strength of its cultural identity, what is remarkable is that its growth was depressed for so long. From 1800 through 1950 Chinese per capita gross domestic product (GDP) probably declined—a staggering result of civil war, mismanagement, corruption, and foreign disaster. The delusional economics and totalitarian fantasies of Mao Zedong continued decades of misery and mass death—Mao was probably the greatest of the twentieth century's killers, beating even Hitler and Stalin. Only with the rise of Deng Xiaoping and the beginning of reform in the late 1970s did China begin the spectacular rise that has, in roughly four decades of nearly 10 percent year-on-year growth, lifted half a billion people out of poverty. That growth has now slowed to less than 7 percent annually, which is remarkable enough. The Chinese economy's deeper problems, including corruption, wasteful investment in infrastructure, excessive government debt, environmental degradation, a mania for secrecy, and the Communist Party's insistence on keeping an iron grip on all means of communication may make matters much worse.[1]

Still, not surprisingly, China's spectacular growth to become the world's second-largest economy has had large strategic consequences. Just how much the Chinese spend on defense remains obscure, and deliberately so, with up to half of the national defense budget being concealed or misrepresented by the Chinese government. The real Chinese buildup began in the 1990s and accelerated in the 2000s, with one expert observer suggesting that year-on-year increases reached nearly 16 percent a year growth—well ahead of even the remarkable growth of the Chinese economy. The upshot is a defense budget that now amounts to $165 billion in 2014 and perhaps $180 billion in 2015—still between a quarter and a third that of the United States, but the second largest in the world nonetheless, and still growing.[2]

And with increased spending and development have come ever increasing military power, particularly in the domains most relevant to the United States—air, sea, and space. The Chinese military of the 1970s and 1980s was a relatively poor, primitive, mass conscript force oriented to territorial defense, and in many cases tied to corporate enterprises remote from the military's real missions. In a series of reforms, the force was reduced in size and internal security hived off to the People's Armed Police (at 660,000 strong, the size of the US Army and Marine Corps combined) and a large, militarized coast guard. China's wealth allowed it to acquire from Russia top-of-the-line air and naval vessels and weapons, and over time it has developed its own robust defense industry. Nor is this merely a case of a newly prosperous country's acquiring weapons that it cannot use. China can now project military power half a world away, evacuating citizens from Libya under protection of its warships in 2011 and from the Yemeni port of Aden in 2015. In neither case did China have to conduct operations under fire, but it was impressive nonetheless. So, too, is the increased ability of the Chinese navy (officially and somewhat confusingly known as the People's Liberation Army Navy, or PLAN) to conduct sustained operations abroad. And on top of this, China has begun moving to establish bases abroad, beginning with Djibouti on the Horn of Africa, which is already home to American and French military bases.[3]

The modernization of the People's Liberation Army (the umbrella term for all branches of the Chinese military) is dramatic. An air force that in 2000 had slightly over one hundred fourth-generation fighter aircraft (that is, airplanes designed in the 1980s and comparable to the American F-16 or F-15) had six times as many in 2015; a navy with no modern diesel electric submarines or destroyers in 1990 had forty such submarines and nineteen such surface combatants twenty-five years later; an army with no modern tanks in 1990 has nearly 2,700 today. To be sure, China's military development has some way to go; and indeed, it has been exaggerated by its government, keen to project an image of the nation's inexorable and irresistible rise to parity with the United States. Some of the PLA's drawbacks remain: it is still a conscript force, limited by two-year military service, and without the kind of strong noncommissioned officer corps that is the backbone of Western militaries. The Chinese inventory contains many obsolescent items, from helicopters to frigates, fighter planes to artillery pieces. Still, not since the rise of the United States as a global power in the period from World War I through 1945 has the world seen such a growth in one country's military spending, and with it, military power. The process of modernization continues, to include a redesign of the PLA's organization and high command.[4]

This dramatic and sudden acquisition of military power has alarmed China's neighbors even as it has intoxicated Chinese public opinion. Its emphasis on the radiation of power outward from China's sea frontiers east and south is historically unusual for a country that has expanded west and southwest toward Asia, and found most of its threats there. No geopolitical challenge to the American world role comes close to that posed by the newly prosperous, nationalistic, and sometimes belligerent Middle Kingdom.[5]

China today is a strategic problem for which there is no real precedent in America's past. In particular, the often raised analogies with the twentieth-century Cold War with the Soviet Union are only misleading. For most of the Cold War—certainly, from the 1960s onward—no one could think that the Soviet economy was more productive than the American one. Although as a system it had pockets of excellence in both civilian areas (e.g., metallurgy) and military manufacture, it became increasingly clear that the USSR was sclerotic. The Chinese economy in the early twenty-first century is very different. By some measures it was as large as, or even slightly larger than, that of the United States by the end of 2014; by others, it had some distance to go.* Even if that moment were deferred, and perhaps indefinitely so, China had clearly become the world's second-largest economy by the second decade of the twenty-first century, surpassing Japan. Chinese enterprises, aided by a mercantilist state, are voracious and aggressive in carving out markets for both export and import.[6]

The Chinese economy's structural weaknesses, such as the rapid aging of its population and the limits of a system built on excessive capital spending, slowed the pace of economic growth from double digits to 7 percent or less by 2015. No matter: an economy worth over ten trillion dollars by 2015 had the wherewithal to produce a great deal of military hardware, and so it did. Modern conventional and nuclear submarines, advanced fighter aircraft, and above all, sophisticated ballistic and cruise missiles are flooding into Chinese arsenals. Moreover, a focused campaign of modernization has left China with a military that is, while still plagued with corruption, increasingly modern, capable, and professional. The upshot, by the early twenty-first century, is a rival whose long-term military potential does not parallel that of the Soviet Union.[7]

China takes a distinctive approach as well to conflict. The Soviet Union, animated by Marxism and Leninism as well as traditional

---

* The critical question is whether one measures "purchasing power parity" (which takes into account, for example, that a haircut costs a lot less in China than in the United States, but is still a haircut) or GDP as measured by exchange rates. The argument is technical, and in this case, not all that important.

Russian approaches to war, became familiar to the United States, particularly once the government and academe had invested considerable
efforts in studying it. Chinese strategy, by way of contrast, has long
seemed (and to some extent is) very different, and has arguably received less attention. Military organizations reflect the cultures from
which they emerge, and Chinese culture is very different from that of
the West.[8]

Understanding Chinese strategy, and the appropriate American response, is made more difficult by myths—some consciously concocted
and spread by the Chinese government, some rooted in American
romantic conceptions of China. Until very recently, the most difficult
problem was the simple unwillingness of American political and military officials to admit that China was a strategic problem. For years,
US military leaders have discounted, or at least put off far into the
future, a Chinese military challenge. Admiral Samuel Locklear, former
commander of the Pacific Command, went out of his way in 2014 to
warn Americans against "talking ourselves into conflict with China,"
after having previously declared that the greatest security threat in Asia
is climate change. General James Cartwright, former vice chairman of
the Joint Chiefs of Staff, declared in 2012 that "Russia and China are
not enemies of the United States." For decades, from the 1990s to the
present, US officials as well as commentators would insist that China's
military was too obsolete, too poorly trained, or too badly supported
to pose a challenge to the United States. In 1999, for example, the
otherwise cautious Admiral Dennis Blair, commander in chief of the
Pacific Command, said that "China would not represent a serious
military threat to the U.S. for at least 20 years." This is palpably no
longer true.[9]

The second, more insidious argument was that to talk about China
as a strategic challenge to the United States would turn it into one.
This, indeed, seems to have been the trap into which Admiral Locklear fell. This form of intellectual folly afflicts contemporary American
strategic thought in a number of ways. It conflates what it is politic to
say in public with what one conceives truth to be in the real world. It
invokes a quest for "strategic trust," as Admiral Michael Mullen put
it, when a colder calculation of interests, intentions, and capabilities

is more in order, particularly from those charged with developing the armed forces. The practice of hoping that if you refrain from mentioning a problem, it ceases to be a problem, is particularly worrisome because few political or military leaders are as capable of doublethink as cynics might think. After a routine of publicly denying that China is in a strategic rivalry with the United States, very few are capable of believing the opposite, and acting accordingly, in private.[10]

The deeper strategic silliness is that the Chinese government and military have no such inhibition in describing the United States. There are the colorful but unrepresentative writings of pundits who are not particularly senior (but popular nonetheless), such as Senior Colonel Lieu Mingfu, who argues that China must be able to contain the United States. Considerably more important are official documents, such as "China's Military Strategy," whose latest version lists the US rebalance to the Asia-Pacific region as the first of "multiple and complex security threats" facing China. The rebalance, an initiative of the Obama administration, does not represent a major military buildup. It has involved some minor deployments (e.g., of Marines to Darwin, Australia), warming ties with the Philippines, arms sales to Vietnam, and closer cooperation with such US allies as Japan in training and the like. The "rebalance" (which occurred under conditions of static or declining US defense spending) in no way compares with the much larger naval shift to the Pacific that occurred in the late 1930s through 1941 under the Roosevelt administration. But still, the Chinese declare it a major threat.[11]

Sensible strategic discourse about China is further hampered by the Communist Party's shrewd and consistent propaganda about the Chinese past. If there is one consistent theme there, it is the unjust sufferings of China during the "century of humiliation" from the Opium Wars through World War II. The sense of outrage and demands for apologies are cynical, in that the Chinese government dials them up and down as needed. For example, in the 1980s and early 1990s the Chinese government was quite willing to forget Japan's depredations on the continent during World War II, so as to secure Japanese investment and technical expertise. But Chinese grievance nationalism, and the insistence on ritual forms of obeisance (apologies and formal acknowledgment of the county's cultural or political superiority) are also part of Chinese strategic culture. There is a certain continuity in contemporary Chinese officials insisting on their country's moral superiority as a victim, and the old imperial court's requirement that foreigners kowtow before securing benefits. Knowing little of China's actual history, many Americans accept these assertions whole, when the reality is far from the morality tale of Chinese government spokesmen.[12]

No country has as rich a strategic culture as China, a civilization molded and wracked by war over millennia. This too poses a challenge, particularly for a United States that is prone to regard China as culturally exotic. In the decade following the Korean War, American popular culture captured a variant of this in such movies as *Pork Chop Hill* (1959) or *The Manchurian Candidate* (1962), in which Chinese skills at psychological warfare were portrayed as little short of fiendish. This tendency to paint China in terms of the mysterious Orient is reinforced by the popularization of Chinese strategic literature, such as Sun Tzu's *The Art of War*, or pithy proverbs ("kill the chicken to scare the monkeys" or "kill with a borrowed knife") that play to what one might call the Fu Manchu conception of Chinese military power. It is easy to construe Chinese military thought as a kind of occult wisdom before which American naïveté and muscle-bound strength are powerless.[13]

The only serious conflict between the United States and China thus far was during the Korean War, which showed the reality and power of the Chinese strategic style, but also its limits for any future contest between the two countries. The war had begun with a Soviet-supported North Korean invasion of the South, and a response by a United Nations force under the command of the United States, which provided the bulk of forces sent to Korea. In the late fall of 1950 Mao Zedong, overcoming the wariness of some of his fellow leaders of the newly created People's Republic of China, launched the People's Liberation Army against American and South Korean forces that had smashed the North Korean People's Army, reversed its invasion of the South, and were approaching the Yalu River on the border between Korea and China. In a sudden blow on October 25, PLA forces struck at isolated American and South Korean units, and then suddenly withdrew into the hills. Following classical Chinese doctrine, they had "agitated the enemy to determine his shape." The sharp, sudden attacks enabled the Chinese to take the measure of both Americans and South Koreans. By using dispensable troops—former Nationalists who had belatedly come over to the Communist side—they helped obscure their own capabilities.

On Thanksgiving Day 1950, the real counterattack began. The Chinese light infantry forces in their hundreds of thousands had denied their enemy knowledge of their real whereabouts through extraordinary march and camouflage discipline. They were, as Sun Tzu would have put it, "without shape." When they attacked, it was not so much in the manner of human waves, as the overheated imagination of newspaper reporters believed, but again, as Chinese military culture would suggest, by surrounding isolated units, harassing and intimidating the American troops at night with grass fires, drums, and bugles, causing them to break rather than be overwhelmed in direct combat.

It was a triumph of the Chinese way of war against a highly mechanized, conventional, road-bound Western enemy, one might think—and so it was, but only up to a point. The Second Infantry Division of the United States Army withdrew in disorder; Regimental Combat Team 31 ("Task Force Faith"), a 3,000-man unit, was destroyed; South Korean units fell apart; and the UN forces withdrew. But when the Chinese came up against the carefully prepared First Marine Division at the Chosin Reservoir, the results were very different. With meticulously coordinated fires and air power, the Marines destroyed at least five Chinese divisions as they withdrew with their supplies, their wounded, and their dead. In the ensuing combat in Korea, the PLA lost as many as a quarter of a million men. Under a new commander, General Matthew B. Ridgway, in the spring of 1951, the American Eighth Army, which did the bulk of the fighting, pushed the PLA back to the 38th parallel—and could have gone farther. It was not coincidental that in the wake of Korea, the PLA invested heavily in the conventional military power—tanks and airplanes in conventional units—that it had dismissed earlier.[14]

This happened more than sixty-five years ago. Neither the American nor the Chinese militaries today look anything like the forces that clashed in the winter of 1950. But the story of the Korean War stands as a double caution. It shows, on the one hand, that there is indeed a distinct Chinese military culture, different from that of the West and particularly of the United States. That war demonstrates, moreover, that that mode of war—indirect, psychological, rooted in camouflage, deception, and patience—can be very powerful. But, on the other hand, it reveals as well the limits of that approach when opposed by an alert, resolute, and well-organized adversary. As Edward Luttwak has pointed out, throughout history Chinese strategists have repeatedly failed to assess their environment correctly, and muster the resources to meet the threats they faced, not despite Chinese strategic culture, but because of it.[15]

China's proclivity for psychologically oriented uses of military force is revealed by other examples—most notoriously, the 1979 border war with Vietnam, in which China took tens of thousands of casualties to "teach Vietnam a lesson," as Deng Xiaoping put it. China's gradual extension of its grip on the South China Sea—by building half a dozen islands, gradually turning them into military bases, issuing extensive claims, conducting ever increasing air and naval operations—is an example of a subtle and effective use of military power to shape political realities. And lest the locals miss one of the key points, the *People's Daily* website noted that the Chinese Coast Guard's newest ship—at 12,000 tons, the size of a modern destroyer—"has the power to smash into a vessel weighing more than 20,000 tons and will not cause any damage to itself when confronting a vessel weighing under 9,000 tons. It can also destroy a 5,000-ton ship and sink it to the sea floor." This last—a celebration of muscle not heard from other Coast Guards, including the American—was a message to such countries as Vietnam and the Philippines, whose coast guard vessels displace 1,000 tons or less.[16]

To come to terms with China's military rise, American strategists must recognize that they confront an opponent with a unique and powerful, but far from invincible, strategic style. Chinese strategy can be subtle, menacing, or downright brutal in ways that are unfamiliar to Americans, whose strategic conduct can have the same qualities, but in different ways. That does not necessarily make it any the more effective: merely different, and requiring understanding as such.

The People's Republic of China is run by a Leninist party, whose chief concern is perpetuating its own hold on power and developing national power. The opening up of China following the death of Mao Zedong and the destruction of radical elements led by his wife came to an end in 1989 with the crushing of demonstrations on Tiananmen Square at the cost of several thousand lives. From that time it became apparent that the Communist Party would tolerate no challenges to its authority, no questioning of its rule, no alternative bases of power, no political or civil rights secured by an independent judiciary and no free expression of opinion.[17]

China's leaders seem to believe, moreover, that their country is on a rising trajectory, while the United States is in decline. Periodically, however, they have been shaken by American resilience and unpredictability, and even more so, by demonstrations of American military power, as against Iraq in 1991, Serbia in 1995, and again in Afghanistan in 2001 and Iraq in 2003. They have studied carefully not only the technological dimensions of these conflicts but also psychological, public opinion, and legal warfare—the soft elements of power that, in their view, paralyzed Iraq by delegitimizing its government and demoralizing its armed forces before the United States defeated it twice. Indeed, not the least impressive quality of the Chinese communist leadership is its proclivity to study large political and strategic problems seriously, including by conducting collective study retreats by senior leaders provided with scholarly reports from which to work.[18]

That leadership's worldview is in important respects at odds with the conception of world order that the United States helped create after World War II. Rather than recognizing a state system based on equality and sovereignty, and an economic system built around globalized free trade supported by the rule of law, it has a hierarchical conception of international relations, particularly in Asia. It may be too much to claim, as some do, that China has a secret, carefully worked out plan to replace the United States as a global hegemon.

Such claims usually minimize China's enormous internal troubles and exaggerate the degree to which any country's leaders can conceive and concert a long-term plan. They also underplay the sense of insecurity that has led hundreds of thousands of wealthy Chinese to send money and family members abroad. More important, they underestimate the degree to which Chinese leaders are preoccupied by internal stability, the immediate security of their borders, the counterpoise of the United States, and broader international challenges—the multiple rings of threat described by Andrew J. Nathan and Andrew Scobell in *China's Search for Security.* But the basic incompatibility between American and Chinese worldviews is real, nonetheless, and may be exacerbated by the rise of a more dictatorial, repressive, and belligerently nationalistic leadership, as appears to be the case today.[19]

Undoubtedly, China's ever increasing openness to the world, its citizens' ability to study and live abroad, and to even, albeit to a limited degree, access the riches of information available in the Internet age, pose a long-term challenge to the regime. The legitimacy of the Communist Party rests on prosperity and national self-assertion, not on an economic doctrine that was false in the nineteenth century, failed in the twentieth, and is ludicrous in the twenty-first. But the party retains control, and having witnessed the demise of the Soviet Union—and having studied it carefully—it will fight to the death to remain in power. It may try to reform itself spasmodically, as recurrent waves of corruption prosecutions have suggested; however, in the end, as some formerly more sanguine observers have concluded, it will not be able to do so. But this is cold comfort from an American point of view, because a Communist Party facing a threat to its existence may well be tempted to play, as it often has in the past, to a belligerent nationalism that it cannot control.[20]

American commentators and decision-makers make much, and perhaps too much, of China's long-term calculations. The story is told of Henry Kissinger's asking Zhou Enlai about the impact of the French Revolution, and being told, "It is too early to tell." In the usual version, this response epitomizes the patience, caution, and even the farsightedness of Chinese statecraft. In fact, Ambassador Chas Freeman, the interpreter for the talks, revealed years later that Zhou had understood the question as dealing with recent French student riots, the consequences of which were as unknown to any Western diplomat as they were to him. As Westerners learn more about the vast failures of Chinese demographic, environmental, and even economic policy, they may moderate their views of Chinese subtle and farsighted shrewdness—which should have been called into question by China's alienation of almost all of its neighbors during the early twenty-first century. There are reasons to doubt the statesmanship that caused China brutally to suppress its birth rate to one per couple and now faces rapid and ruinous aging, whose capital city's air is dangerously unbreathable, and that builds spanking new cities with no employment for those who might live there. This more realistic picture of subtly effective Chinese statecraft, however, does not make China any less problematic as a strategic rival.[21]

Although the Chinese Communist Party's broader goals are troublesome enough, it is its ambitions in the South China Sea that, together with the People's Republic's unrelenting claims on Taiwan, have the most potential to cause direct confrontation between the United States and China. Using the vague "nine-dash line" that would incorporate most of the South China Sea into the mainland's territorial waters, China has made claims that would not only deny other countries access to the riches of the seabed, but would, by constraining commerce, render them vassals to their giant neighbor. It has attempted to consolidate those claims by a vast program of creating island military bases from coral reefs, while using a combination of its militarized coast guard and a fishing fleet—itself, a quasi-civilian maritime militia—to bully and badger lesser naval powers. And it has made clear its determination to disregard rulings by international bodies (such as that of the Permanent Court of Arbitration at the Hague in July 2016) that would restrict its claims to the South China Sea.[22]

China desires, moreover, deference from its neighbors, in a pattern of relationships not dissimilar from those of its imperial past. The point is not to impoverish or subjugate, much less absorb those countries; rather, to ensure that they become part of a hierarchical system at the top of which is the government in Beijing. To achieve this, it is necessary to lever the United States out of east Asia, gradually nullifying its ability to project power there, intimidating its chief allies (e.g., Japan) or seducing them into its own orbit (e.g., South Korea).[23]

This is a multifaceted contest, in which China uses trade deals; the creation of new international institutions (the Asia Infrastructure Investment Bank being the most notable recent example); and "soft power" tools, such as foreign aid and the creation of Confucius Institutes around the world, to influence opinion. But military power rests at the center of the Chinese thrust outward. It was one of the four modernizations—and initially, though no longer, the lowest priority of the four—launched by Deng Xiaoping in 1978, and since the 1990s has been spectacular in scale, speed, and conception.

Some of the Chinese military reforms of the late twentieth and early twenty-first centuries merely laid the groundwork for a modern armed forces—getting the army out of most of its policing functions, for example, as well as out of the management of businesses. Similarly, though less successfully, the Chinese government has struggled with wiping out egregious forms of corruption in the People's Liberation Army. All elements of China's military have been overhauled, as the force has shrunk by nearly half in numbers since the 1980s, while organizations have been consolidated and restructured, and exercises grown larger and more complex.

The larger elements of China's defense modernization are its comprehensive development of four kinds of forces. The first are those that allow China to project force abroad, not so much to contest control of the global commons with the United States, but to show that it has arrived as a global, and not only a regional, power. Beginning with the deployment of a sustained antipiracy patrol in the Gulf of Aden in 2008, the Chinese navy has projected power abroad. It conducts numerous, essentially symbolic exercises and deployments that help create the image of world power. It is in this light that China's acquisition of an old Soviet aircraft carrier, the *Liaoning*, should be understood. The aim here is not to be able to contest American power in some twenty-first-century version of the Battle of Midway—which ended unhappily, after all, for the Asian challenger to the United States—but to deploy one of the great symbols of contemporary naval power. The *Liaoning* will be followed by other ships, indigenously constructed, one of which is already being built.[24]

In one respect, however, China is already a global power, in its ability to conduct cyberespionage and to wage cyberwarfare. While Chinese attacks on American computer networks began in the 1990s, if not earlier, in 2003 several years of the so-called Titan Rain attacks exfiltrated dozens of terabytes of data from American government computers. This was, however, only the beginning. Attacks aimed at stealing the secrets of advanced weapons programs, and American high-tech companies, such as Google, continued. Most recently the personnel records of tens of millions of Americans may have been exfiltrated from databases controlled by the federal government's Office of Personnel Management.[25]

A third element of Chinese military development consists of forces intended to overawe, or simply overwhelm neighbors. An aging coastal defense force has been replaced by an increasingly modernized fleet of ocean-going destroyers, frigates, and submarines. This includes China's coast guard, which operates as an adjunct to the Chinese navy, but chiefly China's land and air forces. In a vast (and environmentally destructive) effort, China has constructed massive air bases on artificial islands in the South China Sea, which it increasingly claims as a form of territorial waters. Nor are such developments confined to the sea frontier. On India's frontier with China in the disputed mountainous region of Arunachal Pradesh, People's Liberation Army patrols periodically enter Indian territory, even as China builds civilian and military infrastructure farther north in Tibet.[26]

Finally, the Chinese have constructed forces designed, in the jargon of defense planners, to "deny access" to American forces operating in the Western Pacific. These include a variety of systems: long-range cruise and ballistic missiles that can target American surface ships and naval bases, as well as advanced torpedoes and mines. The so-called carrier-killer, the DF-21D "West Wind" ballistic missile, with a range of over 800 nautical miles and possibly using stolen American technology, was designed particularly with the United States Navy in mind. Weapons of this kind may make it nearly impossible for the US

Navy to operate close to Chinese territory, and are intended to force the American military (land and air forces as well as warships) back beyond the so-called first island chain (the line running from the Kuril Islands, the Japanese archipelago, Okinawa, Taiwan, and the northern Philippines) to the second (the Pacific Islands, such as the Marianas and Guam) and possibly even to the third (as far as Hawaii).[27]

Experts on the Chinese military sometimes use the term *assassin's mace* for weapons that could disable larger and more complex American systems—antisatellite weapons that could blind American reconnaissance, for example; electromagnetic-pulse weapons that could disable American electronics; and long-range high-speed missiles and torpedoes that could damage or sink American aircraft carriers. Low-tech weapons, such as sea mines delivered by civilian ships, qualify as well. The idea of an assassin's mace is a good example of the strengths and weaknesses of Chinese military thought, its mixture of shrewdness and, in some cases, mysticism. On the one hand, it makes sense to avoid a head-to-head confrontation with a United States using symmetrical capabilities that China does not yet possess, and may never possess. On the other hand, the lure of the assassin is the possibility of defeating an enemy with a single, exquisitely timed and directed blow of an exotic weapon. But military history suggests that such approaches rarely succeed in the way those who conceive them would hope. After all, Japan's massed use of aircraft carriers in the attack on Pearl Harbor did not decide the Pacific War, and Hitler's wonder weapons, including cruise and ballistic missiles and the first jet fighter planes, did not retrieve the fortunes of Nazi Germany in 1944–1945. Of course, China's strategists do not seek war, but hope to deter one. The problem lies in the possibility of their having too much confidence in weapons that are intended to disarm a highly competent opponent at a single stroke.[28]

China, then, is a serious and sophisticated challenger, but has its own weaknesses, misconceptions, and limits, which the United States must understand and can in some measure exploit. In particular, America has three great assets in its strategic confrontation with China: its alliance relationships, the quality of its armed forces, and—if used and explained correctly—its way of war. We have seen that it is difficult to reconcile a belief in masterly Chinese statecraft with the reality that Beijing has done a no less masterful job of stimulating its neighbors into increasingly open hostility to it, and into alignment with the superpower that China hopes to eject from the region. In systematic polling of the populations of Asian countries, Bangladesh, India, Indonesia, Japan, South Korea, Thailand, and Vietnam all viewed the United States as their chief ally. Only Malaysia and the Philippines had a different view, and in the case of the Philippines, the trend of government policy has been in the opposite direction. The most important thing the United States can do—and it is no small task—is to nurture the coalition of countries aligned against China, bolstering their actual strength, their self-confidence, and their ability to work together.[29]

Japan, India, and Australia are medium powers that spend, respectively, $48 billion, $45 billion, and $23 billion each on defense, for a combined total that may be less than half that of China. Still, each has, in the early twenty-first century, embarked on military spending programs aimed (to differing degrees) at countering Chinese hegemony, particularly through expanded submarine fleets. Japan and Australia are close allies of the United States, and India is an increasingly close partner whose range of cooperative activities includes the acquisition of advanced military technology and joint exercises. China has responded by becoming even closer to Pakistan, thereby tying down India and extending Beijing's territorial reach, particularly through its construction of Pakistan's new Gwadar port and a network of roads and rail lines to lead there across Central Asia. But China's deepening relationship with Pakistan, in turn, is just as likely to perpetuate and even worsen the relationship between the two countries with the largest populations in the world.

The Philippines, Vietnam, and Taiwan are much smaller and more vulnerable states directly threatened by China, which claims control of international waters surrounding the first two, and denies the third its right to independent existence. Yet, to a surprising degree, each has been willing to stand against direct pressure. A third category of countries includes Malaysia, Thailand, Indonesia, and Singapore— each with moderate-size militaries, each apprehensive about Chinese ambitions, and each glad to see the United States present in the region to balance Chinese power.

Seen in this light, the only major powers on China's eastern and southern periphery that are on generally good terms with it are South Korea and Russia—and the latter's cooperation with China remains tinged by fear, historical antagonism (Russia, after all, has fought against China more recently—in the late 1960s—than the United States) and xenophobia, which explains Russia's insistence on maintaining a vast arsenal of tactical nuclear weapons directed against its Eastern neighbor. As for South Korea, its animosity toward Japan, driven by history, contemporary rivalry, and some concrete disputes, can be tempered by American diplomacy, and its fear of North Korea keeps it close to the United States to the point of accepting American ballistic missile defense systems that China opposes.

Put together, the counter-Chinese coalition is more than enough to balance the rising power of Beijing. A crude addition of GDPs or defense budgets overstates its strength. There will probably be no formal alliance along the lines of NATO, with its invaluable Article V saying that an attack against one is an attack against all. The interests of the different powers diverge (Australia, for example, has a tremendous economic stake in shipping raw materials to China), and the opportunities for China to drive wedges among its neighbors is considerable. The counter-Chinese coalition is diverse in the size and weight of its members, their political systems (from staid or more rambunctious forms of democracy among the big three to various forms of authoritarian government), and their willingness to openly admit that China is a problem. Still, the opportunity is there for the United States to construct a countervailing coalition that wants to keep it as the counterweight to China, and indeed its overmatch. Moreover, the geography of China's neighbors, constituting a vast island chain off its eastern and southern coasts, means that its access to the sea will always be in jeopardy in the event of conflict. While China has attempted to compensate for this by expanding land routes to Asia and Europe, water remains what it has been throughout history, the main avenue for trade, on which China depends.

That said, there is nothing automatic in the existence of a coalition to balance China, or in its survival. In all of these countries
there are those who favor accommodation with China for a number
of reasons, including the belief that the United States is in decline as
a great power. While few simply wish the United States to throw up
all claims to be an Asian power, there are voices—not all instruments
of Chinese propaganda—who argue that the United States should
choose to "share its supremacy" with China, and that countries like
Australia should try to find an intermediate position between the two
great powers.[30]

In the postwar world, American military diplomacy has become a
separate branch of US foreign relations. Through the creation of regional commanders, to include the Pacific Command (PACOM), the
United States has developed military supremos who play an under-
appreciated role in shaping America's relations with other countries.
Unfortunately, this role, undersupervised by civilian authority, for
decades lent itself to military diplomacy oriented toward the cultivation of good relations with all powers. American military diplomacy in
the Pacific is becoming more avowedly oriented to countering China,
in a way not dissimilar to its role in the Middle East and Persian Gulf
of countering Iran's rising influence. It probably has further to go.[31]

No diplomacy, however, no matter how adroit, can substitute for
real power, which is why the numbers and quality of forces deployed
and deployable to the Pacific matter. A fundamental asymmetry between China and the United States is that the former is in the neigh-
borhood, and the latter projects forces from afar. Even with forward
deployments in Japan, the base at Guam, and the ability to use ports
throughout the region, the fact remains that one ship forward requires
two, and more likely three, back, as crews either prepare for deployments, recover from them, or transit back and forth. Similarly, the
tyranny of distance in the Pacific argues for much greater investments
in long-range aircraft, manned and unmanned.[32]

The American force structure of the early twenty-first century
still reflects the strategic realities of the twentieth. A navy designed
to maintain order globally and to defend the sea lanes to Europe in
the event of war with the Soviet Union is not the same thing as a

navy designed to thwart Chinese aggression. The US Navy has, for example, foregone the long-range strike capabilities that its carriers had through the 1980s, opting instead for a versatile but short-range fighter bomber, the F-35. An air force oriented chiefly on maintaining air superiority in the congested and compact European theater is not one designed to project power across the expanses of the Pacific and into Asia. Although numerous adjustments have been made, more will be required: a navy with many more submarines and an air force with more long-range bombers are the beginning of it. The Navy has assumed that it would not need long-range antiship missiles for its surface combatants, and that more of those combatants could be light vessels, such as the Littoral Combat Ship. For a long time, the Air Force has assumed that its bases would not come under direct enemy attack. Neither set of assumptions should apply in a potential contest with China; and indeed, the Navy is moving hurriedly to put long-range antiship missiles back on all of its surface combatants.[33]

If US strategic success rests on coalition management and force structure, it requires as well an application of—and curiously, an argument on behalf of—the American way of war. That way of war has been shaped by centuries of varied combat in all the domains of conflict; it derives chiefly from Western traditions and is different from that of China. How the two differ may be described in terms of the differences between the two master thinkers of each culture: the Napoleonic-era Prussian officer Carl von Clausewitz and the ancient (and perhaps apocryphal) Chinese general Sun Tzu.

Sun Tzu's theory of war is still widely taught and studied in China, where the Chinese Academy of Military Science holds a roughly biennial conference on the master's thinking. It is an approach that puts a premium on knowledge:[34]

> He who knows the enemy and himself
> Will never in a hundred battles be at risk;
> He who does not know the enemy but knows himself
> Will sometimes win and sometimes lose;
> He who knows neither the enemy nor himself
> Will be at risk in every battle[35]

Sun Tzu aspires to victory without bloodshed ("to win a hundred victories in a hundred battles is not the highest excellence; the highest excellence is to subdue the enemy's army without fighting at all"), and he predicates success on careful positioning, a concept that is deeply rooted in Chinese thinking about the world. The idea of winning at little or no cost persists in top-level, authoritative documents such as *The Science of Military Strategy*, although as history suggests, China can and will accept losses if necessary.[36]

Clausewitz is very different. "War is the realm of uncertainty; three quarters of the factors on which action in war is based are wrapped in a fog of greater or lesser uncertainty." Most information that comes to a commander is false, and in any case, "Truth in itself is rarely sufficient to make men act." Hence, what matters in the fog of war (a phrase he coined) is the ability to size up a situation rapidly, make decisions under conditions of radical uncertainty, and persevere. Although Clausewitz is a sophisticated thinker, he argues for the limits of calculation in war; and he is grim in his description of the limits of human knowledge. Most important, he rejects the notion that actual fighting can be avoided by superior knowledge. "While in war many different roads can lead to the goal, to the attainment of the political object, fighting is the only possible means." It was the Clausewitzian style that stopped the Chinese offensive in Korea, and had Americans been willing to resume the offensive, would probably have allowed them to push the Chinese all the way back to the Yalu. However, the Clausewitzian way is not mere doggedness and brutality. Indeed, Clausewitz begins the very first chapter of the first of the eight books of *On War* by saying that "the maximum use of force is in no way incompatible with the simultaneous use of the intellect."[37]

The key to success of the Sun Tzu way of war is exquisite intelligence about, and understanding of, one's enemy; it must be accompanied as well by operational virtuosity, by a combination of proper positioning (*hsing*), so that one's advance is as effortless and fluid as water running downhill, and deception: "Warfare is the art (*tao*) of deceit." Chinese military thought seems to assume that this can be achieved. In contrast, the key to the success of the American way of war is energy and mass: the ability to mobilize forces; adaptability in their application (it is a Western notion, expressed by Clausewitz's countryman Helmuth von Moltke, that no plan survives contact with the enemy); and resilience in dealing with the inevitable shocks, surprises, and stresses of combat. This way of war has become attenuated in some ways as all militaries have become voracious consumers of data (hence the ungainly Chinese term *war under informationized conditions*). But there remains much in it.[38]

Clausewitz is more correct than Sun Tzu. The first step in balancing China, therefore, is not only to follow the Western way of war, but to proclaim its superiority. Indeed, there is a Sun Tzu–like game to be played against Chinese leaders: making the case that their psychological shrewdness, extensive espionage, and supposed operational virtuosity will not compensate for the depth and resilience of the American approach to battle.

Behind this, of course, must lie substance: an American military system that is, in fact, capable of generating large quantities of military power. This requires no small change in how US political and military leaders approach defense. For most of American military history until World War II, the defense of the United States depended on mobilization: a relatively small active force that could be expanded by conscription or mass induction of volunteers. That system was astonishingly successful during the Second World War, in part because of the attention to the challenges of mobilization of material and manpower during the 1920s and 1930s.[39]

This changed in the years after World War II as the United States deployed, for the first time in its history, a very large peacetime standing force, manned first by conscript forces and then, from the mid-1970s onward, by volunteers. As military technologies became more and more complex and exotic, as the armed forces themselves became increasingly comfortable with a smaller force composed of volunteers (the United States had almost 2.5 million under arms in 1960, 2 million in 1990, and fewer than 1.5 million in 2010), the concept of mobilization slipped away. To grow the United States Army during the wars of the early twenty-first century, for example, was a strenuous effort that yielded little more than 100,000 additional soldiers over a decade.

To the extent that America's deterrent power in Asia rests on others' appreciation of its latent, as well as its actual, power, it will need to show its ability to generate large forces in relatively short periods of time—say, within a year or two of the beginning of a conflict. This will not be the same thing as in World War II, to be sure, but parts of it might have the same feel. For example, if demonstration contracts were let that would enable the United States to obtain advanced missiles or unmanned aerial vehicles from US companies not hitherto in the defense business, the Navy and Air Force could show that their standing forces were far from all they had available. The same might be said of the ability to generate space power quickly, by launching large numbers of smaller satellites to replace constellations of larger, more capable systems damaged or destroyed by China's growing anti-satellite systems. The larger point must be that the United States understands that a shooting conflict could last much longer than a week, and that it is prepared for such a possibility.

The Chinese way of war puts a premium on surprise; the temptation that American planners must therefore deny Beijing is one to which the Japanese succumbed in December 1941—that is, the lure of a sudden surprise attack to disable its larger opponent. To the extent American forces are concentrated in mega-bases in the Pacific well within the range of Chinese missile and air forces (particularly in Okinawa and Guam), this becomes a greater danger. It will become even more so if China can develop weapons that are particularly suitable to Pearl Harbor–type attacks—hypersonic missiles, for example, that can travel several thousand miles per hour and be almost impossible to intercept, at least in their final phases of flight.

The key to American strategy in the Asia Pacific region is a powerful navy and air force that can reassure, strengthen, and protect its allies, and cripple China by blockading its ports and disrupting its commerce. The former is essential to the challenge of balancing China with a coalition, the latter to threatening China's critical weakness—the legitimacy of a regime dependent on economic prosperity. Moreover, in light of China's interest in attacking space-based systems (including a test reported in 2007 against one of its aging weather satellites), the United States must retain the ability to use space, while denying it to an opponent that is increasingly dependent on access to the heavens. Yet even as the PLA has embarked on its extraordinary buildup, there has been a steady decline in US forces deployed in the Pacific since 1990: from 170,000 service personnel down to 130,000, but more important, a decline in naval forces, particularly aircraft carriers (7 to 5); cruisers and destroyers (51 to 45); and attack submarines (44 to 30). Given the deployment cycles of ships (one forward, one recovering, one transiting), the raw numbers of vessels matter, no matter what their individual capabilities are. A substantial naval and aerial buildup in the Pacific, along the lines envisioned by the bipartisan National Defense Panel, is urgently needed.[40]

To raise the issue of whether a war between China and the United States could occur is often confused with wanting one. That is a logically absurd and strategically irresponsible proposition. Wars become more likely when one side decides that the possibility is so awful that it will refrain from thinking seriously about them. That said, it is difficult to imagine why either country could deliberately choose a large-scale war, with all of its attendant costs and perils. As a status quo power, the United States is averse to large-scale warfare; so, too, in a different way, is China, which tends to use force to signal and coerce without crushing. A strategic culture that talks about leaving a "golden bridge" upon which an enemy may retreat is unlikely to choose a head-to-head conflict.

But war may come without either side willing it from the beginning. The political conditions for conflict begin with atmospherics: Chinese decision making that might be shaped by nationalism that has been stoked in a controlled press and educational system, and without the benefit of internal domestic opposition. Moreover, Chinese leaders, and to some extent its military, intoxicated by their newfound capabilities and the vast quantities of fresh hardware at their disposal may make more belligerent choices. This risk is all the greater because China has not fought a war since 1975—a smallish border conflict with Vietnam. That costly, limited war achieved its main purpose of signaling to a weaker neighbor that it should not trifle with the giant to the north, but it in no way prepared China for contemporary war. China's lack of real experience of war may facilitate more than inhibit Beijing's propensity to use force.

On the American side, a prolonged period of reticence in supporting its allies, followed by a hard or even desperate swing back to Asia, could set the stage for a forceful response to Chinese provocation. In some cases, it is the United States that is the least predictable of opponents, shifting, as it seems, between weakness and strength, withdrawal and firmness. It may be easier to miscalculate Washington's intentions than Beijing's.

What might trigger conflict? Perhaps an incident akin to the collision between a Chinese fighter plane and an American signals intelligence–gathering aircraft in 2001. In such cases, however, the instinct on both sides has usually been to tamp down an immediate clash and, in a frosty but reasoned way, to prevent a descent to war. Still, it should be recognized that the opportunities for an escalating clash of arms are there—over American ships and aircraft in the vicinity of China's coast or its claimed man-made islands in the South China Sea, as a result of the destruction or damaging of American spacecraft, or through a cyberattack of the kind that is increasingly prevalent from China.

Considerably more consequential might be a clash between China and its neighbors that brought the United States into play. In particular, should China decide to directly challenge Japan's claims to the Senkaku Islands (known to the Chinese as the Diaoyu Islands), and should Japan resist, the United States would be bound by treaty obligations to come to Japan's aid. Similar obligations bind the United States to other allies—for example the US-Philippine Mutual Defense Treaty of 1951. A Chinese attack on Taiwan—improbable but not inconceivable—would similarly bring the United States into a conflict. The credibility of American power throughout Asia would be at stake; nor would the material consequences be trivial. With a superior technological base and a GDP that puts it in the top twenty world economies, Taiwan is an important geopolitical prize.

China's relentless encroachment on the maritime and aviation rights of others in the South and East China Sea is probably the most worrisome potential trigger of global war in the early twenty-first century. Its steady pushing of island creation and base building; its militarization of those bases with surface-to-air missiles, antiship missiles, and combat aircraft; and the extension of efforts to control the air space in the East and South China Seas could breed a shooting war. The issues of sovereignty are weighty enough in themselves. Upon them depend not only the economic independence of such countries as the Philippines, but in some measure a global order of free use of the great commons of humanity for the purposes of peaceful trade. Behind them, moreover, is that great intangible of international politics: credibility. A United States that allows smaller allies to be bullied into submission by China will have very little left.

An accidental or nearly accidental clash between American and Chinese forces at sea, in the air, or in space, would have its reputational dimension; but the consequences of a conflict between China and an American ally or partner would be far more perilous because the stakes would be higher. American leaders are likely to believe, and with reason, that a failure to back up Japan, the Philippines, or even Taiwan could lead to a complete collapse of the American position in Asia, and forceful measures would need to be taken.

A Sino-American war would be deeply dangerous to both sides: it could even conceivably escalate to the nuclear dimension (Chinese generals have issued nuclear threats to the American homeland), though that is unlikely. What is more probable would be a conflict quite different from American wars of the twentieth century. The United States would have no conception, as it did during World War II, of conquering and occupying its enemy, while China would know that a war that damaged its economy severely would endanger its regime. The United States would probably choose to limit the war's geographical dimensions and functional scope (no cyberattacks on civilian targets, for example); China would conceivably attempt a disarming stroke along the lines of the Pearl Harbor attack, if it believed such were possible, or otherwise attempt to use its military power to split the anti-Chinese coalition.[41]

It is not preordained that such a war would be short or long. One can imagine a contest for control of the first island chain interspersed by Chinese sallies against the opposing coalition, with spasms of violence intended to intimidate or split apart the opposing forces. American strategy might rest chiefly on disrupting Chinese commerce (particularly oil imports) in the hope of affecting Chinese domestic politics—but it is unlikely that such a conflict would be confined. US forward bases, and even in some ways the American homeland, would be under attack—through cyberwarfare, if nothing else. How such a conflict would interact with instability in China itself, and with domestic opposition to the war in the United States, is unknowable.

The outcome of such a war is, at this time, also impossible to forecast. A reasonable observer in 1941 would probably have concluded that a Japanese attack on the United States was likely to end as it did, in a catastrophic defeat for a country that had barely 15 percent the GNP of the giant it had attacked. The imponderables here are much greater: even the coalition that might come to bear is uncertain. Russia, which has provided China with much of its most modern military technology, might openly side with China—but it might also hesitate in contributing to an outcome that would leave China dominant in Asia, with Russia left alone and vulnerable.

Obviously, the best outcome is to avoid war altogether. But the deterrent posture necessary to do so will be something very different from that for the Cold War in Europe. The challenge here is quite different: to convince a rising, assertive, and yet vulnerable peer of the United States that attacks on its neighbors would in the end not only fail, but endanger the regime that launched them. And that will only be accomplished by an American force structure, alliance system, and mobilization capacity that makes such attacks self-evidently unwise.

At the same time, American strategists will have to counter—to include by lampooning—China's relentless psychological warfare, which attempts to project an image of power that is beyond China's realities. The greatest danger of Sun Tzu–like thinking lies precisely in its reliance on deception; and if history teaches us anything, it is that those who believe most in the power of fooling others are eventually fooled themselves, particularly by those they understand as naïve or gullible. That fact, coupled with the infectious nature of America's core political warfare capability—the lure of its freedoms and securities of life, liberty, and property, on the one hand, and the undeniable realities of corruption, cover-up, and abuse of power by the Chinese Communist Party—mean that even on Sun Tzu's home turf, so to speak, the United States can play a winning hand.[42]

CHAPTER FIVE

JIHADIS

The hard power challenges posed by America's conflict with various jihadi movements—al-Qaeda, the Islamic State, al-Shabaab, Boko Haram, and others—is in many ways the obverse of those with respect to a rising China. Thus far, the standoff with China has been almost entirely nonviolent; it is a relationship between states; it involves primarily (though not exclusively) conventional forces; and its stakes are prestige, territory, and state influence. It is, in a word, traditional. America's fight with Islamic extremists—let us call them jihadis, as they call themselves—could not be more different: it has been dramatically violent since before the 9/11 attacks; it involves a state taking on nonstate actors and movements; and it spills over into law enforcement domestically and counterinsurgency and counterterrorism abroad. It is anything but a familiar problem.

But what kind of conflict is this, which takes up so much of America's attention to foreign news on the one hand yet, on the other, consists chiefly of a muted staccato of air strikes and commando raids so routine that Americans barely notice them? The first, and nontrivial, question is what to call this conflict. In the wake of the attacks of September 11, 2001, some maintained that the United States—and in some measure, the larger Western world—was at war; others vehemently rejected that term. What was, and remains, at stake in the choice between two monosyllables—*war* versus *crime*—is how we conceive of a conflict that has taken thousands of lives, that did not begin with the attacks of September 11, 2001, and did not end with the killing on May 2, 2011, of Osama bin Laden, the man who inspired and directed the attacks on New York and Washington nearly ten years earlier. The underlying differences in approach and understanding of those on either side of this question remain relevant today.

The issue arose almost immediately after the 9/11 attacks. For example, then secretary of state Colin Powell, at a press conference two days after the attack, had the following exchange with a journalist:

QUESTION: You spoke about building a coalition and you talk about tools such as the NATO Article V and the UN resolution, are you speaking about war in a legal sense? Are you ready to declare war on this candidate, Usama bin Laden? Or another candidate? And are you expecting these organizations to join you much as you did during the Gulf War in such a war? And are you worried that using the language of war would carry with it specific guidelines as per war that you're not willing or able to follow?

SECRETARY POWELL: I am speaking about war; the President is speaking about war as a way of focusing the energy of America and the energy of the international community against this kind of activity. And war in some cases may be military action, but it can also be economic action, political action, diplomatic action and financial actions. All sorts of things can be used to prosecute a campaign, to prosecute a war. And we will be looking at every tool that we have, every weapon that we have to go after terrorism and to go after these specific organizations.[1]

A case for the term *crime*—or at least something other than *war*—was made at the time, however, and it was put most powerfully by the dean of English-speaking military historians, Sir Michael Howard. One line of argument (not so much Howard's) held that simply to use the word *war* was to run the risk of generating a generational conflict between believing Muslims everywhere and the United States. In a similar vein, careless use by American leaders of the word *crusade*, some argued, would play into the hands of Islamic radicals who hope to recruit others to their cause.[2]

Howard's take was different: that what happened on 9/11 was not war but some other kind of conflict, much more akin to crime—an "emergency" perhaps, the term British officials used for the communist insurgency in Malaya the 1950s, but not war. That is to say, it should be viewed as a conflict waged by police and intelligence agencies, far less so by armies and air forces; a conflict waged by states against an organization, or perhaps a web of organizations, not a fight between recognizable political entities. A variant on this approach is thinking of Islamic terrorism as analogous to a chronic medical condition to be limited and alleviated, but not as a war in which victory is even the right way of thinking about success. More than one writer on this subject believed that using the term *war* played into the hands of the terrorists by making them out to be a bigger problem than they really were or could ever be. In 2001, 42,000 Americans died in traffic accidents—fourteen times as many as perished in the 9/11 attacks. And indeed, President Obama is said frequently to remind his staff of this fact.[3]

In the post–Cold War world, it is common to argue that calling something by its name is to risk inflaming the problem, a contention put forward with respect to China as well. Even if one thought this were true, however, the prior question has to be, "what *are* we actually dealing with?" Conceivably a prudent statesman might then decide not to call something by its true name, but it would be folly not to allow oneself to *think* about it. First, we must understand the world as it is, and then decide whether it is safe to describe it according to that understanding. As we shall see, there is a stronger case to be made that one should publicly describe things by their names.

The argument that the conflict with radical Islam is simply not a war, from the analytical point of view, is wrong chiefly because it assumes an excessively narrow conception of war framed by the history of Europe from the mid-seventeenth century onward. It is a notion of war in which states predominate, in which conflicts have clear beginnings (often through a formal declaration of war) and endings (usually through some negotiated peace), and in which even insurgencies aim at the creation of states conceived like other states. Thus, the Irish revolt against Great Britain at the end of World War I aimed not at

protracted turmoil or revolution per se, but at the creation of an independent country, which is one reason why the Irish Republican Army
adopted all the trappings of the military against which it fought, to
include military ranks, organizations (brigades), and a general staff. It
was planning on creating a new state.

There is indeed something to the proposition that jihadi terror
is crime. It can be countered by some of the tools of law enforcement. The courts have an undoubted role to play in prosecuting those
who engage in it. There is certainly a need for the kinds of programs
(known by the unwieldy term *counterradicalization*) akin to community crime prevention efforts. But in the end, to shy away from the
term *war* is to misunderstand the nature of this conflict. The violence
used by such groups as al-Qaeda, or the Islamic State, or Boko Haram,
and others has some elements of sheer sadism and blood lust, but it is
ultimately purposive, and has a political aim. Criminals may join such
movements, but they have been known to join regular armies as well.
What distinguishes war from crime is whether the participants have
objectives that go beyond the desire to either hurt or achieve material
gain. By this standard, the jihadis are very much at war. And far from
being cowards (an epithet often thrown at them), many have been
exceptionally courageous and self-sacrificing in the pursuit of their
cause. It does no good to pretend anything else.[4]

Nor does it do any good to use such words as *extremist* while
avoiding the term "Islamic" in characterizing the enemy. Jihadis' self-
understanding is wrapped in religious faith, and it is both strange and
presumptuous to assert that agnostics, atheists, Christians, and Jews
understand their enemies' beliefs better than they do. Accepting that
this is, in fact, a religiously rooted conflict is profoundly unsettling
for today's Western elites, who much prefer to understand conflict
in purely secular terms. (Even during the Troubles in Ireland during
the 1970s, there were those who insisted that the struggle could not
be between Protestants and Catholics, but had to be understood as
a product of class.) Jihad is holy war, and although it may be desirable for Muslims and non-Muslims alike to redefine or reinterpret
it as a struggle for self-improvement, holy war it has been since the
earliest days of Islam. As Bernard Lewis, one of great students of the

contemporary Islamic world, wrote in 1988, "The overwhelming majority of classical theologians, jurists, and traditionists, however, understood the obligation of *jihād* in a military sense, and have examined and expounded it accordingly." For hundreds of millions of Muslims, *jihad* means an internal struggle rather than bloody encounters with unbelievers. But indubitably, for many of those who waged and continue to wage war in Afghanistan, Bosnia, Chechnya, and later in Iraq, Syria, Yemen, and indeed Europe and the United States, *jihad* means just that: holy war.[5]

Religious war is war, but the Western world's near-paralytic fear of using the word *crusade* inhibits it from learning the lessons of that gory struggle. The Crusades, after all, were a series of wars that went on for generations, indeed very nearly two centuries. They involved curious alliances and coalitions, including some that spanned the religious divide (there were Christian lords and Muslim vassals, and vice versa, in the Holy Land), yet some of the bitterest conflicts were within common faiths (the brutal Crusader sacking of Christian Constantinople during the Fourth Crusade in 1204 being the most notorious case). It was a conflict that involved states and statelets, mass mobilization, and new transnational organizations; crusading orders, such as the Hospitalers and the Knights Templar; as well as the sect known as the Assassins, who bequeathed that word to following centuries. It invoked high ideals and realpolitik; it was war, and it was also banditry, plunder, rape, and massacre. It was, in short, a highly complex set of conflicts that roiled the politics of Europe and the Mediterranean for nearly two hundred years. Today, a Christian West (which no longer really exists, in any event) is not crusading against a Muslim East; still, the historical events are worth studying, and some of the parallels worth considering.[6]

The current war will probably be shorter and simpler than the events of 1096–1272 but will incorporate many of the same ambiguities. The former chief of the Australian Army, Peter Leahy, matter-of-factly told his countrymen in August 2014 that Australia was engaged in a hundred years war with radical Islam, a sentiment subsequently echoed by the French prime minister Manuel Valls after the Charlie Hebdo massacres of 2014 in Paris. It is a kind of war that is still not

taught in the war colleges of the West, which tend to focus their curricula on conventional conflicts or traditional kinds of insurgency that
last six days or longer but six years or shorter.[7]

To wage this war wisely, or even with a modicum of success, will
require understanding its roots and its logic. This requirement makes
it different from other wars. In January 1942 it really did not matter to
American strategists planning operations in Europe or the Asia-Pacific
what the imperfections of the Versailles Peace Treaty were, or the psy-
chopathologies of Adolf Hitler, or how the clash between American
and Japanese interests in the Pacific had paved the way for Pearl Harbor. For this war, however, consideration of its roots is as important
as understanding what our situation is now. One of the great failures
of both the Bush and the Obama administrations was the insistence
on caricaturing the enemy as criminals who had "perverted a great religion," as evildoers whose actions were inspired by no recognizable
creed, and whose sole motivation was destruction. An enemy portrayed
this way has no ideology to be understood. Further, if an enemy's
deepest beliefs are also characterized as "bankrupt," we will continue to
underestimate the power of its creed. The enemy's actions will remain
mysterious and its ideology's appeal baffling, unless we take that enemy
seriously—and only then will an effective counterstrategy emerge.[8]

One must therefore begin thinking about this war from the other
side of the hill, seeing the enemy, or rather enemies, as they see themselves. That being the case, one has to understand the motivation
behind the claims of those who are waging holy war in the name of Islam. That faith, like all of the great belief systems, is complex, and has
many streams. It is divided between Sunni and Shia, among the great
legal schools of religious interpretation, and has within it sects that
are austere and others that are tolerant; traditions that are legalist and
rationalist in outlook, and others that are mystical and otherworldly;
and approaches to the rest of the world that are peaceful and accommodating, and others that are belligerent, aggressive, and lethal. It is
an extraordinarily diverse faith. What concerns us here are the violent
and menacing streams, which are as authentic as any others.[9]

Modern jihadi movements tap two sources for their motivation.
The first is a fundamentalist stream of Islam going back at least to early

fourteenth-century theologian Taqi ad-Din Ahmad ibn Taymiyyah, who fled to Damascus from the Mongol armies that had invaded Mesopotamia. He resolutely opposed traditional practices such as pilgrimages to saints' tombs, and was a relentless advocate of the application of religious law. Jihadism is a strand in Sunni Islam, in particular, that was shaped by the conflict with both the invading Mongols in the East, and the Christian world in the West. Nor was ibn Taymiyyah alone in medieval times: the Almohad movement that swarmed from North Africa into Spain in the twelfth and early thirteenth centuries was, like ibn Taymiyyah, as keen to wage holy war against "peoples of the book" as on true pagans, destroying or driving out most of the Jewish communities of Spain that had flourished under the Almohads' far more tolerant Muslim predecessors.[10]

There is a far more modern set of precursors to and ideological exponents of the contemporary jihadi movement. They include modern Islamist movements, such as the Deobandi in India (founded in the nineteenth century) and more recently modern Islamists, such as Sayyid Qutb and, on the side of the Shia, Ayatollah Ruhollah Khomeini. Qutb, an Egyptian intellectual and author whose writings laid the groundwork for much of the modern Islamist movement to include al-Qaeda, was hanged by the Egyptian government in 1966, refusing offers of clemency while saying, "My words will be stronger if they kill me."[11]

Khomeini, who led the revolution that swept away the modernizing monarchy of the Pahlavi shahs in Iran in 1979, was a Shia theologian, and hence, from the view of Sunni extremists, a schismatic, but there is no question that his Islamic revolution inspired even those who loathed his religious creed. For this, among other reasons, the relationship between al-Qaeda and the Islamic Republic of Iran has long been complex, and not entirely conflictual. The 9/11 Commission identified a number of connections between Iran and al-Qaeda, to include sharing of tactics developed by Hezbollah (the Iranian-sponsored Lebanese Shia Islamist movement), but the patterns of wary cooperation go much deeper than that.[12]

Modern Islamists may draw on medieval and earlier inspirations, but in its modern incarnation radical Islam has much to do with the ills of an Islamic world that has felt, with reason, that history had taken a path radically different from that which it believed it had been promised. A Qutb or a Khomeini saw a Muslim world either defeated or humiliated by the West in outright battle, or worse, subjugated by its ideas, its lifestyle, culture, and political ideas. It was not just that Egypt's Gamal Abdel Nasser or Iran's Reza Shah Pahlavi were tyrants whose secret police were brutal; it was that they were unabashedly secular. And in long, roiling waves, from the mid-twentieth century on, the jihadis turned against both heretic regimes and the Western opponent that had, in their view, inspired them. "For a long time now," wrote one scholar in 1990, "there has been a rising tide of rebellion against this Western paramountcy, and a desire to reassert Muslim values and restore Muslim greatness." It was an argument echoed in Samuel P. Huntington's prescient (and highly unpopular) *Foreign Affairs* article "The Clash of Civilizations," several years later.[13]

There can be no accommodation, other than a purely tactical truce (of the kind that the Islamist movement Hamas periodically accepts with the state of Israel) between the radical Islamists and the West. Similarly, the government of the Islamic Republic of Iran can never desire truly friendly relations with the United States; the sources of conflict are existential in nature. And Americans must accept that as long as the United States is the largest and most powerful Western country, it will be squarely in the sights of Islamist groups.

The Islamist groups see themselves as rooted in the Arab world, and indeed, most of their leaders come from it. Certainly, most of the funding for Sunni Islamist movements comes from the oil-rich kingdoms of the Persian Gulf. But they are not confined to there. Their numbers have swelled with recruits from many non-Arab lands, from Afghanistan to Chechnya, from Nigeria to Bosnia, as a result of local conflicts that may have originally been only partly religious in nature, but which have been transformed over time. In 2013, for example, one Norwegian expert estimated that Sunni jihadists from eighty nations numbering between 5,000 and 7,000 had already streamed into Syria to join the war against the largely secular regime of Bashar al-Assad. Meanwhile, Iran has been no less active in recruiting its own "foreign legion" of Shia holy warriors to do battle there as well. In total, by

2015 some 20,000 foreign fighters were estimated to have traveled to Iraq and Syria. This is a larger number than journeyed to Afghanistan in the 1980s for the ten-year jihad against the Soviet Union and its puppet (also secular) government there.[14]

Like the great totalitarian parties of the twentieth century, radical Islam is an international movement. And as was true in the Spanish Civil War of the 1930s, when communism and fascism collided, true believers—as individuals and on behalf of states—came to fight for their cause in a distant land. But where there was only one (if symbolically powerful) Spanish Civil War in the 1930s, here there are several such conflicts. And unlike communism before World War II, radical Sunni Islamists are not dominated by a single state that is entirely cynical in its willingness to sacrifice local interests for the needs of a state. The case of the Shia is somewhat different because of the dominating role of Iran, but arguably, Iran is less willing to sacrifice local Shia interests for Persian national objectives. In short, the international Islamist ideological movement is extensive, varied, and persistent—and has shown a remarkable ability to recruit fighters to battle for its cause.

The Islamist movements are vanguard organizations; that is, they view themselves as an elite among a much larger and supportive public. And they have some limited evidence to support their self-understanding. While most Muslims have a negative view of al-Qaeda, for example, percentages ranging from 5 percent in Turkey to 23 percent in Bangladesh have a favorable view of that group. Overwhelmingly a minority in absolute terms, yet percentages like these indicate that millions of the world's Muslims are at the very least susceptible to the jihadist message of al-Qaeda, let alone those of other, more successful groups.[15]

Perhaps most disturbing of all, the jihadists have reason to believe that they are winning. This has been the hardest notion for Western, and particularly American, leaders to accept. Indeed, for a time in 2011–2013 the president of the United States and his senior advisers declared that al-Qaeda was on the verge of strategic defeat, and President Obama went so far as to tell an audience at the National Defense University that "this war, like all wars, must end," and implied that it was about to do so.[16]

Nothing could be further from the truth. The United States and its allies have racked up a long list of tactical successes, chiefly through the systematic assassination of senior leaders of al-Qaeda and its off-shoots, including in the Arabian peninsula. But on the larger view, the Islamists have reason to think that in fact the world is going their way. Such movements as Boko Haram in Nigeria and al-Qaeda in the Arabian Peninsula are probably larger today than they were in 2005. The Islamic State controls large swaths of Syria and Iraq and is inspiring others as far away as Afghanistan and the United States itself. Indeed, in 2015 FBI director James Comey described the Is-lamic State as a bigger threat than al-Qaeda. Islamist terror attacks in Europe have produced episodic public revulsion, but no less, a quiet intimidation of their enemies. Editor in chief Carsten Juste of Den-mark's *Jyllands-Posten* newspaper, which published a set of cartoons of the prophet Muhammad in September 2005, was asked a few months later about the torrent of threats and intimidation that followed:

> It is almost with a sigh that I say, well, they've won. The fear of trig-gering the things we've experienced: the death threats, people who burn the Danish flag in the West Bank, it is terrible. If you have to look quite soberly on it, then they damn well won.[17]

Islam is now the world's fastest growing religion, on course to overtake Christianity in the next thirty-five years. More important, its growth comes in the context of minority but substantial support for conservative interpretations of religion, to include the support of over four fifths of South Asian and over three quarters of Southeast Asian Muslims for making sharia the law of the state. More chilling are the numbers who favor the harsher provisions of sharia, to include executing apostates from Islam. This does not mean that the majority of conservative Muslims are eager to wage jihad against the West, or that they approve of the activities of those who do. It is to say, how-ever, that the minority that does issue the call to holy war has a very large pool, in absolute terms, from which to recruit and receive other forms of support, such as funds, sanctuary, and information. Fur-thermore, as state structures come under pressure in some countries (e.g., Pakistan) and disintegrate in others (Syria, but other parts of the Middle East as well), it is likely that religion will gather strength as a source of cohesion, meaning, and social organization. It was, after all, by providing basic social services in Lebanon and the Palestinian territories, respectively, that Hezbollah and Hamas established their dominance in both places.[18]

This said, the radical Islamist movements have tremendous—and over a period of decades, crippling—disadvantages. What makes them terrifying also renders them ineffective: their intoxication with violence, embodied in the slogan "You love life, we love death." That saying reflects the sick fascination with killing (to include beheading with a knife, stoning, throwing prisoners off buildings, or burning them alive) that characterizes these movements, and their inability to build much that is constructive or likely to last. Great Muslim conquerors of the past, such as Tamerlane, may have exterminated their enemies, but they were, as well, great builders of empires and the patrons of scholarship and high culture. Today's jihadists offer nothing more than bleakness, paranoia, and a volatile avidity for violence. Where they do gain consent, it is because they provide some kind of stability or protection from schismatic sects, or simply, as in the case of the Taliban's conquest of Afghanistan in 1994–1996, relief from anarchy. In the long run, however, this lack of an ability to build modern societies makes it easier to construct coalitions against the jihadis, and to foster lethal splits among leaders and cliques to whom moderation, tolerance of differences of approach, and accommodation are heresy.[19]

The peculiar nature of the war against radical Islam has led the United States government to fall back on a limited set of military tools, chiefly the targeting of individual leaders. "The tacticization of strategy," the coinage of shrewd strategic thinker Michael Handel, is an ungainly phrase, but it captures well the American response to the jihadi threat. It is the reduction of a large strategic problem to a matter of mere tactics; in this case, the fetishization of one tool, manhunting chiefly with missile-armed drones, took the place of a deeper strategic response. Growing from the experimental mating of low-yield antitank guided missiles with reconnaissance drones, to the systematic arming of large unmanned aircraft with a dozen purpose-built weapons or more, lethal attacks went from several a year before 2008 to a program of over one hundred strikes a year in 2010, before being ratcheted down again in 2013 and after. Complementing such precision attacks were raids for the purpose of killing or capture conducted by US and allied special operations forces.[20]

The technical skill of the air strikes in Pakistan and Yemen, and the virtuosic raid that killed Osama bin Laden in 2011, required a remarkable combination of comprehensive intelligence gathering, rapid analysis, and precision action, all of which were provided in abundance. The experience of waging protracted war in Iraq and Afghanistan honed skills that were already latent: in the United States military the key was not only technology (being able to exploit geolocation of telephone calls, long-loitering drones, precision-guided weapons), but the creation of organizations that could bring intelligence and action together. It was a remarkable achievement in the history of arms: never before had the art of systematic, surgical elimination of individual opponents been conducted on anything like this scale.[21]

Unquestionably, the killing of senior and midlevel leaders of al-Qaeda helped disrupt plots. But it also lulled American decision-makers into complacency. President Obama's counterterrorism adviser, John Brennan, who subsequently became director of the Central Intelligence Agency, declared in 2011 that

> al-Qa'ida and its ilk have been left on the sidelines, watching history pass them by . . . as we approach the 10th anniversary of the 9/11 attacks, as Americans seek to understand where we stand a decade later, we need look no further than that compound where bin Laden spent his final days. There he was, holed-up for years, behind high prison-like walls, isolated from the world. But even he understood the sorry state of his organization and its ideology. . . . We are left with that final image seen around the world—an old terrorist, alone, hunched over in a blanket, flipping through old videos of a man and a movement that history is leaving behind . . . we have put al-Qa'ida on a path to defeat. . . .[22]

Brennan turned out to be wrong on several counts. Bin Laden was in touch with his organization around the world roughly a week before his death, following eagerly the wave of popular demonstrations that overthrew Arab governments from Tunisia to Egypt; moreover, his subordinates described for him "these days of consecutive revolutions" (what some Westerners called "the Arab Spring") as "a great and glorious event" from the point of view of jihadists. Al-Qaeda leadership, according to press reports, were even able to hold undetected conference calls. And even as the future CIA director foresaw al-Qaeda headed to defeat, a new movement that had originated within it—the Islamic State—was taking shape. President Obama subsequently dismissed it, saying, "If a jayvee team puts on Lakers uniforms that doesn't make them Kobe Bryant." Five months later, the triumphant "jayvee team" seized the Iraqi city of Mosul.[23]

If the history of warfare has one lesson to offer, it is that there are no decisive weapons, tactics, or operational concepts. Rather, the law of action and reaction applies, what the British general and historian J. F. C. Fuller called "the constant tactical factor." US leaders were reluctant to acknowledge this, but discovered, over time, that the surgical strikes from unmanned aerial vehicles (UAVs) were unable to do more than temporarily disrupt terrorist organizations. By hard experience, those jihadist movements most closely under the scrutiny of American tacticians learned to conceal the physical and electronic signatures their enemy could target—chiefly by staying far away from anything that emitted on the electromagnetic spectrum. They hid among civilian populations, knowing that drone strikes were unlikely if the Americans believed that large numbers of innocents would perish along with terrorist leaders. And they simply moved into areas that the US military and intelligence communities had less access to. The terrorist assassination campaign worked in countries that put up with it (Pakistan, to some extent, and Yemen) or areas in which there was no effective government. Drone strikes in London, by way of contrast, would be unthinkable, and were less likely even in such countries as Syria, at least until that country disintegrated into chaotic civil war.

The preference for killing terrorists rather than capturing them had something to do with risk and convenience—a snatch operation

being far more difficult than the firing of a missile—but also with
the squeamishness Americans developed over handling prisoners. The
construction of the Guantánamo Bay detention center by President
George W. Bush attracted controversy; despite his frustration with it,
President Obama could not close it, but he sought to winnow down
its inhabitants to the smallest possible number. By treating some terrorist leaders as criminals, with all the rights and procedures associated
with criminal law, and others as targets for mere killing, the United
States lost the opportunities that capture would have offered. In Iraq,
the use of prisons for the gathering of intelligence, for recruiting turn-
coats, and for sowing dissent in the ranks of the other side appeared
only late in the war.

In the case of the greater war with the jihadis, however, American leaders could not bring themselves to make a convincing case
for a policy on incarceration and the systematic and prolonged use
of similar techniques. The controversy over maintaining a prison at
Guantánamo Bay for jihadists too dangerous to let go, but not susceptible to trial in American courts, obscured the larger issue: the need to
use detention facilities as a front in a broader war. At the same time,
assassination brought its own uncomfortable dilemmas, as when in
2011, US missiles killed the charismatic preacher Anwar al-Awlaki, an
American citizen, in Yemen. "An execution without the formalities of
indictment, trial, and sentencing," a journalist called it and so it was.
An inevitable watershed, but a troubling one.[24]

Edward Luttwak has observed that often in war, success breeds, of
necessity, a certain kind of failure. In April 2015 the White House acknowledged that a drone strike that killed several al-Qaeda operatives
also killed an American and an Italian relief worker who had been
held prisoner for three and four years respectively. Journalists depre-
cated the program's mistakes and the president apologized profusely.
America's successful scrupulousness had boomeranged upon it. No
war can ever be waged with exquisite precision, and as a result, civilians, hostages, and innocents will always die. Neither President Bush
nor President Obama had attempted to condition public opinion to
inevitable blunders and loss of life—in part, perhaps because they
themselves were seduced by the promise of perfect warfare—so such

events were misunderstood and misinterpreted. The US military's tremendous strength and skill had been turned into a vulnerability.[25]

The United States waged the counterjihadi campaigns of the early
2000s with one impressive but limited tool, targeted killing, even as
it avoided any larger campaign of political warfare against the jihadi
enemy. This resulted from Washington's reluctance to identify the
enemy correctly to begin with, as discussed earlier. As a result, such
public opinion campaigns as were waged by the Department of State
and other agencies were weak, underfunded, and worst of all, uncon-
vincing. The themes of these programs were ineffective: attempting
to prove that the United States was not hostile to Islam, for example. And thus, in August 2015, the Department of State's Twitter account, @ThinkAgain_DOS, had all of 22,000 followers—compared,
say, with the 316,000 followers of Islamist thinker Tariq Ramadan.[26]

There was a need here for a very focused kind of soft power. The
difference between the confused and ineffective ways in which the
United States waged political warfare against jihadists in the twenty-
first century, and the way in which it had combatted communism in
the mid-twentieth century, could not be more pronounced. There were
no new organizations here comparable to the US Information Agency,
Radio Free Europe, or Radio Liberty. There was no cultivation of intellectuals to attack the opposing ideology directly. There was nothing, in
fact, other than a plaintive desire across two administrations to prove
that the United States was not as bad as many in the Muslim world
thought. And the result of this war unwaged was reflected in public
opinion polling in the Muslim world. In Egypt, for example, only 30
percent of the population had a favorable view of the United States in
2006—bad enough. By 2013 only 16 percent did. A real political warfare campaign would have done more to stir internal divisions in the
radical Islamist camp, turn factions upon one another, and sharpen the
revulsion most Muslims felt for the barbarity of the jihadists.[27]

Failing to treat the war as war, and tackle it as such, led to fateful
strategic misconceptions, and even more fateful choices. One example
was the United States government's misreading of events in the larger
Middle East in the wake of the so-called Arab Spring. On September 11, 2012, American embassies throughout the Middle East were

suddenly attacked: in Benghazi, Libya, which had been liberated from the Gaddafi dictatorship by an American-supported operation led by France and Great Britain. The attacks there on the US consulate culminated in the death of the American ambassador and three contractors. Government spokesmen suggested that the attack was the product of a bizarre six-month-old Internet video, a trailer for a movie that was never made, about the prophet Muhammad—a highly implausible notion, to put it mildly. Having declared repeatedly that al-Qaeda was on the verge of strategic defeat officials could not interpret the black flags flying over American installations for what they were: the emblems of a movement that was very far from dead.[28]

By 2015 the war that one president had hoped to win (in part) through a shock delivered to the Arab world and an appeal to representative government, and that another president had hoped to secure by routine, if selective and exquisitely precise, killing, was not close to success, save in one key respect—preventing another mass attack on the American homeland comparable to 9/11. This owed a great deal to the hardening of US borders and to the antiterror campaigns abroad. But in the rest of the world it could not be said that the war was going well. The United States having disengaged from the region—hastening to leave Iraq, and refusing to engage in the Syrian civil war—chaos crept in behind, as jihadi groups attacked an increasingly authoritarian Shia government in Iraq and the minority regime in Damascus. As Emma Sky, an experienced Iraq hand put it: "[The Islamic State] feeds on a Sunni sense of disenfranchisement and grievance and claims to offer a better future in the form of an idealized past—an unmoored, postmodern Caliphate with globalized ambitions and a new territorial base." In Iraq, the Islamic State established effective control of several major cities, including Mosul, while extending its reach to Europe and beyond. Elsewhere in the Arab heartland of Syria and Iraq, al-Qaeda-like movements were attracting and training terrorists from around the world. In small but growing numbers those foreign fighters returned to their homelands and—as in the Charlie Hebdo attacks of January 2015 and the much larger attacks on the Bataclan theater and other sites in Paris in November of that year—gained the occasional spectacular publicity and success. Similar movements were burgeoning in Libya and in Nigeria; in Pakistan, which had long used jihadist movements as a weapon against India and first Russia and then the United States in Afghanistan, the state itself was threatened by movements it could no longer control. In a larger Middle East whose state structures have in some cases collapsed, and in other cases are at risk, the possibility of serious internal violence remain large.[29]

The jihadists have only intermittently struck in the United States since 2001—the attacks of both Major Nidal Hasan at Fort Hood in 2009 and the bombing of the Boston Marathon in 2013 were the acts of individuals who were not simply loners, but had been radicalized by others, mostly located abroad. Something similar seems to be true of the terrorists who attacked a local public health center in San Bernardino in December 2015. As horrific as these attacks have been for the individuals concerned, they did not affect daily life or endanger the fundamental values of the United States. Still, such attacks, in and of themselves, would be enough to require some kind of governmental response acknowledging that the country was indeed under attack. It may be illogical for citizens to fear terrorist attacks more than car crashes, but it is a psychological and therefore political fact that they do.

What makes the jihadist threat a greater strategic problem, however, is chiefly the possibility that a terrorist movement could acquire weapons of mass destruction, as well as the probability that such movements would disrupt parts of the world whose stability is in America's interest. We know that al-Qaeda has made multiple efforts to acquire chemical and biological weapons—in 2008, for example, one of its experts, an Egyptian chemist with a $5 million bounty on his head, was killed in an American airstrike. He was hardly alone. Home-brewed ricin or anthrax are not inconceivable, although less easily manufactured and handled than is sometimes suggested in the news media. More dangerous and troubling is the possibility of nuclear weapons ending up in the hands of jihadi movements, perhaps with the aid of radicalized technicians or guards, or through an Islamist revolution or coup d'état. Unlikely, perhaps; implausible, by no means.[30]

How, then, to fight such a war? The first and most important step is to shake off inhibitions and misconceptions and speak the truth about this war: that it will go on for decades, if not most likely generations; that it results from a deep cultural and political crisis in large parts of the Muslim and specifically the Arab world; that it is further fostered by the collapse of the Middle East state system; and that it is complicated by the diffused nature of authority in the Sunni world; that the jihadis are brave and determined adversaries, who are very good at what they do, including the arts of propaganda.

Strategic thinking about this war will require a different mind-set than that of other, more conventional conflicts. Military and intelligence officials will have to think about success in the long term; and political leaders will have to accept that they will not rack up dramatic or enduring successes during their tenure in office. Such an honest appraisal itself will test the character of politicians who, naturally enough, hope to end their tenures having won, or at least finished, the wars that they have begun or inherited.

This will be a long war against a dangerous minority element of a major religious faith. Recognizing this, curiously, should reduce some of the pressure to focus excessively on jihadi terrorism at the expense of America's other strategic challenges. For now, the terrorist organizations are too weak to attack the United States directly and systematically. They threaten the stability of important parts of the world, however, and, if armed with weapons of mass destruction, which is conceivable, they could become much more dangerous. Still, part of a new strategic approach to the war with extremist Islam is to reestablish a sense of proportion, treating it as neither a minor threat comparable to traffic accidents, nor an apocalyptic confrontation between cultures.

The direct disabling of terrorist organizations that attack the United States and its allies will have to continue. This means the continuation of targeted killing; it could mean far larger-scale action if such groups are about to acquire weapons of mass destruction or seize control of a state. Otherwise, however, the purpose of lethal operations is to tamp down, disrupt, and limit a virus that cannot, however, be destroyed in this way. The operational purpose is attrition; and although the tactics are offensive in nature, this is an essentially defensive aspect of strategy.

At the same time, what is also needed is a return to capturing and where possible turning leading terrorists. This requires a different approach to incarceration of individuals who may be neither subject to civilian trial nor yet to handling as conventional prisoners of war. In this respect, a strong case remains for keeping the Guantánamo Bay facility open, and for leading other liberal democracies in creating new conventions for handling prisoners in this new and strange form of war. The war with Islamic radicals is in some ways an insurgency, and captured figures on the other side are not only a source of intelligence, but eventually a way to cause splits on the other side.

That leads to the second line of effort: if an enemy cannot be destroyed, to at least divide it. Terrorist movements in general, but the jihadists in particular, are vulnerable to internal division, splits, and intramural violence. In the past there have been spectacular successes using this approach. The most interesting publicly known case is the dismantling of the violent and dangerous radical Palestinian Abu Nidal organization in the early 1970s, which Western intelligence agencies helped turn on itself by fostering lethal paranoia about penetration and betrayal from within. Secretive, violent movements that are prone to squabble about esoteric points of religious faith and doctrine, led by imperious and ruthless men with aspirations to lead hundreds of millions of believers, are vulnerable to brutal internal purges. It is in our interest, through whatever overt or covert means are available, to encourage and enhance those fights.[31]

A third component of strategy involves political warfare—a war of ideas waged on a completely different scale than any conducted thus far. Indeed, if there is a need for soft power understood as something active (rather than the mere presumed attractiveness of the American system), it is here. Until now the purpose of propaganda programs against jihadism has been either "outreach" designed to persuade Muslim communities abroad that the United States is not hostile to their faith, or an effort to persuade individual young Muslims not to join such organizations as the Islamic State. An alternative would be to tackle the ideology of jihadism more directly—its brutality, its bigotry, its misogyny, and its utter inability to deliver a better life. The purpose would be to denounce that ideology, but it should have a positive dimension as well. The themes would not be a preemptive apology for the United States; rather, it would be an assertion of American values—to include tolerance, rights of women, and rule of law—that are inimical to jihadi ideology. This campaign would have the advantage of supporting similar efforts to weaken and undermine other ideological opponents, most notably China and Russia. It would probably mean a mobilization from the private sector not dissimilar to President Kennedy's recruitment of the legendary broadcaster Edward R. Murrow to lead the United States Information Agency during the Cold War. If targeted killing is strategically defensive, this would mean taking the strategic offensive.[32]

Finally, in a few cases, the United States and its allies may have to consider participating in operations designed to secure and stabilize countries won back from, or on the verge of succumbing to, jihadi movements. The bitter aftermath of the Iraq war would seem to prohibit this, but the chaos that ensued when the European powers overthrew Libyan dictator Muammar Gaddafi with American help and then failed to stabilize the country is a counterpoint: even more so are the consequences of the protracted, brutal Syrian civil war.

When—and no less important, how—the United States should intervene are large questions that cannot be decided a priori. It will do no good to pretend, in the wake of Iraq and Afghanistan, that America will never undertake such operations again. Indeed, such self-inflicted amnesia will only ensure that it shall make the old mistakes, or new and worse ones, when it finds itself compelled to intervene again in Muslim lands.

Future interventions will have to take account of the lessons of Iraq and Afghanistan, including the limits on America's ability to reshape foreign societies. What the United States can do, however, is help provide security, develop the armed forces and police that can sustain it in our absence, and provide limited assistance to the reconstruction of government institutions. Expeditions of hundreds of thousands of soldiers will neither be required nor tolerated by the American public, but there are lesser forms of intervention that will. The United States and its allies would have been well advised, for example, to put some thousands of American and European troops into Libya to help stabilize that country after the overthrow of Colonel Gaddafi.

In one large respect, strategic thinking for this war will resemble that of other conflicts: setting priorities, making choices, employing an economy of force—the minimum effort needed to contain a foe in one place—while delivering decisive blows elsewhere. The logic of strategic choice is discussed in this book's final chapter, but for now one can observe that it will require the US government to decide which foreign governments it will bolster, and which it will help only up to a point. A kind of strategic opportunism will be required as well: where it is possible to deliver highly visible and crushing setbacks to the jihadis, those must be seized. Targeted killing at a low level will probably not suffice: the fact is, thousands, perhaps tens of thousands of jihadis will have to be taken off the world's battlefields for good.

This is a coalition war. Many of the allies are unproblematic—France, for example, or Australia. But the question that the United States has always confronted is the extent to which it will turn, on the one hand, to authoritarian regimes, such as that of President Sisi (and previously, President Mubarak) in Egypt, or to the monarchies of the Persian Gulf whose citizens have supported the religious seminaries that incubated jihadist movements; or, on the other hand, to such rivals as Russia and China, which face their own internal Islamist movements but deal with them with a harshness that Americans cannot approve. Here, too, a truthful account to the American people and to others of the compromises that the United States must make is the best insurance against strategic misjudgment on its part—either putting too much trust in allies or having impossible scruples in working with potential partners. Decisions will have to be made case by case: it is entirely likely that in some cases this will involve cooperation with odious regimes, such as that of Russia's Vladimir Putin. The key is to make such choices carefully, acknowledging that values are being sacrificed in some cases, or interests jeopardized in others.

These elements of a strategy—wearing down terrorist organizations, dividing them, waging political warfare against their base, as a last resort intervening to help stabilize countries threatened by them, and working in a coalition—are not new, but until now they have not been executed effectively. They will not, in and of themselves, end the jihadist threat. But they may reduce it to the point that it becomes a nuisance rather than a threat to world order.

The strategists of al-Qaeda, the Islamic State, and Boko Haram, among others, have mastered the theater of fear—it is why they cultivate spectacular attacks on places of entertainment and carefully orchestrated executions of helpless individuals. It is for a reason that one of the key jihadi texts is Abu Bakr Naji's 2004 book *Management of Savagery: The Most Critical Stage Through Which the Islamic Nation Will Pass*. But at the end of the day, they can only achieve success if we persist in a willful misunderstanding of who they are, what their ideology demands, and whence it comes. Their chief ally is America's unwillingness to tell the truth about them—indeed, even to admit it to ourselves. When the United States describes the problem forthrightly, and accepts that this will indeed be a very long war, the challenges will, in truth, look more manageable than they now appear.[33]

CHAPTER SIX

Dangerous States

China is, by virtue of its size, wealth, and aspirations, the great geopolitical challenger to the United States; the jihadists are, by their murderous convictions and practices, the most immediate threat. Only the former, by dint of its wealth, population, and rapidly growing military power, can challenge America's status as the sole superpower. Only the latter are, at the moment, waging open war against the United States.

But a third strategic challenge emerges from a set of hostile states: Russia, Iran, and North Korea. They cooperate often, but are neither an axis nor a coalition. They have in common several features: authoritarian and lawless governments that rely on coercion to retain control and are therefore particularly threatened by liberal-democratic ideas; nuclear arsenals or nuclear aspirations; a high tolerance of risk; and willingness to use force in covert or disguised ways. The first two are revisionist powers, seeking to establish (or in their view, recover) international positions that they believe they have unjustly lost to the United States and its allies. The third is increasingly a loner, a client of China that finds itself neglected by its former patron, yet willing to undertake reckless acts to maintain or raise its status.

All three states are led by regimes predicated on opposition to the United States, a hostility that derives largely from their understanding of their recent past, be it the collapse of the Soviet Union, the defeat of Iran in its war with Iraq in the 1980s, or their isolation in the international system. Their hostility, rooted in an abiding and often irrational resentment, is unlike that of China, which reflects rather the antipathy of a rising power for a state that has dominated the international system. Nor does it resemble the animus of the jihadis, which is blind ideological hatred. In all three cases, to be sure, anti-Americanism is a genuine sentiment, but it is also a useful tool for repressive and even illegitimate regimes to maintain their hold over populations that might otherwise turn on their rulers for their own shortcomings. Because all three are, in essence, dictatorships, senior leaders are not easily replaced and, more important, are not likely to hear divergent views or robust policy disagreements. They are, in other words, susceptible to making very bad decisions. All three display a paranoid style in politics that makes them prone to misjudge both American behavior and the nature of the outside world. These are dangerous states, and dangerous not only by virtue of how they understand their own interests, but how they interpret the actions of others.

The word *rogue*, often used to describe these governments, is misplaced. These are not, from the point of view of international politics, outlaw regimes—they have normal interstate relationships with many nations. Nor is it indeed possible to isolate them very much. India, for example, is friendly to the United States, yet wishes nonetheless to have good relations with Iran not only to secure oil supplies but also because of deep cultural connections, the strength of which the United States cannot ignore. Persian, after all, was for centuries the court language in much of South and Central Asia. In a similar vein, many countries feel a connection to Russia that is rooted either in historical friendships, common religious faith, or sympathy for an empire done down by its rivals. And even North Korea has had, if not friends, then partners, such as Pakistan and Syria, with whom it has shared expertise in manufacturing ballistic missiles, fissile material, and ultimately nuclear weapons.

These characteristics affect the way in which military power contributes to American foreign policy toward them. The global balancing effected by large air and naval forces against a rising China, or the continuous grind of precision attacks and special operations against the jihadis, are less relevant here. Because their interests are chiefly regional, these opponents require regional rather than global responses. The American response must further take into account that one critical element of their menace lies in their actual or desired possession of nuclear weapons, to which they turn precisely because their strength has fewer dimensions than that of China. All are economically fragile, depending either on oil exports in a flooded market, or having nothing in particular to sell other than arms (in the case of North Korea). But they are more immediately dangerous than China, because unlike their Chinese counterparts, Russian, Iranian, and North Korean leaders are waging low-level war against their neighbors, and are willing to take risks that Beijing will not. Against them, a different approach to military power is necessary.

Let us consider each opponent in turn, beginning with the most important, Russia. In Senate hearings before becoming chairman of the Joint Chiefs of Staff, General Joe Dunford declared that "Russia presents the greatest threat to our national security." In one way, this seems like a case of old habits dying hard. After all, Russia is no longer a superpower. Its military, despite the recovery of the early 2000s, is a fraction of its former self. At the height of the Cold War, in the late 1980s, the USSR may have spent the equivalent of $392 billion (in 2015 dollars) on defense. In the aftermath of the Soviet Union's collapse, defense spending shrunk to the equivalent of $65 billion, and then barely a third of that in the late 1990s.[1]

But Dunford's assertion reflected Russia's partial military recovery, and more importantly, what Russia has done with the resources it has. Today, Russia's defense spending has rebounded, to over $96 billion in 2015. This puts Russia's military expenditures at something like two or three times those of Germany and larger than those of Great Britain, as inexact as these measures must be. With this recovering but still limited expenditure, it has refurbished its nuclear arsenal with new long- and short-range missiles and improved warheads, modernized key elements of a much smaller army, and invested heavily in unconventional warfare. On the one hand, the Russian hand is poor: a shrinking population; an economy unbalanced in its reliance on raw materials and weapons exports; a corrupt and dictatorial government;

and huge expanses of territory to defend against a range of potential enemies, including radical Islamists. On the other hand, it has the vast inheritance of conventional and nuclear weapons as well as bases from the late Cold War, professional and adroit military and clandestine services, and a ruthless leadership.[2]

This reviving Russia is a problem, as became clear first in its invasion of Georgia in 2008, and then its seizure of Crimea in 2014 and its intervention in Ukraine since then—a war that has cost Russia at least 2,000 dead, or more than the United States suffered in its first decade in Afghanistan. As is often the case, domestic politics offered some indication of the direction that a country's foreign policy would go. As former KGB officer Vladimir Putin has secured undisputed power, his rule has witnessed a wave of assassination of troublesome figures, such as journalist Anna Politkovskaya and politician Boris Nemtsov; the incarceration of political opponents; the smothering of independent organs of free speech; and the ferocious crushing of a revolt in Chechnya in a siege that lasted into early 2000 and leveled the largely ethnic Russian capital, Grozny.[3]

The United States and other Western powers, and in particular Germany, had hoped that this would not be so. They hoped that Russia would find its way into a larger European and international state system; they believed that by engaging in trade and relatively free travel to and from the West, Russia would liberalize. They thought that having abandoned communism, Russia had no ideological alternative to liberal democracy and free enterprise. And they believed that if there were rough edges left, it must have been because Russia had been driven into a corner by an overbearing West triumphant in the Cold War.[4]

These were profound misjudgments going back to the 1990s, rooted in a combination of wishful thinking and misreading of history. In fact, the George H. W. Bush and Clinton administrations went out of their way to soften the blow to Moscow of the collapse of the Warsaw Pact and the Soviet Union, through policies involving substantial economic assistance and symbolic gestures, such as cooperation in building and operating an international space station. They underestimated the power of nationalism and Russian exceptionalism as an ideology, particularly when manipulated skillfully by Vladimir Putin. They hoped, incorrectly, that domestic political behavior, to include the brutality and repression described above, would not reflect a similar approach internationally—a general tendency of so-called realist thinking about international politics that can be found in other cases, most notably Iran. And they underestimated the way in which the resources generated by material wealth, and in particular the export of oil, could fund a resurgent Russian state in its desire to reassert its role in Europe, while temporarily preventing corruption and state control of key industries from sinking the economy.[5]

There is no doubt that Russian aggressiveness abroad is, in some measure, a defensive reaction by its leaders to their fear of democratic contagion. Ukraine, its neighbor and home of the original Russian state, experienced the so-called Orange Revolution of 2004–2005 and then, a decade later, threw out of office a Kremlin ally, Viktor Yanukovych. Other real or incipient "color revolutions" threatened the Kremlin's hold on other countries in the so-called Near Abroad. But Russia's international behavior also reflects the views of a leadership that was not and is not willing to accept a demotion of Russia's international status. Russia's rulers may have accepted the end of the Cold War, the disappearance of the Warsaw Pact, and even the breaking off of some (not all) elements of the former Soviet Union, but they do *not* accept the shattering of the old Russian empire and the persistence of NATO.

It is these two issues that explain Vladimir Putin's behavior: the desire to restore Russian prestige and control—be it through formal annexation, or informal but effective rule—in the Russian periphery; and the desire to weaken and perhaps ultimately destroy NATO. Putin's quirks and personal history are no doubt important, but barring a transformation of Russian government, the United States and its allies have to expect that a revisionist Russian state will continue to pursue those ambitions even after he passes from the scene.[6]

Russian revisionism, like that of Iran, is a threat for a number of reasons. By virtue of its actions already undertaken, it threatens norms of interstate behavior, particularly in Europe, that underpin the post-1945 order. The borders of Ukraine, in particular, were assured

by the United States, Great Britain, and Russia itself in a solemn declaration in Budapest in 1994, when Ukraine acceded to the Treaty on
the Non-Proliferation of Nuclear Weapons (NPT). Those commitments have been broken, in the first changing of international borders
in Europe by forceful aggression since 1945. Russia's willingness to
export dangerous military technologies to such countries as Iran and
Syria poses other hazards for American interests. Its dramatic military
intervention in the Syrian civil war, accompanied with extensive shell-
ing and bombing of civilian targets, indicates its willingness to use
force to expand its geopolitical reach. Yet as striking as the sight of
Russian bombing runs in Syria have been, what has been more threatening is its clever use of semicovert coercion.[7]

The invasion and subsequent annexation of Crimea in 2014 was
undertaken by thinly disguised Russian special forces and eventually
regular units. At first Russia blandly denied any formal intervention,
and then equally blandly acknowledged that units of its armed forces
had done just that. It was remarkably effective in defusing an immediate crisis, lulling the United States and its European allies into
confused paralysis. The Russian way of war, to include provocations
against far weaker opponents that evoke a reaction to which it can
react in turn, is powerful against opponents who do not have the
stomach to threaten open war against Moscow. It is entirely reasonable to expect that such techniques, which are still evolving under the
guidance of a Russian general staff that retains its Cold War intellectual sharpness, could be turned against the Baltic states, in the hope
that those states will fruitlessly invoke the collective defense provisions of the North Atlantic Treaty, and in effect, be abandoned by
the states of Europe and even the United States, whose armed forces
could find themselves disconcerted, if not blocked, by advanced Russian cruise missiles, mines, and torpedoes from operating freely in the
Baltic Sea.[8]

This could happen. The steady decline in European defense
spending in recent decades reflects a larger decline in Europe's understanding of itself as a potential zone of conflict. Of the major European states, only Britain has hit the 2 percent of gross domestic
product (GDP) target set for defense spending by NATO members

in recent years, while some have failed to spend even 1 percent; and although this trend is beginning to reverse itself, European budgets have a long way to go to make up for years, and in some cases decades, of shrinkage. The Europeans' apathetic response to the Ukrainian crisis of 2014–2015 revealed a deeper unwillingness to stand up to a revisionist Russia. While European states favored economic aid to Ukraine, majorities of public opinion even in the United Kingdom (and a far greater percentage in Germany) opposed providing military aid to Ukraine. Most troubling of all, large percentages, and in some cases majorities, of the populations of several founding members of NATO no longer accept the fundamental premise of the alliance, embodied in Article V of the North Atlantic Treaty, that an attack against one is an attack against all. By margins of 53 to 47 in France, 51 to 40 in Italy, and 58 to 38 in Germany, populations told pollsters in 2015 that their country should *not* use military force to defend a NATO ally in a military conflict with Russia.[9]

At the same time, some members of NATO are vulnerable domestically, as authoritarian right- or left-wing parties emerge that are willing to do deals with Moscow. Hungary and Greece are examples of this. The upshot is that a canny Russia can use sympathetic governments in the West to block united action by NATO in response to its ambiguous aggression; and without unity, NATO is paralyzed.

What makes Russia all the more dangerous is its strength in select military areas (nuclear weapons, special operations, incursions by small conventional forces); the subtlety of its doctrine for using force short of all-out war; the ruthlessness with which it uses force and diplomacy to achieve its ends; and its cunning use of propaganda through well-funded media, such as the television network RT. Paradoxically, Russia's very weaknesses—its paranoia, its faltering economy and falling birthrates, the closing down of civil liberty and civil society, and its thuggish, highly personalized politics—make it even more dangerous. Russia has the appetite for global power—hence such stunts as deploying warships off Australia and flying long-range bombers around the coasts of the United Kingdom and even in the vicinity of American ports—but lacks the ability to sustain it. As Bismarck said long ago of Austria-Hungary, it has a strong appetite and weak teeth. Its illusions

about its own capabilities are matched by its skills at some of the arts
of subconventional war, including propaganda, its military's reliance
on tactical nuclear weapons, and Russian politicians' willingness to
contemplate their use. The result is a power that can act provocatively,
aggressively, and dangerously while courting disaster. Since Russia
poses a threat to the very heart of America's alliance system, NATO, it
has to be thwarted.[10]

━━━━━

Iran resembles Russia in some ways. It exhibits a perplexing mixture
of strength and weakness, whose leaders' fundamental views of the
United States are deeply hostile. On March 21, 2015, as Secretary
of State John Kerry was celebrating progress in the nuclear negotiations with Iran, the nation's supreme leader, Ayatollah Khamenei, was
speaking to an audience that repeatedly chanted "Death to America!"
Khamenei responded, "Death to America, of course." It was neither
the first nor the last time. Why did he do it?[11]

American observers of Iran have often dismissed such expressions
of hostility to the United States as a necessary sop to "hard-liners," as
opposed to the "moderates" in the Iranian regime; others view them
as a mere nervous tic, meaning nothing. It is wiser to take such cries
seriously, as an expression of a hostility that is not merely real, but
fundamental to the regime. The crowds doing the chanting may have
had little choice about what they were called upon to shout, but on
the part of the Islamic Republic's elite, the sentiment is real.[12]

The Islamic Republic of Iran was born in opposition to the United
States; its defining moments included the confrontation with Washington during the hostage crisis of 1979–1980. Moreover, it was born
of opposition not just to the corrupt and brutal rule of Khomeini's
predecessor, the shah, but to the program of Westernization that he
undertook. The revolutionary theater of pouring alcohol down the
drains, abjuring neckties, and installing a morality police was about
confronting the secular society of the West, which had taken such a
hold (and that still in some ways persists) on the elites of Iran. This
theocratic revolution has often proven itself unpopular at home, rest-
ing as it does not only on indoctrination but coercion, to include

hundreds of executions annually (including public hangings from construction cranes), stoning, and routine use of torture, for crimes that include adultery and heresy.[13]

At the same time, the rulers of Iran are the inheritors of Persian pride and imperial aspirations. In this case, as in the past with Russia and China, commentators who thought that a revolutionary state had to choose between ideology and national interest are wrong. It is possible to blend the two, and although at one time or another these elements may come into tension, interest can serve ideology and vice versa. As Stalin used the international network of Communist Parties, the Comintern, to serve Soviet foreign policy in the 1930s, Iran can, and has, used Shia insurgencies to further Iranian state ends. As Stalin was willing to cut deals with capitalists and sacrifice local communists, so, too, has Iran been willing to shelter the terrorists of the Sunni al-Qaeda and come to arrangements with all kinds of regimes, including those run by atheists. But as in the case of the Soviet Union, ideology has created a lens through which the regime views the world, and provided useful tools for war waged by subversion and terror.

As of this writing, Iran exercises great, and in some cases preponderant, influence in four Arab capitals: Damascus, Beirut, Baghdad, and Sanaa. Iran does not rule those cities or control their governments; rather, it has local clients who may, in some cases, have their own interests. It may not, for example, be entirely in Hezbollah's interest to immolate itself and the Shia of Lebanon to serve Iran by waging war against Israel. And Iran's presence has stimulated the opposition and hostility of other groups in each of those societies, chiefly among Sunni populations.

Iran waged quasi-conventional war against Iraq from 1980 to 1988 and failed: the human-wave attacks of revolutionary militias crumpled in the face of Iraqi guns and poison gas. But since then it has waged covert war brilliantly, using the Quds Force of the Revolutionary Guard Corps to support and train Arab militias and terrorist organizations at war with the United States in Iraq, the minority government of Bashar al-Assad in Syria, and others. Iran's conventional military is weak, although clever engineering on its part, and the willingness of other actors to ignore sanctions on the Islamic Republic, have given it pockets of real capability, including a broad array of missiles and speedboats, and a wide variety of explosive devices and mines to attack armored vehicles. But the heart of Iran's emerging military potential lies in its nuclear program.

The Iranian nuclear program began in 1957, when the government of Reza Shah Pahlavi signed an agreement for nuclear cooperation with the United States under the Atoms for Peace program. It expanded considerably in the mid-1970s, with plans for the construction of a score of nuclear reactors. After a pause resulting from the chaos of the Iranian revolution in 1979, the nuclear program restarted in 1984 and, with help from Abdul Qadeer Khan, a Pakistani scientist, acquired nuclear centrifuges. With the designs in hand, Iran could build thousands of these machines to enrich natural uranium to U-235—the raw material for atomic bombs. In 2002, an Iranian dissident group broke the news of a vast clandestine nuclear enrichment program. And indeed, in ensuing years, despite sanctions and cyberattacks, Iran emplaced thousands of centrifuges, perfected the technique of enriching uranium to 20 percent U-235—just one step from weapons grade–developed ballistic missiles, and pursued research into warhead design. Moreover, it pressed the construction of reactors that would allow it to pursue a plutonium (in addition to an enriched uranium) path to nuclear weapons technology.[14]

From a strategic point of view, the Iranian nuclear program makes eminent sense. One of the lessons many countries drew as early as the Gulf War of 1990–1991 was to not engage in confrontation with the United States without nuclear weapons handy. The Iranian regime's hostility to Israel is profound and blatant: the day after the British foreign secretary Philip Hammond visited Tehran in 2015 to restore diplomatic relations, remarking that Iran had a "more nuanced" view of Israel than he had realized, the Iranian Parliament's foreign policy adviser declared, "Israel should be annihilated." Even so, Tehran would probably not use nuclear weapons recklessly to obliterate Israel for fear of being incinerated in return, but it likely believes that nuclear arms would provide the Islamic Republic with a shield against violent Israeli or American behavior, particularly if its weapons are fitted to intercontinental ballistic missiles.[15]

Assuming there is no successful cheating on the part of Iran, the arms control agreement negotiated by the Obama administration in 2015 would defer an Iranian nuclear weapon until 2025 or perhaps 2030, a short time in the life of states. More likely, it will stave off that eventuality for a shorter period of time, given that the Iranians have always had a clandestine program, and given the profound unwillingness of the signatories of the agreement to resume a policy of sanctions and threatened use of force. Once Iran does have nuclear weapons, or even if it is merely seen as having them, the world will have changed dramatically. Among the consequences would likely be a drive for nuclear weapons on the part of other Middle Eastern states (e.g., Saudi Arabia, Egypt, the United Arab Emirates, and Turkey), so as to counteract Iran's ability to threaten them or to match the prestige that nuclear weapons confer. Iran's having broken through a remarkably unanimous international sentiment that it should be blocked from having such weapons, it is highly unlikely that other states—particularly those more necessary to the West, such as Saudi Arabia—would face anything like the opprobrium Tehran has. If nothing else, the precedent would have been set. A nuclear-armed Iran would face a nervous Israel, which takes language such as "the destruction of Israel is nonnegotiable" to be a statement in deadly earnest.[16]

Finally, a nuclear-armed Iran would be an Iran that felt itself empowered to assert itself even more boldly in the Middle East and beyond. In this connection, it is worth noting that even without nuclear weapons, Iran was willing to conduct a massive terrorist attack in Buenos Aires against the Jewish community center there in 1994, and to attempt the murder of the Saudi ambassador to the United States in 2011. Given that the Islamic Republic has embarked on campaigns of assassination and sabotage abroad, it might feel more of a sense of impunity than ever before in doing so once it has nuclear weapons. It could, as well, be willing to attempt to intimidate or even overthrow some of the Arab Gulf states through direct but semidenied means, to include mining and naval guerrilla warfare. The danger, in other words, is that Iran will follow the Russian playbook even more than it already has.

Iran threatens American interests in multiple ways. The containment of the spread of nuclear weapons through the Nuclear Non-Proliferation Treaty since the 1970s has been breached in a number of ways, most notably by the Indian and Pakistani nuclear tests in 1998. An Iranian bomb, however, would raise the stakes immeasurably. Iran directly threatens the stability of important states allied to the United States, and its activities in Iraq and throughout the Levant have been conducive to a rapidly metastasizing conflict that pits Sunni against Shia, Persian against Arab, and that in turn breeds further radicalization and conflict. It is waging a proxy war against the Gulf states in Yemen, with the potential to further destabilize the Arabian peninsula. Finally, a nuclear-armed Iran will, eventually, pose a direct threat to the continental United States if it masters the technology for an intercontinental ballistic missile—a technology that is, after all, more than half a century old, and which the director of national intelligence, James Clapper, has said Iran has the "means and motivation" to develop. The technology in those ballistic missiles comes from a third "dangerous state," North Korea.[17]

═══════════

North Korea without nuclear weapons would merely be a ludicrous and appalling relic of the Cold War, brutally oppressive to its own people, but no threat to world peace. It does, of course, pose a conventional threat to its prosperous southern twin, with its artillery in range of the outskirts of Seoul. But South Korea is now rich and strong enough so that it could probably defeat North Korea in a conventional conflict, even though the price might be devastatingly high in terms of material damage and the loss of life. Even so, the United States would be engaged in such a war, because of the forward presence of its own troops and its treaty commitment to the Republic of Korea, which dates back to the end of the Korean War.

Isolated, vicious, and yet shrewdly calculating, the government of Pyongyang has proven skillful in extracting concessions from other states, and from the government of South Korea. It periodically engages in violent acts such as the murderous surprise attack that sank the South Korean corvette *Cheonan* in 2010, which may be the result of standing orders that put its forces on a hair trigger, or a more cunning attempt to encourage others to appease it. But the heart of the North Korean security problem lies in its possession of nuclear weapons, the product of a program dating back to the 1950s, when the Soviet Union agreed to provide North Korea with nuclear technology. After three nuclear tests in 2006, 2009, and 2013, its arsenal remains uncertain, but it has both a plutonium reprocessing and a uranium enrichment program. Although its military is obsolete and poorly equipped, its one area of strength is an extremely active long-range missile development and testing program, which resulted in over one hundred tests in 2014 alone.[18]

For decades, the United States persuaded itself that North Korea could be negotiated out of its nuclear program. In the 1990s the Clinton administration attempted the "Agreed Framework," and in the 2000s the Bush administration initiated the "Six Party Talks." Both efforts were fruitless, and predictably so. North Korea's rulers understood perfectly well that in the absence of their scary nuclear program, they would be merely a miserably poor, failed state, an irritant that was utterly unimportant to the rest of the world, isolated and ignored by countries far more interested in South Korea, which, though poorer than its northern cousin in the 1950s, now has a GDP more than thirty-five times greater. Without a nuclear program and nuclear weapons, North Korea would never have been more than the destitute cousin of the South. With them, it is a country to be appeased, pacified, and above all bribed. It was, and remains, in the regime's strategic interest to acquire nuclear weapons, to brandish them, and to be able to deliver them against all of its neighbors and the United States.

North Korea is a strategic problem, and not a nuisance, for multiple reasons. It has no compunctions about the export of nuclear technology, as was vividly demonstrated in 2007 when the world learned of the construction of a North Korean–style nuclear reactor in Syria that had been demolished in a precision strike by the Israeli Air Force. North Korean experts have also been sighted in Iran, whose missile technology bears more than a family resemblance to that of Pyongyang. Indeed, it is clear that Iran and North Korea have collaborated on many aspects of ballistic missile design. With the thousand-odd missiles in its inventory, North Korea can hit many targets in North Asia, particularly in Japan and South Korea, and very much including the large array of American forces stationed in those countries, as well as farther out in major bases, such as Guam.[19]

North Korea's nuclear arsenal may, at some point, lead its neighbors to acquire nuclear weapons, particularly if they doubt that they can trust an American guarantee to defend them. Most notably Japan, which has a robust nuclear industry that includes the ability to produce large amounts of plutonium, could move swiftly to acquire nuclear weapons should it so choose. While South Korea has no desire to live next door to a nuclear catastrophe, it has, in the past, explored a nuclear option, until US pressure led it to sign the NPT in 1975. A nuclearized Asia is a more dangerous, not a safer Asia, and the United States has long attempted to forestall that.

There is an even more disturbing side to the North Korean nuclear arsenal. While it would be a mistake to think of North Korea as a "crazy state," it is clearly capable of reckless behavior and wild misjudgments. Its internal politics are obscure but most certainly violent, involving the murder of senior officials at the whim of the Kim family that has ruled since the end of World War II. It is by no means inconceivable that Pyongyang, at some moment of desperation or exuberance, would think it in its interest to conduct a nuclear demonstration shot in the proximity of a close American ally, or even the United States itself.

The North Korean problem is not going away, a point punctuated by its fourth nuclear test, on January 6, 2016. It used to be conventional wisdom that North Korea's collapse was imminent; that no longer appears likely. With even a modicum of reform (e.g., the creation of some two dozen economic development zones, and some easing of restrictions on economic activity), and an ever vigilant and brutal police apparatus, the rule of the Kim family may last a very long time, and with it, the threat posed by Pyongyang to world peace and American interests. Not the least dangerous aspect of North Korea has been its willingness to sell its nuclear and ballistic missile technology to other countries, including nominal friends of the United States, such as Pakistan.

Which brings us to a category of dubious friends—states that are nominally aligned with the United States but that are in some respects deeply hostile to it. The most important of these is Pakistan, a nominal ally in the war against al-Qaeda but in fact a state that has long played a double game, including turning Taliban and similar movements against American forces in Afghanistan. It is not inconceivable that the Islamist government of Tayyip Erdogan in Turkey could take a similar path.

Pakistan is, if not a failed state, then a wretchedly constructed one. With a huge and growing population—177 million, or roughly half that of the United States—it has the forms, and to some extent the reality, of civilian government, but the real power lies with a vast army whose active duty and retired generals dominate its public life, aided by a shadowy intelligence organization, ISI (Inter-Services Intelligence). Pakistan has a large and growing nuclear arsenal with at least enough material for one hundred nuclear weapons. To one reactor at a military facility to produce plutonium in the 1990s, it has added three more between 2002 and 2011, suggesting a plan to ramp up the production of nuclear weapons. Like Russia, Pakistan is expert in the use of covert warfare, which has been part of its arsenal since its founding. It is locked in a hostile standoff with India not merely because of unresolved territorial issues but for more profound reasons. A Pakistan that comes to terms with India is a Pakistan that no longer needs a vast military whose leaders dominate its society; the institutional interests of the army trump the national interests of the country. Moreover, a Pakistan that recognizes India as a peaceful neighbor loses some measure of its very reason for existence. Despite the migration of many Muslims to Pakistan during the Partition of 1947, India's Muslim population is nearly as large as Pakistan's population altogether (about 172 million vs. 177 million, respectively): why, then, does Pakistan, with the same or eventually fewer Muslims and which was carved out of India, need to exist? Pakistan's rulers are desperate to avoid that question.[20]

Pakistan, like Russia, Iran, and North Korea, has a paranoid style in politics. Its newspapers are filled with stories of American, Indian, and Israeli (often, merely Jewish) plots. It sees enemies and double-dealing everywhere, acts accordingly, and has its suspicions confirmed when the United States reacts. Having successfully used militants against India (in Kashmir), Russia (in Afghanistan), and the United States (also in Afghanistan), it finds itself gripped by its own Islamist insurgencies. It is, in short, a state in perpetual crisis. What is dangerous here is that—as in 2008, when Lashkar-e-Taiba militants abetted, and in some measure controlled, by the Pakistani intelligence service launched a horrific set of simultaneous attacks in Mumbai that killed over 150 people and injured hundreds more—Pakistan may do something foolish. A second Mumbai-type operation would probably elicit a violent Indian response. New Delhi demonstrated extraordinary self-restraint in 2008; but no country, and certainly not one of India's size and importance, could tolerate a second such attack. Indian military and civilian officials believe that their retaliation for such an attack could be limited; they may misjudge the potential for escalation.

Pakistan will become more dangerous yet because of its growing relationship with China, including large arms sales of jet aircraft, tanks, and submarines, and the construction of a large port at Gwadar on the Arabian Sea, thereby relieving in some measure the Indian threat to the port of Karachi in the event of war. The problem is as much psychological as it is material: a Pakistan that believes that it has a friend who will give it a blank check is more likely to make stupid mistakes.[21]

Russia, Iran, North Korea, and even Pakistan are all potential challengers to the United States, and there could be others. The question becomes, what is the role of hard power in coping with the foreign policy challenges they pose? Iran, North Korea, Russia, and Pakistan have in common a number of qualities: their discontent with the international system, their deep mistrust of and antipathy to the United States, and their proficiency in subconventional war. Confronted, as they believe, by states that overmatch them in conventional terms, they have repeatedly used, and honed, their skills at using proxies and cutouts backed by special forces; exploit guerrilla and terror tactics (even at sea: the Iranian revolutionary guard corps flotilla of small attack boats); relentless propaganda; and in the shadows, a nuclear deterrent to prevent a crushing conventional counterblow. It is a powerful combination, which emerges from combinations of weakness and strength. In each case it is now a preferred style of war, and one which the United States finds difficult to cope with.

But cope with it the United States must. The threat posed by dangerous states is a different kind of subversion of the post-1945 order than that threatened by China, which would be the emergence of a hegemonic power in Asia and possibly major interstate war, or by Islamist militants, which would be mere bloody chaos. What is at stake here is a more dangerous erosion of norms, a routine simmering of war along numerous disputed borders, and the potential for the escalation of conflicts into much bigger and unanticipated disputes in which nuclear weapons could eventually come into play. Moreover, the dangerous states threaten the security of America's most important allies (Japan, the European states) and security partners (the Gulf states, and increasingly India).

American military power has four purposes in dealing with the dangerous states. The first is to deter them from large military adventures, which would be dangerous in their own right, or which run the risk of leading to broader conflicts. Second, the United States has to reassure anxious allies and partners, both to preserve its own alliance system and to prevent those allies from turning to more drastic measures—in particular, acquisition of nuclear weapons—to ensure their own security. Third, because the dangerous states rely heavily on subconventional or hybrid war—that is, warfare characterized by subversion, propaganda, clandestine operations, and the use of proxy forces, as well as conventional operations—the United States needs to be able to wage this kind of war effectively in response. Finally, in extremis, America has to be able to use force preemptively, to disarm the smaller dangerous states—Iran and North Korea in particular—if they ever seem likely to make use of their nuclear weapons.

The first response, deterrence, is one with which Americans became comfortable, and perhaps dangerously so, during the Cold War. Like some incantation of bygone times, it is believed to ward off catastrophe. After all, it is generally believed the very presence of US forces in Europe warded off the possibility of a ruinous third world war fought on European soil. Over time, however, deterrence in Europe became something formulaic. By the 1980s it was a bizarre combination of serious preparation for war, and a deep-seated conviction that it would never occur. The US nuclear umbrella over Europe unnerved some, but in their heart of hearts, the large majority of European and American politicians never thought that they would ever have to deliver thermonuclear devastation on the Soviet Union. American military units (and to a lesser extent, their European counterparts) trained hard, but very few soldiers in the 10,000-soldier Berlin Brigade really thought that they would have to die in the ruins of Germany's divided capital as waves of Soviet armored divisions rolled over them.

It was not thus at the outset of the Cold War, when the possibility of hot war was real. Contemporary deterrence, if it is to be effective, will need to convince friend and enemy alike that those making threats are willing to go to war with all of its terrors and havoc, so as to make good on their promises to their allies. How one speaks about the use of force, then, may be as important as the tools one has to apply it. The paradox is that to avoid the worst, politicians must not only say but do things that deprive them of what they crave most—freedom of action. As the famous game theorist Thomas Schelling put it, "Often we must maneuver into a position where we no longer have much choice left."[22]

Deterrence by denial ("We will stop you") and deterrence by punishment ("We will inflict terrible pain on you") are different things. Both require the country or leaders being deterred to understand that we ourselves will not be deterred by the costs of war. In that way, the United States often operates at a disadvantage. Its leaders are unwilling, as a matter of principle, to say, "Our military will slaughter thousands of your soldiers," or "Fight with us and your cities will be devastated." As one Middle East expert remarked during the 1990 crisis following Saddam Hussein's invasion of Kuwait, there is a rhetorical asymmetry between those who say, "We view these actions as profoundly destabilizing and therefore unacceptable," and those who say, "Drink from the chalice of death, infidel." This rhetorical asymmetry is unfortunately reinforced by American decisions not to follow through on deterrent threats. In this connection, the failure of the

Obama administration to follow through on its "red lines" about the use of chemical weapons in Syria in August 2012 has done long-term damage to American credibility—according to, among others, two of the secretaries of defense who served in it, Robert Gates and Leon Panetta. Repairing that impression will take some time.[23]

Americans often believe that foreign powers judge a particular administration; that is true, but the degree to which those abroad make their judgments about the United States as a whole, and not just about a leader at a given time, is often underestimated. America overall is easily misjudged, in part because of the seeming, and deceptive, transparency of its culture and its politics. And by both admirers and critics, friends and foes, its resolve and strength are often misjudged.[24]

Indeed, repeatedly, from the early nineteenth century (when foreign powers expected the United States to fly apart) through the twentieth century, America has been underestimated. As Churchill later recalled his thinking on hearing of the Pearl Harbor attack in 1941:

> Silly people—and there were many, not only in enemy countries—might discount the force of the United States. Some said they were soft, others that they would never be united. They would fool around at a distance. They would never come to grips. They would never stand blood-letting. Their democracy and system of recurrent elections would paralyze their war effort. They would be just a vague blur on the horizon to friend or foe. Now we should see the weakness of this numerous but remote, wealthy, and talkative people. But I had studied the American Civil War, fought out to the last desperate inch. American blood flowed in my veins. I thought of a remark which Edward Grey had made to me more than thirty years before—that the United States is like "a gigantic boiler. Once the fire is lighted under it there is no limit to the power it can generate."[25]

This tendency to underestimate the United States did not end with the explosion of American power during the Second World War. Raymond Aron was one of the wisest of twentieth-century European intellectuals, and a good friend of many Americans as well as of the

United States; yet he, too, succumbed to this view. In his 1973 work *The Imperial Republic,* he concluded that American hegemony was finished, a position he reaffirmed, a bit more cautiously, in his philosophical memoir published ten years later. It was an understandable, if altogether incorrect, judgment following the debacle of Vietnam and the decade of civil strife and domestic upheaval that left American cities burning, American campuses in chaos, and the American economy seemingly buckling before new challenges from Japan and Europe. Fifteen years after Aron published his memoir, the Cold War was ten years over, the Soviet Union long since vanished, and the French foreign minister, Hubert Védrine, was fretting about the United States as not a superpower, but as something even more gigantic—a hyperpower.[26]

America's credibility is not at quite as low a point now as it was then, but it has declined, reflecting in part a loss of self-confidence about its own position in the world, and the decline of US military capabilities relative to other powers. A recovery of credibility about the use of force, and thereby the power to deter, will probably occur only when the United States actually does something to someone—wiping out a flotilla of Iranian gunboats attempting to seize an American-flagged merchant ship, for example. Arguably, the recovery of American credibility in the wake of Vietnam and the disastrous Iranian hostage rescue mission in 1979 owed something to the shooting down of Libyan jets over the Gulf of Sidra in 1981, and the invasion of Grenada in 1983. Still, it was only after the Gulf War of 1991 that the impression of overwhelming American military power and the will to use it was fully recovered.[27]

Yet even if the US Navy sank some Iranian gunboats (a precedent being Operation Praying Mantis in 1988, when the United States sank an Iranian frigate and destroyed a number of smaller vessels following Iranian mining operations in the Persian Gulf), the challenge of maintaining credibility in an increasingly nuclearized world will remain. That problem is in some ways unsolvable. Effective defenses against ballistic missiles, on the one hand, and a much more robust and modernized nuclear force, on the other, will help, but there is a danger that states with small arsenals will believe that they can get away with a lot. The Pakistani decision to launch a major military operation against India in 1999—the Kargil crisis—is a good, and scary, example of how the sense of nuclear immunity can liberate countries' leaders to do risky things.

Reassuring allies is chiefly a matter of presence, and in particular, presence on the ground. In this respect Cold War deterrence is indeed a model. When a country puts its soldiers on the front line, then it has a power that words alone do not. But the forces deployed have to be considerable. The Allied decision to maintain a large garrison in Berlin—which was completely surrounded by the Soviet Union's client, East Germany—meant that any attempt to take the city would involve real, protracted fighting. In 1990, immediately after the invasion of Kuwait by Saddam Hussein, the United States sent the ready brigade of the Eighty-second Airborne Division to the Saudi border. Composed of a few thousand soldiers, it could not have stopped Iraqi armored divisions, but it was large and strong enough to put up a fight. By contrast, the tiny British garrison in the Falklands in 1982—a couple of dozen Royal Marines—did not deter Argentina from lunging at the islands, just as US Marine guards could not deter Iranian revolutionaries from seizing the American embassy in Tehran three years earlier.

In the current case, the most urgent need is for the permanent deployment of substantial US forces in Eastern Europe, particularly in Poland and the Baltic states. A rotating rather than a permanent presence resulted from consideration for Russian sensibilities after 1990. While better than nothing, it was considerably less forceful. Against Iran, the issue is less ground forces than a powerful air and naval presence in the Persian Gulf, and forceful action against attempts to harass American or other countries' shipping. Against North Korea, it remains, as in the past, nearly a division of US forces along the front lines in South Korea. The temptation to shrink America's military presence abroad and to attempt to reassure allies by rotational deployments is understandable; but the fact is that there is something uniquely reassuring about permanently stationed US troops.[28]

Adequately countering subconventional war is a trickier proposition. The United States is very competent at some elements of it:

special operations, for example. But America has fallen woefully be-hind of late in its ability to rapidly train and support effective allies or aligned parties. This is in some measure a question of capabilities, but also of will. In the Syrian crisis since 2011 and the Ukrainian crisis since 2014, American decision-makers were unwilling to order the military and CIA to intervene quickly to provide arms, training, and logistical support to those parties to whom we were offering political sympathy and support. The announcement by Secretary of Defense Ashton Carter in 2015 that hundreds of millions of dollars and over a year of effort had yielded the training of precisely sixty Syrian rebels, indicated how feeble American capabilities had become in this field.[29]

It is the nature of subconventional conflict that it usually provides no conclusive victories, that it lasts a long time, and that it is obfus-cated by denials and misrepresentation. It is therefore easy for the United States to ignore it, as it did in Iraq, when Iran's Quds Force persistently supported groups attacking American forces with ever more lethal improvised explosive devices (IEDs). Only near the end of the American involvement, in early 2007, did US special forces nab five Quds Force operators in Irbil, and even then, only to let them go. This, too, was a mistake. Those who wage subconventional war do so chiefly because they hope to achieve gains on the cheap, and because they know they cannot prevail in conventional conflict. All the more reason to respond forcefully, to make the gains more expensive, and to confront opponents with risks that they do not wish to bear. This re-quires being able both to meet an opponent measure for measure, and to escalate quickly to forms of conventional conflict that they wish to avoid.

One dimension of subconventional warfare consists of becoming able to rapidly arm, train, and organize proxy or client forces. Another dimension is propaganda and political warfare—soft power, albeit not of the type usually discussed in the literature on that subject. During the Cold War the United States was remarkably creative in its efforts to wage a war of ideas; since then, it has failed miserably to do so. In some cases, what is called for is simply publicizing what the other side is doing; in others, what is needed are more creative efforts to weaken an opponent and throw it on the defensive. To that end, for example, anything that can be done to help undermine the authority and legitimacy of the Iranian regime, including by enabling Iranians to safely access the Internet and get access to programming that undercuts the regime, is worth doing. It must be remembered that other countries do this all the time to us—most notable is Russia's RT television, which provides a constant diet of anti-American programming to audiences around the world, but also Chinese outlets, such as *Global Times*. More modern versions are needed of such organizations as the old United States Information Agency or the Eisenhower administration's Psychological Warfare Board.[30]

Finally, in some cases, America must accept the necessity of using force preemptively. This will be particularly true in those cases where weapons of mass destruction might be used, or are about to fall into utterly irresponsible hands. While it is generally believed that the United States has some such capabilities, they will probably become of greater importance in the future. They will probably involve a combination of long-range precision strike weapons (e.g., through very long range, conventionally armed ballistic and cruise missiles and stealthy manned and unmanned aircraft) and special operations. More to the point, the possibility of preemption of some kinds of threats needs to be publicized, both at home and abroad, so that if the occasion for it ever arises, public opinion will be ready.

And although one hesitates to say it, it is conceivable in the future that the United States will have to be ready with precise, low-yield nuclear weapons. This is a horrifying possibility. A North Korean hydrogen bomb landing on Tokyo (let alone Los Angeles), however, would be infinitely more horrifying. The actual use of nuclear weapons by the United States is not a last resort—accepting the detonation of a nuclear weapon in a great American or allied city is.

The dangerous state problem competes for attention with the two great challenges discussed previously: the rise of China and the Islamist threat. It also feeds into and interacts with them. It is not coincidental that in differing ways and to different degrees, China has reached out to each of these dangerous states, and increasingly so—through oil and military technology deals with Russia, large infrastructure and arms projects with Pakistan, a warming relationship with Iran, and the long-standing patron-client relationship with an admittedly troublesome North Korea. Iran was the original home of contemporary Islamic revolutionary spirit, and Pakistan has both used and suffered from Sunni jihadi movements.

But there are opportunities as well for shrewd American statecraft to exploit these multiple conflicts for our ends. Here too, US military power must operate in cooperation with diplomacy, both together serving American foreign policy. Russia is as threatened by Islamic extremism as the United States is—more so, in some ways, because of its brutal repression of Islamist movements in the Caucasus. China finds itself increasingly attracted to North Korea's rival, South Korea, as an economic partner, and is, perhaps, not entirely comfortable with a violent, nuclear-armed, and bellicose dictatorship on one of its borders. Iran, as a Shia state, can never be entirely comfortable with Sunni jihadi movements. Russia, deeply mistrustful of China's vast population and economic energy, harbors a stock of 5,000 tactical nuclear weapons to defend thinly populated Siberia (Russia's vast Far Eastern Federal District, with an area of 2.4 million square miles has roughly six million inhabitants) against its neighbor to the southeast.

The United States has or will develop military capabilities to deal with each of the challenges described in this chapter. In the long run, however, it is highly unlikely to be able to handle all of them at once, even with a revived set of alliances. All the more important, then, that it find ways to expose, enhance, and exploit splits among its opponents, which are vulnerable to them, and to subvert governments that are dictatorial and often deeply unpopular. This will be easier (not, as some might suppose, more difficult) if the United States has the military power to cope with each of these threats to a greater degree than it now does. To the extent that coalitions of convenience on the other side look like losing propositions, it is more likely that they will fall apart. It is the job of American diplomats to make that more likely; here too, American military power is the handmaiden of American statecraft.

CHAPTER SEVEN

UNGOVERNED SPACE AND THE COMMONS

The three previous chapters have examined threats—states or organizations whose interests and, in most cases, values are opposed to those of the United States. Conventional thinking about foreign policy is usually framed that way: who are our friends, who are our enemies, how do we strengthen our relations with the former and balance or push back or even wage war against the latter? But there is another set of challenges to which hard power is relevant: the broader concept of the commons and ungoverned space. Vast areas, both physical and virtual, are not under the sovereignty of any state or aspiring state, and yet must play a large role in the military policy of the United States.

One of the foundational concepts in the work of Alfred Thayer Mahan, the late-nineteenth-century naval officer turned historian turned theorist of sea power, was the idea of the oceans as "the great commons of mankind." His analysis of the uses of sea power, and of its nature, stemmed from his insight that naval power, unlike its land component, operated chiefly in areas where no one ruled. To the extent that naval power could use the commons, and deny its use to a hostile power, it was valuable. Barry Posen of MIT has updated this concept in modern form, although pressing it too far by making it the centerpiece of American strategy.[1]

American foreign policy has always had as a central feature the belief that the free transit of people, information, and goods was valuable to the country and broadly beneficial to humanity. To be sure, like many developing countries in the nineteenth century, the United States indulged in various forms of protectionism; and its compunctions about the interruption of free trade by blockading squadrons were reversed when the Union suppressed the South's effort to secede in the 1860s. But on the whole, American leaders, and certainly since World War II, have seen an open trading order, and free international movement as a desirable "milieu goal," as scholar Arnold Wolfers once put it. In the twenty-first century, the commons have expanded beyond the oceans to space, the Arctic (as melting opens it up for transit and mining), and cyberspace. These are the realms in which many, if not all, nations have an interest, and whose control or disruption by hostile actors would be a threat to the United States. One function of US military power in support of American foreign policy must be to help protect and insulate some aspects of the commons from attempts to seize or dominate it, and to be prepared to deny its use to hostile entities, states and nonstate actors alike.[2]

In addition to the commons, American strategists face the problem of ungoverned space. These are areas of the globe nominally under state control but in fact dominated by substate actors, such as clans, tribes, or gangs. Parts of Africa (e.g., Somalia), Syria, Yemen, and the Pakistani border areas are examples of ungoverned space. Sketchily governed areas exist, too, some close to the United States, such as Venezuela, which teeters on the edge of complete state failure. The ungoverned spaces of this world arise for many reasons—state collapse, or perhaps the creation of states that never had much to hold them together to begin with, usually fragments of old European and Asian empires slapped together in the process of decolonization.[3]

That some kind of order, even if it is that imposed by warlord or religious sect, exists in such places is not always a consolation. Those groups may be unwilling or unable to control terrorists, pirates, or states that wish to use their territory for their own purpose. In general, American interests are best served when functioning states exist. It is possible to manage turbulent frontier areas with an adroit combination of threats, bribery, coercion, and local accommodations; from the point of view of international order, however, that is only a second-best solution. Al-Qaeda flourished during the 1990s in the exceptionally weakly governed or semigoverned borderlands of Afghanistan and Pakistan. One of its successors, the Islamic State, did so in Libya, taking advantage of the turbulence following the overthrow of Muammar Gaddafi in 2011.

From one perspective, ungoverned, or chaotically governed, physical space was a large cause of Europe's expansion into large parts of Asia and Africa in the nineteenth century. Unlike the more straightforward plundering, looting, and conquest of Latin America by Spain, British and French expansion in other parts of the globe resulted in part from the weakness or even the collapse of local governments from a variety of causes, some of which had little to do with direct European action. Chaos on the periphery often draws foreign powers in, partly in hope of gaining economic advantage, partly to secure the gains they have already made. This was the argument famously made by British historians Ronald Robinson and John Gallagher, who explained British expansion into Africa in the late nineteenth century in this manner: "Crises in Africa, no less than imperial ambitions and international rivalries in Europe, have to be taken into account."[4]

Arguably, it was weakness at the periphery that drew the United States into Vietnam in the 1960s, and into the Persian Gulf in the 1980s and 1990s. In both areas the United States previously had relied on allies—France in Indochina in the 1950s; Britain, then Iran, in the Persian Gulf during the 1960s and 1970s—to hold the line against Asian communism, on the one hand, and various hostile local powers (Egypt, then Iraq) on the other. When those allies withdrew or collapsed (indeed, in the case of Iran, becoming the new problem), the United States was drawn in. A similar process occurred in Afghanistan following the withdrawal of the Soviet Union in 1988–1989 and the protracted civil war that ensued. The shaky Taliban regime that ruled much of Afghanistan did not plan the 9/11 attacks on the United States in 2001, but it tolerated (and benefited modestly from) the presence of al-Qaeda, which did. In 2015 President Barack Obama, who had strongly opposed the 2003 American war with Iraq and had prided himself on having brought that conflict to an end, reintroduced thousands of American troops to that country. It was done with deep reluctance, as a necessary response to the collapse of Iraqi state rule in large swaths of the country. The logic of peripheral chaos was too strong to be resisted.

———

As the Robinson-Gallagher thesis suggests, there is nothing new about the problem of anarchy at the periphery. State collapse takes many forms and occurs in states from large to petty. It may result from a variety of collisions with the outside world, or from more generally internal problems, such as civil war or economic catastrophe. The ensuing disorder can be something as minor as the proliferation of drug cartels in Caribbean nations that lack the policing power and financial control institutions to disrupt or apprehend them. Or it can be altogether more significant, such as the 1991–1992 collapse of the Somali state, which occasioned a humanitarian intervention by both the Clinton and George H. W. Bush administrations. In the 1990s such disorder came to be viewed as warranting intervention by the dominant powers in the system, as the United States led coalitions twice in interventions in the collapsed state of Yugoslavia, first to secure Bosnia in 1995 and then to protect the population of the breakaway state of Kosovo in 1999. Jurists and diplomats began to describe an international "responsibility to protect"—a concept whose allure was diminished when it became clear that the price in blood and treasure of such interventions might be higher than it had been in the former Yugoslavia.[5]

The relative ease of these interventions in the immediate aftermath of the Cold War obscured the limits of military power in conducting them. The European imperialists of the nineteenth century had the appetite, self-confidence, and (internationally, if not locally) legitimacy to follow up intervention with formal governance by colonial rule. Today, by and large, the United States and its allies do not. They derive neither pleasure nor prestige from planting their flags in dusty lands. In some cases (Bosnia, most notably) it was possible to hand off the challenge of governance to a multinational organization, although even in that case the inevitable consequence was muddled or ineffective administration. In some cases, governance can come through a local power acting through the medium of the United Nations—the Australian intervention in East Timor in 1999 followed that model. Providing nearly half of the troops and all of the strategic direction, Australia eased Indonesia out of its former colony. But it found itself sending several thousand troops back to East Timor in 2006 to stabilize a country that remained poor, barely literate, disorderly, and malnourished.[6]

The age of protectorates and mandates has passed, less from geopolitical necessity than from a shift in attitudes and beliefs. Military intervention in a zone of chaos is now usually followed by a quick restoration of the semblance of local rule, with the frequent result (think: Haiti after the US intervention of 1994–1995) of corruption, dysfunction, and again, state collapse. In the last several decades, moreover, well-meaning Western governments have learned that showering vast sums of money on collapsed societies and economies does little good, and often considerable harm by undermining local institutions. While much improvement can be made to the management of governance in failed states, and to the recruitment and training of those who do it, little can substitute for the willingness of outside powers to persevere in such tasks. For now, such perseverance is lacking, nor is it clear that in most cases external powers know how to successfully conduct state-building.[7]

Understandably, the United States would like to avoid such adventures, and in a number of cases it has done so. The horrific violence of the Great Lakes region of Africa (Burundi, Rwanda, the Democratic Republic of the Congo, and Uganda) since 1998 has probably taken millions of lives, and yet America remained aloof. During the brutal Sudanese civil war of 1983–2005 the United States did not engage, despite the arguments of a small but vociferous minority insisting that it should—again, the dead can be measured in the millions, the destruction vast, and the conflict continuing. The cost, in each case, was born by the locals; in none of these instances, however, did chaos on the edges of the international system involve a setback to US interests, however wounding they were to American values or appalling in human terms.

In other cases, however, the United States will pay a cost not only in terms of its conscience, but its interests. The Syrian civil war since

2011 is a case in point. Although America belatedly made efforts—
none substantial, all half-hearted—to support the moderate elements
of the movement that first demonstrated, and then revolted, against
the regime of Bashar al-Assad, it refrained from direct military intervention against the regime, even after Damascus had used chemical
weapons against its enemies. The result was a crisis that has bred instability and violence throughout the Levant and into Europe itself.

The choice in Syria was not, as some supposed, a weary acceptance
of an authoritarian regime aligned with Iran versus the alternative of
mere chaos; it was between a civil war that would overwhelm that regime if external aid were provided, and prolonged internecine warfare.
The United States and its allies did not support the former, and the
latter is what resulted. The humanitarian cost was enormous: at this
writing a half-million dead, and roughly half the population refugees
at home or abroad—over four million alone having fled the country.
Other states saw an opportunity to intervene and did so: Russian air
power, coupled with Iranian special forces and Hezbollah light infantry, stopped rebel advances and recovered territory for the embat-
tled regime. This, in turn, began to embroil other states—Turkey,
whose forces shot down a Russian fighter plane in 2015, and Gulf
Arab states that began supporting the rebels. Syria became home to
several jihadist movements and a magnet for foreign recruits in the
thousands. The Syrian conflict abetted and broadened the Iraqi conflict and the metastasis of the Islamic State, which did not recognize
the Iraq-Syrian border and operated comfortably on both sides of it.
Meanwhile, the flood of Syrian refugees into Lebanon, Jordan, and
Turkey altered the population balances of the border regions of all
of these countries, and created breeding grounds for future generations of angry, traumatized young people, poorly educated, unem-
ployed, and thirsting for revenge. By 2015, hundreds of thousands
of refugees from the war-torn Levant were streaming into a Europe
torn between pity for suffering families and a deep-seated fear of
unassimilable strangers, bringing fresh strains to a Europe caught in
its own economic and political crises. Chaos in Syria has serious consequences for the state system as well as for American humanitarian
sensibilities.[8]

American leaders may have refrained from intervention in Syria in part because of the lessons they drew from Libya in 2011. In that case, the United States reluctantly supported an Anglo-French–led coalition of some European and Arab states in the overthrow of the brutal regime of Muammar Gaddafi, who faced a similarly fierce domestic opposition. Neither the coalition nor its American backer were willing to do more than provide air strikes and indirect support to the insurgent groups. In the chaos that followed, no external power committed a sizable effort to the rebuilding of the Libyan armed forces, or to the consolidation of governance. For a time, in 2012, that restraint seemed to offer the prospect of intervention on the cheap. In the following years, though, as Libya was again gripped by war, the consequences of the overthrow of Gaddafi became clear. Looted arsenals of arms built up by the former regime diffused weapons around the region; mercenary veterans of Gaddafi's armies fueled internal wars in central Africa; jihadist groups deepened their presence and turned on other groups in a debilitating civil war; and thousands of economic refugees swarmed through its uncontrolled ports into leaky boats headed for an appalled Europe that alternately sheltered them or ignored their plights until hundreds died at sea of drowning or exposure.[9]

Thus, intervention on the chaotic territorial periphery is not simply a matter of humanitarian impulse, or a "responsibility to protect." Those dimensions are important, but often, so, too, is the consideration of interest. What those interests are varies by case: in the Great Lakes of Africa the humanitarian dimension was large, but the interests at stake small; in other cases, the interests are substantial. How, then, should the United States go about the business of intervention in the violent periphery, understanding that in each solution much depends on circumstances that cannot be anticipated in advance?

In recent years the United States has attempted to preempt the problem of military intervention to secure a chaotic periphery by quietly deploying military assistance teams, often drawn from the armed services' special operations forces, to train local militaries. Such efforts, however, are intrinsically limited in scope: US Army Special Forces were initially created to train guerrillas to operate behind Soviet lines in the event of a war in Europe. Their basic organization has not changed: units of roughly a dozen officers and sergeants who, in the field, can train units up to the battalion level—say, six to seven hundred soldiers. As valuable as this may be, however, it does not substitute for everything that goes into building effective military organizations on a much larger scale. Special forces soldiers rarely have experience themselves at managing large-scale logistics, the various supporting functions of intelligence and transportation, let alone everything that goes into the business of operating a ministry of defense. Other elements of the military do, of course, and are often dispatched, together with defense contractors, to that end.

The limits of such advisory efforts can be seen in a number of countries, most notably Yemen, when in 2014 the Yemeni state, such as it was, collapsed before the advance of Houthi rebels, aligned with (certainly supplied by and possibly guided by) Iran. Moreover, although special forces units can revert to their original mission of training rebels, as can CIA paramilitary units, they have even less to offer in terms of state building in such cases.[10]

Intervention in the ungoverned periphery will not disappear as a mission of the US military; in some ways it is the oldest mission of the United States Army, which throughout the nineteenth century was committed to controlling a turbulent frontier. It is rendered more difficult by the skepticism of the American people and political elite in the wake of the Iraq war. A decade following the beginning of that conflict, the American public was evenly split about whether it had succeeded and whether it was the right decision to begin with. Such doubts about the possibility (as well as desirability) of attempting prolonged governance abroad are now being expressed by leading politicians from both parties.[11]

The pacification of peripheral areas is not necessarily overly taxing in terms of funding or numbers of manpower: the United States has quietly attempted to build up the police forces of Central American states, for example, at a fraction of the cost of a war. The stabilization mission requires skills and capabilities that are only partly to be found in the military, and above all, sound strategic judgment about when and in what way to address the challenge of the chaotic periphery. What is needed is less new organizations (all that are needed already exist) or equipment (although in this area as in others, technical innovations are constant), than a different strategic approach, which has four elements.

The first is simply a recognition that intervention without follow-up of some kind, as in Libya, is as likely to produce calamity as not intervening at all. That follow-up may take years or even decades, not of fighting necessarily, but of the commitment of forces and resources. Colombia would not have been the qualified success it is today had American leaders not committed to aiding its government for two decades or more. Similarly, in retrospect it is clear that the United States withdrew too hastily from Iraq in 2011 and that it would have been better to maintain a military presence of some 10,000 to 20,000 troops, if that could have been negotiated with the Iraqi government.

The second element goes to the nature of that follow-up: not full-bore nation-building, so much as more focused assistance on developing security institutions and basic rule of law. As we have seen in the discussion of Iraq and Afghanistan in a previous chapter, the pouring of vast sums of money and the presence of large numbers of foreign aid workers, all with the best intentions, is often counterproductive. It is the locals' jobs to build schools, dams, and power plants. The foreigner may help train and mentor their police, soldiers, and in some cases their jurists and administrators, but the business of economic and social development is best done by those on the ground.[12]

A third requirement for such interventions is a coalitional component, both to secure legitimacy and for greater effectiveness. Politicians understand this intuitively, but they often turn to formal alliances (NATO) or the United Nations when they would be better advised to use a coalition of the willing, allowing America to take a lead in most cases, and without the cumbersome politics, bureaucracy, and inefficiency we have discussed earlier. In the future, the United States will find new partners, as it already quietly has with Colombia, which now trains Central American police and military forces to standards that the United States helped set.

Finally, although in the wake of the Iraq war it is tempting to say that the United States will never engage in such efforts again, the fact is that it probably will. Indeed, in some ways it already is in places like

Iraq. In other cases—Libya may have been such a case—the United States may come to discover that the choice was not between stable dictatorship and anarchy, but among different kinds of anarchy, some worse than others. When that is the case, willy-nilly, the United States will be back in the intervention business.

That being so, political and military leaders must make it clear that stabilization remains, as it has ever been, a potential mission of the US military, for which it must prepare in times of relative peace. In retrospect, the United States Army was unprepared for the Afghan and Iraq war missions because it had painted a picture to itself of what war is, modeled on the blitz against Iraq in 1991, and had renounced its experiences in Vietnam nearly a generation earlier as an anomaly. The logic of geopolitics being what it is, the only real choice is whether to wage such conflicts well or poorly, successfully and efficiently or badly and wastefully.

It would be better if ungoverned space were not; but the commons we wish to preserve outside the sovereignty of any state. Yet the commons too requires the exercise of hard power. The United States has long understood the importance of keeping the high seas open to commerce. Its Navy, following the Royal Navy, helped put down slave trading and piracy in the early nineteenth century. Its squadrons guarded American commerce in the Mediterranean, and in the second Barbary War of 1815 forced the release of European as well as American prisoners of North African states. In 1835 it created the East India Squadron (renamed the Asiatic Squadron in 1868) to protect American trade in the Pacific. Indeed, throughout the nineteenth century the US Navy not only protected American interests narrowly understood, but undertook a larger mission of maintaining order, to include creating an African squadron (chiefly engaged in antislavery patrols) in the 1840s. Not until the middle of the twentieth century, however, when the Royal Navy had receded from its international police role and the US Navy had become an overwhelming force, did the latter become the chief guarantor of the freedom of the seas. It has continued to fulfill this role, including by taking on and disabling Iranian naval forces in the Persian Gulf during Operation Praying Mantis in 1988, following Iranian mining of international waters.[13]

This role occasionally led to clashes with countries claiming substantial territorial waters beyond the general consensus of international law. In 1981 the US Navy, as part of its extensive program of passage intended to demonstrate freedom of navigation, sailed into the Gulf of Sidra, waters claimed by Libya. Two Libyan fighter jets scrambled and were promptly shot down off the Libyan coast.

Freedom of the seas rests in part on an agreed legal framework, and partly on the enforcing presence of naval power. To the first, paradoxically and some believe damagingly, the United States has refrained from ratifying UNCLOS, the international agreement resulting from the third UN Conference on the Law of the Sea in 1982. Political and military leaders alike believe that UNCLOS would help regularize the exploration and exploitation of the seabed outside of countries' exclusive economic zones, as well as in neutral waters. The argument against UNCLOS holds that the navigational rights it protects existed before UNCLOS, that it provides no benefits beyond those of customary international law in terms of exploitation of the seas, and would expose the United States government and American companies to suits and penalties. Although administrations have supported the ratification of UNCLOS for twenty years, the Senate has yet to comply with their wishes.

Law is one thing; naval power is another. The United States continues to patrol contested waters, including through what's known as freedom of navigation operations, or FONOPS. The challenges to the freedom of navigation, however, have grown in seriousness over time. The most troubling emerges from China's claims to the vast expanse of the South China Sea embraced by the nine-dash line—a line on Chinese maps that, breathtakingly, reaches to the territorial waters of neighboring states, such as Vietnam and the Philippines. China has attempted to assert its territorial rights through aggressive patrolling by its coast guard, navy, and air force, and by the construction of half a dozen large military bases built on reclaimed land (and ruined coral reefs) in international waters.[14]

Piracy, the oldest scourge of maritime traffic, has been reduced in recent years—a decline of almost 50 percent in the last few years, if statistics are to be believed. International naval patrols, better procedures for avoiding or thwarting attacks, raids against some pirate bases (in Somalia), and increased use of private maritime security forces have all helped. Piracy can be contained relatively easily by coalitions of maritime powers. Still, hundreds of pirate attacks occur every year, particularly in Southeast Asia, and to some extent off the African coast. Despite the best efforts of littoral nations, pirates still plague the areas around Malaysia. The United States Navy, Coast Guard, and intelligence services all play an invaluable role in coordinating and informing antipiracy efforts, and American leadership of an allied naval operation designated as Combined Task Force 151 in 2009 was critical in terms of providing intelligence and coordination in the counterpiracy fight off Somalia.[15]

Terrorist attacks at sea have been relatively few, the most notorious being the hijacking of the Italian cruise ship *Achille Lauro* by Palestinian terrorists in 1985 and the murder of a crippled passenger on it. The enormous growth of the cruise ship industry, however, presents an array of appealing targets for groups that, with a suicide boat crammed with explosives, or even conceivably some kind of cruise missile, could inflict appalling loss of life on ships that routinely carry thousands of passengers. This has yet to happen—but it easily could.

Future threats to oceanic freedom will emerge from the melting of the polar ice cap and the discovery of substantial mineral deposits in areas that will be increasingly accessible as a result. In the Arctic, Russia has begun to aggressively assert its claims to the exploitation of the mineral wealth below the ocean, and control of navigation lanes through it. This will open up a new sphere for maritime competition.[16]

Maintaining freedom of the seas will be a greater problem in the future; while some of the threats, such as piracy, are very old, they are abetted by modern techniques, to include the ability of pirates to monitor traffic and conduct sophisticated ransom negotiations through intermediaries in the developed world. Far more serious, though, are the challenges to free transit on the ocean and above it from states. When China in 2013 established an Air Defense Identification Zone (ADIZ) over a large part of the South China Sea, it was also extending its claims. Nominally, the ADIZ only requires airplanes flying through it to identify themselves to a country's air defense system, but in this case, extending as it did over Japan's Senkaku Islands, it represented one more step in China's effort to establish sovereign control over disputed waters.

Naval superiority, of the kind the United States has taken for granted for many years, no longer provides unlimited reach into disputed waters. If they acquire modern land-based cruise missiles and the means of targeting them, even weaker countries can sink ships at a considerable distance from their shores. In 2006, the Israeli corvette *Hanit*, operating off the coast of Lebanon, was struck and nearly sunk by a Chinese C-802 Silkworm missile fired by Hezbollah, an Iranian-backed militia. Silkworm, its successors, and like missiles have ranges of hundreds of kilometers, can be launched from air, sea, and land, and are in the hands of such countries as Iran that have small conventional navies but extensive coasts. By and large, however, the real threat to maritime freedom will come from large states with powerful navies, supplemented by land-based systems, such as ballistic or cruise missiles cued from space or land-based long-range radars or other sensors. The power of competing fleets has grown, particularly the Chinese navy, which in the early twenty-first century began conducting missions (starting with counterpiracy) halfway around the world, and, more important, has the ability to deny most maritime nations the ability to operate in the international waters that it claims.

The maritime realm, then, is a source of risk, not chiefly because of the presence of outlaws, but because of the appetites of states eager to acquire territory or assert claims by force. If they do so successfully, we risk a competition for the seabed and rights of transit as fierce as the European competition for Africa in the nineteenth century. In such an environment, the security of free transit, upon which the global economy rests, will be in danger. While America has allies who share not only an interest but an approach to maritime law that would safeguard free passage, few besides the United States are willing to assert those rights by force. This is why American decisions beginning in 2015 to sail close (within 12 miles) of the artificial islands built in the South China Sea were so important. As China builds air and naval bases on these islands, deploys armed forces there, and insists that they are sovereign territory, however, the struggle to maintain freedom of navigation will require strong nerves. Other countries (Australia, most notably) may follow, but the United States has to lead.

In short, with the exception for now of piracy, the challenges of keeping both the high seas and confined waters (e.g., the Persian Gulf) as well as critical bottlenecks (e.g., the Straits of Hormuz) open to commerce and free passage are increasing, not dwindling. This problem comes on top of the rise of the Chinese navy and the partial recovery of the Russian navy, both of which pose more traditional great power challenges to the United States. And this means that the need for American naval power is at its greatest since the end of World War II. Even minor opponents can pose a greater threat, even to the United States, and certainly to other countries and their commercial shipping. At a time when long-range precision weapons at sea and the ability to detect targets on the oceans have grown, this means the need for a qualitatively larger force to project power on, above, and below the sea surface. A shipbuilding program that reverses the shrinkage of the fleet is urgently needed; so, too, is a more overtly navalist strategy, articulated as clearly as it was at the turn of the twentieth century, and again shortly before World War II. After decades of the US Navy being chiefly a supporting service, it needs to be understood as taking the lead, particularly in the Pacific. Indeed, it, and other branches of the US armed services with oceanic reach, requires a very large expansion, and not merely increases to stop the shrinkage of the fleet.

This is also true for outer space. The heavens are also the commons, and no less important than the maritime domain. The United Nations Office for Outer Space Affairs lists a dozen major fields in which the modern world depends on space. All nations, in one way or another, rely on remote sensing, telecommunications, and space-based navigation. Nearly 1,300 satellites are in orbit, some two hundred are launched every year, and nearly sixty countries operate satellites of one kind or another.[17]

Space, or at least the part inhabited by satellites in low earth orbit, is increasingly a crowded and even a dangerous place. In 2013 NASA reported that more than half a million pieces of space debris the size of a marble or larger—and even more much smaller items—were traveling at speeds of up to 17,500 mph. Such objects can do serious damage. Windows on space shuttles have had to be replaced, for example, after getting hit by paint flecks. Satellites have collided with one another, and a number of countries, including China, Russia, and the United States, have conducted antisatellite tests.[18]

Antisatellite technologies are, and will be, increasingly available to countries other than the United States, Russia, and China. Satellites can be intercepted physically, blinded with lasers, or interfered with in other ways. Mere reckless behavior, such as the Chinese antisatellite test in 2007 that destroyed an old weather satellite, can endanger satellites by creating clouds of space junk, small fragments of man-made objects (over 3,000, in that case) that can smash other satellites.

Space warfare is controlled by a number of international treaties—most notably, the 1967 Outer Space Treaty—including a ban on testing and deploying nuclear weapons in outer space. Whether those treaties will actually inhibit countries from waging war in space is, however, a different matter. As with the London Naval Treaty of 1930, which prohibited unrestricted submarine warfare, when the first shots are fired, treaty obligations have a way of falling apart.[19]

Weaker powers, in particular, may be tempted by the notion of disabling the United States through attacks on its space systems. In practice this may prove more difficult than they expect, but something in the notion of being able to blind and cripple America is strategically appealing to, say, North Korea. Chinese writers have explored this theme as well, and it fits into their concept of "assassin's mace" technologies.

Among the great powers, mutual vulnerability in space is probably the surest guarantee of our continued ability to function there, although the United States is more dependent on outer space than any other. It may be assumed that American antisatellite capabilities are as advanced, and probably more advanced, than those of any other country, and that that in itself should prove a deterrent, particularly as such nations as China themselves become more dependent on the peaceful uses of space. But a country that for years, however, has been relying on a hostile state to provide launch vehicles for its most sensitive payloads (as has the United States, which has had to stockpile Russian RD-180 launchers) may not appear to be completely serious about dominance in that realm. Moreover, human nature being what it is, that will be no guarantee that human folly will not lead, step by step, to a reckless escalation in space. Indeed, the very fact that lives will not be immediately at stake will make it easier to unleash space warfare.

In war, unintended consequences predominate. In 1991 American airplanes disabled the Iraqi power grid with the then novel weapon of carbon fibers that shorted out the transformers in Iraqi power stations. Planners did not anticipate, however, that by shutting down the electrical grid they would not only hamper the Iraqi military and air defense system, and deliver a psychological shock to the regime's supporters, but also knock out the power systems of hospitals that did not have backup generators. The result was a propaganda coup for the Iraqi government, which could point to the suffering of patients in hospitals suddenly thrown into the dark. On a much greater scale, space war could shut down transportation systems that rely on the US global positioning system or its Russian, European, or Chinese competitors. Having no experience of space warfare, of its unpredictable second or third-order consequences, no state can be sure whether it will be catastrophic or controllable.

The various space regions, from low earth orbit to geosynchronous orbit (the distant region where satellites can remain opposite one place on the earth's surface) are essential for surveillance, communications, warning (by detecting the heat of missile launches, among other things), and navigation; it is a physical environment that must be conceived in ways entirely differently than the terrestrial. At least a dozen states can launch satellites on their own; most countries, one way or another, either operate satellites or have some large stake in them. While commercial use of space is increasingly sophisticated and part of the global economy, the military side of space is unusually obscure: programs to monitor other nations' satellites, and even more so, American programs to disable, destroy, or interfere with other countries' satellites are deep black. There is simply not a lot to be said about it publicly, beyond acknowledging its critical importance.[20]

Space, however, should also be understood as theater. As a realm it is often understood in metaphors—in particular, the notion that it is the ultimate high ground. Throughout the history of conflict, from the Greeks and Romans to the present day, soldiers and civilians alike have had a visceral feeling that it is better to be higher up. This has not always been true (there is a whole set of tactical ruses that involve hiding behind a slope rather than perching oneself on top of it), but that does not invalidate the psychological fact. The power that dominates the high ground is assumed to have an advantage over everyone else. If that power loses the high ground, conversely, it will be seen to have lost more than a few extremely expensive pieces of machinery, but something much deeper.

American power, like all power, rests on aura, reputation, and image as well as upon raw physical capacity. To the extent that the United States is understood to be the world's dominant power in space, capable of using it and denying it to others, it will have a real edge in the conduct of diplomacy. To the extent that it no longer controls the high ground, it will have lost much more than the ability to send bits of information through the heavens. For that reason programs that suggest America retains space dominance are important for what they convey as well as what they can actually do.

Outer space is not easy for earth-dwellers to imagine. Although we all live in cyberspace, it is almost equally hard to understand it as a venue of conflict. There are those who speak about the possibility of conflict in cyberspace in terms better suited to the apocalypse than strategy, "cyber Armageddon" being the most egregious term. Periodically, one reads in newspapers accounts of exotic cyberattacks, be they the so-called Stuxnet virus that plagued but—very importantly—did not stop Iran's development of nuclear centrifuges, or the attacks, supposedly originating in China, that compromised the records of tens of millions of US government employees in 2015. Cyberwarfare has clearly been waged by North Korea (attacking American companies) and Russia (attacking neighbors Estonia, Ukraine, and Georgia).[21]

Cyberspace is a peculiar blend of ungoverned, or perhaps semigoverned, space and the commons. In this area the United States has exerted a loose kind of control, or rather, supervision: the Internet grew out of an American advanced defense research project (the so-called ARPAnet, a system to allow communication within the defense community). American companies have dominated the technologies that underlie the Internet, and the United States has hosted ICANN, which controls the allocation of domain names. Here, too, other countries and nonstate actors have attempted to undermine the American policing function. At great effort, for example, China has managed to wall off much of its population from unrestricted access to the Internet, albeit at considerable direct and indirect cost.

Cyberspace is surely a rich realm for espionage and potentially for sabotage. It is also a place for conflict. As in the case of outer space, no one knows for sure what cyberwar will really look like, partly because so many of the tools of cyberwar are highly technical and understandably secret, and partly because so far as we know, no country has really unleashed more than harassing kinds of attacks such as those suffered by Estonia in 2007, when hackers, presumably operating directly or indirectly for the Russian government, swamped the websites of the Estonian parliament, banks, and other organizations, but did no lasting damage. Many other kinds of cyberattacks occur every day, but it is hard to see what lasting or lethal damage they have caused.

There is some reason to think that cyberwarfare may be somewhat less to be feared than is often thought. In the cyber realm, it is not only governments that build defenses. Some of the largest and most sophisticated companies ever created by human beings are on the front lines, at least of defense, and they have resources (including the ability to hire the best talent available) that even government does not. Moreover, particularly in developed economies there can be a kind of redundancy and complexity created by the very nature of the free enterprise system that prevents single points of failure.

If cyberattacks were as potentially destructive as often claimed, why have they not been more successful? Why have there not been attacks that have involved enduring physical damage and loss of life? If, as is reasonable to suppose, Iran has been subject to cyberattacks on its nuclear program, particularly from Israel, why has it nonetheless been able to build a nuclear program involving thousands, and possibly tens of thousands of centrifuges, and the undisputed ability to manufacture as much fissile material as it would need for a large nuclear arsenal?

This is not to dismiss cyberwarfare as a problem; it is certainly that. But it is to suggest that as has often occurred in the past, it opens up a new dimension of war without supplanting the others. For sure, the ability to exploit cyberspace for intelligence gathering is extraordinary, although who benefits most is unclear. In any event, it is in the American interest not only to look to its defenses and retain its ability to launch its own attacks but, insofar as is possible, also to enhance its ability to keep the cyber realm available to all. Populations that can freely access the Internet are also populations that can find alternatives to government versions of the truth, coordinate protests, and propagate the values that help ensure a world order that Americans want. What this means as a matter of policy is for the United States to do everything it can to maintain cyberspace as a commons, even if that means sacrificing some element of control. It has already done this by (indirectly) sponsoring secure browsing systems, such as Tor. This is one realm where soft power—the American ability to preserve individuals' freedoms—is important.

Hard power is relevant to cyberspace as well. At some point the United States needs to make it clear that a cyberattack (as distinct from espionage) is every bit as much an attack as a physical action. Causing an industrial accident by meddling with a SCADA (supervisory control and data acquisition) system—for example, the kind of system that controls processes in a chemical plant—is an attack, as much as firing a cruise missile at that plant. For that reason, the United States should make it clear that it reserves the right to respond with kinetic force to cyberattacks. There are two reasons for this. The first is that cyberwarfare evens up some of the disparity between large and small powers—a North Korea or an Iran can mount a credible cyberattack, but not (yet) a physical assault on the continental United States. Governments need to know that they cannot choose the means and location of such battles. The second reason is that tit-for-tat responses will often be unacceptable for legal or moral reasons. America will not wish to blow up an Iranian chemical plant in an urban setting if the Iranians do the same to the United States. Likewise, if it has effective cyberweapons at its disposal, it will probably wish to keep them in reserve for a very large crisis. Cyberwarfare is one domain where to show one's strength is to immediately elicit countermeasures.

―――

In all of these dimensions of ungoverned space and the commons—territorial, maritime, space, and cyber—traditional military power relationships continue to exist. States assert interests, and other states seek to cooperate with, balance, or thwart them. But in ungoverned space those relationships are complicated, and in some cases threatened by nonstate actors, be they terrorists, guerrillas, pirates, or even enterprising hackers. That is, the use of force in ungoverned space often has low barriers to entry. This is true for allies of the United States as well its opponents, and indeed in a certain way the "order of battle" in ungoverned space is much larger than that in territorial warfare. In effect, the research and security branches of huge companies, such as Google, Microsoft, and Apple, are working on the same side (most of the time) as the United States government on cyberdefense.

The term *ungoverned* is always qualified. International agreements cover various forms of conduct in the great commons of mankind; but ultimately, the question is whether anyone can effectively police those agreements. In the end, that comes down to the United States.

The best way to understand the importance of the contemporary great commons is to imagine what the world would look like if American dominance were withdrawn, and these became ungoverned in the fullest sense, an arena for conflict in which there were no rules. The result would surely be a great deal more conflict, much of which would spill over and affect the United States. At the moment, smashing another country's satellite, using cyberattacks to cause massive industrial accidents, or declaring that one's territorial waters reach 120 miles rather than twelve does not happen, chiefly for fear of an American reaction. If the United States is not prepared to react, proportionately or disproportionately as the case requires, the situation could easily change. This is particularly true if, in some domains, the lines between piracy, commercial espionage, sabotage, and state uses of power were to become blurry. In some parts of the great commons it is easier than elsewhere to use power anonymously or ambiguously. Invasions across borders, or air or missile strikes, have unmistakable "return addresses." Not so in cyberspace; and even in the maritime realm, it is easier to hide behind the facade of private companies or individuals. Some states—China most notably—have adroitly exploited the possibilities of creating blurred identities, such as China's use of its fishing fleet as a maritime militia.[22]

The great commons is also the likeliest venue of strategic surprise. The United States knows what it is to fight in both governed and ungoverned terrestrial space: both are old and familiar challenges. By contrast, maritime warfare on a large scale has not occurred for over seventy years; cyberwarfare, if it has occurred, has done so at a relatively low level; and space war has yet to happen. Even territorial ungoverned space can generate surprise: the emergence of the Islamic state from the chaotic provinces of Syria and Iraq in 2014 came as a shock to American leaders.

Even as the United States has to monitor and prepare responses to its opponents, real and potential, it must be able to monitor and shape places that are not parts of states. In dealing with the challenges of ungoverned space, many civilian agencies of government will play the leading role; the private sector and nongovernmental organizations will as well. But military power remains the ultimate guarantor that the diverse great commons of mankind remain accessible to all. Having thrived for so long in an age in which the oceans were policed by the Royal and then the United States Navies, in which space was the preserve of a few and cyberspace was more dream than reality, it would be unwise for today's American leaders to think that such openness is self-policing.

Many of the military capabilities discussed in this chapter overlap with those discussed elsewhere: the United States needs a strong navy to balance China; it has to pursue cyberwarfare against jihadi propaganda, disabling e-mail accounts and even sabotaging servers. But it needs as well a strategic concept that informs its approach to those areas of the world that no state commands, which it does not aspire to control, but in which chaos would threaten US interests. From a purely intellectual point of view, it is not the least of America's strategic challenges.

CHAPTER EIGHT

THE LOGIC OF HARD POWER

Thus far we have made the case that the United States should continue to play its leading role in international politics, which in turn implies military primacy. We have examined the lessons of our recent military past and the nature of the resources and abilities that America brings to international politics. We have explored as well the four distinct challenges that loom ahead: China, the jihadi threat, several hostile states of different size and intention, and the problem of the commons and ungoverned space. This, the final chapter, explores how the United States and its government should think about the actual use of hard power: the rules of thumb and strategic aphorisms that do not make sense and those that do.

America needs a substantially larger military than the one it now has. The case has been made by a bipartisan national defense panel, and the detailed recommendations may be found there. It is not enough to have an ample arsenal, however; one needs to know how to use it wisely.[1]

Despite American wealth and power, the multiple strategic problems it faces are rendered more complex in several ways. These challenges do not operate in entirely separate spheres. China's assertion as a great power is felt most in the maritime realm, particularly in the South China Sea; its national strategy asserts as well that "outer space and cyber space have become new commanding heights in strategic competition among all parties." Jihadi movements flourish in ungoverned space; to the extent they succeed, they often create more of it, and in the extreme case have contributed to the dissolution of pre-existing states in the Middle East. Iran, Russia, and North Korea all make use of the cyber realm for espionage and sabotage.[2]

The necessary American approach to any given strategic problem is to narrow it down, chiefly to make it manageable. But although the United States may prefer to divide up its problems, focusing upon one at a time, the fact remains that there is only one United States. What it does or does not do with regard to one area of the world, or one strategic problem, will be noted in and affect others. When President Obama declared that the Syrian use of chemical weapons on its own population would be a "red line," and then failed to use military power once that red line was crossed, Russia and China noticed. After a chemical weapons disarmament agreement was reached, brokered by Russia, Vladimir Putin published an op-ed in the *New York Times* in which, after lying about the regime's use of chemical weapons ("there is every reason to believe that it was used not by the Syrian Army, but by opposition forces"), he proceeded to dismiss President Obama's assertion that the United States is exceptional as "extremely dangerous." It was probably not entirely coincidental that barely six months later, after having informed his American readers that "force has proved ineffective and pointless," he launched the seizure of Crimea and after that a Russian-directed rebellion in eastern Ukraine that brought thousands of deaths and de facto annexation there as well. Subsequently, he introduced Russian air power into the Syrian civil war, temporarily tipping the balance to the Assad regime and its Iranian allies, at the cost of much more civilian devastation.[3]

Credibility can rarely be segregated issue by issue. Politicians know this viscerally, which is why they may choose to take firm stands on matters that are seemingly of second-order importance. They are making a point, hoping to prevent challenges on other fronts.[4]

Yet although these challenges may be linked directly in some cases, and are almost always unified by the element of credibility, they nonetheless require differing responses, particularly in terms of hard power. To disrupt and counterbalance jihadi movements, the best response may be some combination of surveillance, precision strikes (often from drones), special forces raids, and extensive training missions to assist local forces. To balance China, the United States requires exceptionally strong naval forces, long-range air power, and the ability to both defend in space and deny China access to it. Against Iran or North Korea, America requires the ability to launch preemptive strikes against small nuclear arsenals. In extremis, it may even need to use nuclear weapons to do so, if the alternative is to see the capital of a major ally incinerated.

The problem here is not just that each of the kinds of armed forces requires, in effect, its own defense and intelligence budget. The difficulty, rather, is that the kinds of people and organizations suited for one kind of conflict are often radically unsuited for another. The pattern is an old one in military history. Because of their experience in colonial warfare, the French and British armies of 1914 had much more combat experience than did their German counterparts. But the German military, which had remained resolutely focused on large-scale operations in Europe, was better prepared for the mass battles of the opening phases of the First World War. Or closer to our time: the US Army that went into Vietnam was very much an updated version of that which had fought in North Africa, Italy, France, and Germany—hard hitting, extremely aggressive, and inclined to mass, speed, and violence. It was not the right approach for a complex war of jungle fighting, urban terror, and rural counterinsurgency.

The tools of warfare shape military organizations as much as the other way around. Navies, for example, necessarily have a different attitude toward risk than armies do, because they have fewer major units—dozens at most—to put into harm's way. When an organization of several thousand soldiers is defeated, the unit may withdraw in some disarray, but will still exist; when a ship or aircraft carrier is lost, it will sink, and disappear totally. Conceptions of time may differ as well. The war against terrorist organizations is long, and in some ways never ending, which is why such organizations as the National Counter Terrorism Center have been, in effect, operational headquarters for years. The right strategic time horizon for the anti-jihadi war is decades, even longer. The two wars to evict Saddam Hussein from

Kuwait, and then to overthrow his regime, on the other hand, were measured in terms of weeks.

Civilian leaders who have not dealt much with the military may tacitly assume that senior generals and admirals are interchangeable with respect to their professional expertise. They are not. Secretary of Defense Robert Gates recognized this when he relieved General David McKiernan as commander of US forces in Afghanistan in 2009. McKiernan was an able leader of heavy ground forces, the product of a US Army that had spent decades preparing for all-out conflict with the Soviet Union in the heart of Europe. He was simply not the right leader for a counterinsurgency campaign in the wild mountains and valleys of Afghanistan. But Gates's action was exceptional in the postwar history of American civil-military relations, precisely because so few civilian leaders have recognized that a good general may simply be the wrong fit for a given war; and fewer still, ready to act on that insight.

The president of the United States has one principal military adviser, the chairman of the Joint Chiefs of Staff. Of necessity, the chairman cannot be equally expert—indeed, probably cannot be conversant—with all forms of warfare. And this raises a further problem: the simultaneity trap. In all states, be they a city-state like Singapore or the United States, decisions about the use of force are made by a very small number of politicians, military leaders, and their principal advisers. Countries have but one president or prime minister, one secretary or minister of defense, one chief of defense staff or (as in the case of America) chairman of the Joint Chiefs of Staff. The services have but one military chief each. Each, in turn, has but a handful of principal assistants, such as the national security adviser, or the officer responsible for plans or current operations, or the civilian in charge of policy matters in the department of defense. At the end of the day, somewhere between five and fifty personnel—and the real number is a lot closer to five than to fifty—have an important role to play in deciding on the use of military force. And it really does not matter how large the country is, or how complicated its military challenges may be.[5]

Despite what their political rivals at home, and worried allies or dismissive enemies abroad might think, American decision-makers are generally at least as talented as their counterparts, and often better served by their staffs. The problem lies in that they are overwhelmed by the need to direct military operations in different parts of the globe, using different means, and to different ends. This is one of the greatest obstacles to the coherent use of American military power to support America's foreign policy. In theory, political and military leaders at the top of the US decision-making pyramid should establish national security priorities and devote adequate time to the most important of them. In practice they find themselves dealing with multiple problems—about many of which they have only superficial knowledge—at the same time. They have too little time to learn, and less ability to set priorities.

The problem gets worse. For much of the Cold War, American power served American foreign policy less by its exercise than by its potential; less by its action than by its menace. This is no longer the case. Any candidate for the US presidency after 2001 has had to assume that he or she would be a wartime president, actually using violence to serve the ends of policy. But whereas wartime presidents in the past could concentrate exclusively, or nearly so, on the task at hand, American leaders in the twenty-first century must think both about actual operations and the use of military power for deterrence and to shape a troubled peace. That is, they must think about how to use hard power to deter Russian aggression in eastern Europe, while waging war against jihadi movements. They may have to plan very hard for a shooting war with Iran, while hoping to induce China not to push too hard in the South China Sea against US allies.

American military power is thus often caught between opposing poles—actual use versus deterrence; achieving immediate objectives versus creating order, norms, and rules; and, of course, defending interests and asserting values. The complexity of American strategic purpose in the twenty-first century, and the intrinsic limits of any system of using it, makes the challenges of wielding hard power as daunting, from the intellectual point of view at least, as they have ever been. A well-organized staff, particularly in the White House and key agencies, such as the Defense and State Departments, can ameliorate the problem, but it is existential in nature.

As overburdened American leaders wrestle with the multiple demands on the military hard power at their disposal, they face a layered strategic problem. Old forms of conflict, and the military power associated with them, do not vanish. Few strategic problems are ever completely solved; they may diminish in intensity, but will continue to exist in parallel with old ones. The Troubles in Northern Ireland go back nearly fifty years: they are not quite over yet. The insurgency of the Revolutionary Armed Forces of Colombia (FARC) against that nation's government is of a similar age; it, too, is yet unresolved. And while the older threats often survive, new variants emerge alongside older problems. Thus, the traditional problems of nuclear deterrence as understood in the Cold War continue to exist today. Russia retains a somewhat modernized version of its twentieth-century nuclear force; China may have a substantially larger force. In both cases, however, the operational and strategic requirements are familiar. But now a new dimension appears. A nuclear Iran and even more so, a nuclear North Korea, cannot be expected to act as the Soviet Union or the People's Republic of China has. They may not be deterred in the same way; American allies threatened by these states may require different kinds of guarantees and aid than did the Federal Republic of Germany in the second half of the twentieth century.

———

The nearly half-century of the Cold War created, as any prolonged standoff does, a set of axioms, principles, and catchphrases that made sense in that context, but much less now. Indeed, that jargon and those concepts, learned by rote by two generations of strategic thinkers, is now dangerously misleading to them. When they leach out into public discourse, as these ideas inevitably do, they also mislead the American public.

Take, for example, containment, the master strategic concept for the Cold War. As originally described by George Kennan in his famous "X" article in *Foreign Affairs* in 1947, it suggested that the United States should meet Soviet aggression by blocking it; over a period of time, Kennan believed, the Soviet system would mellow. Even Kennan's diagnosis of Soviet communism looks slightly naive in retrospect: he thought Lenin might have moderated the terror (in fact, Lenin was its prime theorist and architect), and he doubted that communist leaders desired absolute power (they did). Still, containment was a useful idea, although even in the Cold War context it provided no guidance about whether, for example, to fight communist movements in Indochina, how to exploit splits in the communist camp, or what kind of nuclear posture was the right one. When the Soviet Union did crack up, it was as a result of a misplaced reform effort from within, and the general failure of the Soviet economic model, as well as the debilitating effects of an arms race that the Soviet Union was convinced it was losing.[6]

Containment had its difficulties even in the Cold War. Simply to duplicate it as a policy vis-à-vis a nuclear-armed Iran, for example, or a rising China, is to ignore the completely different contexts. The front line of containment against the Soviet Union was Western Europe, where several hundred thousand American soldiers stood on the very frontier between the two systems. They were stationed in a continent culturally and politically compatible with the United States. They were up against a system that, after the 1950s, had lost much, though not all of its revolutionary fervor, and a state that had long acted within an international system in which it had been a major player. By contrast, with the exception of Israel, the states of the Middle East and Persian Gulf are not culturally hospitable to the United States, and do not want large numbers of American forces permanently deployed on their territory. The source of the US-Iranian conflict lies in the nature of Iran's religio-sectarian regime, which retains many of its revolutionary characteristics, and whose founding myth hinges critically on animus against the United States. Most important, European statesmen could say (all of the time) that the United States was prepared to threaten nuclear war if they were attacked; and some of the time, they believed it. They had the evidence of two world wars to back up the notion that the United States would risk a great deal to rescue the Old World. That is a much harder proposition for Saudi Arabia.

Containment was a strategic concept born of the early Cold War. The concepts of end states and exit strategies were born of the late Cold War, of the Vietnam war and its aftermath, and in particular, of the American military's repudiation of that experience. Periodically these terms creep into public discourse; they are more often found in the deliberations of government, and they were pervasive in the war colleges of the American armed forces from the 1980s and for thirty or more years thereafter. Born of frustration with the Indochina War, the term *end state* suggests that military planners can have a very concrete understanding of what they hope to achieve by waging a war, the completion of which is just that—completion. The term *exit strategy* means that once the war is won (and it implies that winning is an unambiguous concept), one can safely extricate oneself from conflict, and that how to do so can be known in advance.

Upon close examination, these ideas disintegrate. Politics is fluid and continuous; there are no end states in politics—win an election and now you have to govern; govern and before you know it, you are planning your reelection. Politics, writes French statesman and novelist Maurice Druon:

> has no end and permits the mind no rest. . . . The victorious general enjoys the honors of his victory for a long while; but a prime minister has to face the new situation born of that very victory itself.[7]

War is, as Clausewitz taught, a continuation of politics by other means, and what applies in plain politics applies even more forcibly when it comes to war. Defeat Nazi Germany and find yourself in a Cold War with your former ally, a standoff that takes place in large measure on the territory of your defeated former enemy, now an ally. Watch in astonishment as the Soviet empire, and the Soviet Union itself, dissolves; then cope with the small wars that break out as European communism collapses; and then react to a Russia seething with resentment over the post–Cold War settlement.

In a similar vein, exit strategies conceived in advance have very little bearing on what really happens. American forces remain in South Korea, Japan, and Germany, even though the wars that brought them there were fought by men, most of whom are retired or dead of old age. To "exit" a war requires the cooperation of friend and foe alike: the fatal conceit of an exit strategy, like that of an end state, is that it conceives of war as a kind of engineering enterprise, which it is not, rather than a contest of opposing wills conducted in the murk of politics, which it is.

These tired and shallow concepts have real consequences. An American military imbued with the notion of end states and exit strategies fought two stunningly swift conventional wars against the Iraqi state led by Saddam Hussein in 1991 and 2003. In neither case was there a real end state: the contest went on in different forms. In neither case was there a well-conceived exit: in the former case American forces lingered to protect nearby Kuwait as well as the Kurdish population of northern Iraq; in the latter, a vicious, and generally unanticipated set of insurgencies and civil conflicts broke out.

Containment, end state, and exit strategy are a kind of strategic pixie dust, the sprinkling of which over the complex problems of contemporary policy problems may seem to make them manageable. In fact, they do not manage them. They oversimplify them, and because their intended results are often unattainable, these concepts paralyze decision-makers rather than inform them. Understanding strategy in the years to come will require walking away from these concepts and devising new ones in line with the political and strategic realities of our times.

British political philosopher Isaiah Berlin once observed that "what makes statesmen, like drivers of cars, successful is that they do not think in general terms. . . . Their merit is that they grasp the unique combination of characteristics that constitute this particular situation—this and no other." But as Tocqueville once observed, mediocre politicians resort to general explanations of events to relieve themselves of responsibilities. And timid or unimaginative politicians, and generals, will thrash about, hoping for pat formulas that will relieve them of the burden of sizing up particular circumstances. Intellectuals will often oblige those questing for an intellectual nostrum. In recent years one such comforting notion is grand strategy. It is a soothing concept; yet not merely illusory, for the most part, but dangerous.[8]

The idea of grand strategy was given currency by the editor of the most influential modern American textbook on strategy, *Makers of*

Modern Strategy, a work published in 1943. In an essay published in early 1941, as the United States began edging into the greatest war of the twentieth century, Edward Mead Earle defined *grand strategy* as "the science and art of controlling and utilizing the resources of a nation, including its armed forces, to the end that its vital interests (as interpreted by its de facto rulers) shall be effectively promoted and secured against all enemies." For most of us the term *grand strategy* connotes a kind of architectonic concept of ends and means in foreign policy; the highest level of integrated thinking about what a country wants to do in the world, and a sophisticated, elaborate conception of how it intends to go about it.[9]

The lure of grand strategy reflects the frustration of military officers at the intractability of the problems they are assigned, and at what often seems to them the slackness of the rest of government. It also emerges from academic writers who sometimes misconceive policy as depending chiefly on the development of great ideas rather than the drudgery of implementing them. In any case, grand strategy is an idea whose time will never come, because the human condition does not permit it. A simple thought experiment will confirm this: try leaping ahead by decades from, say, 1910 onward. The statesmen of that year could not have anticipated that in 1920, they or their successors would be rebuilding an utterly shattered world, in which two great multinational empires had been wiped off the map while a third, Russia, was in the hands of a marginal group of political fanatics. In 1920, who would have anticipated the seeming reconciliation of France, Britain, and Germany, and then the onset of the Great Depression by 1930? In that latter year, would it have been plausible to foresee, in a decade's time, the emergence of Hitler, the reconstruction of Germany's military might, and the shattering of France in 1940? From that dark vantage point, the world of 1950—complete with a prostrate Germany and Japan, American armies battling in the Korean peninsula, and nuclear weapons—was almost as unimaginable. As would have been the world of 1960, relatively stable, with a Europe well on its way to recovery, with Japan not far behind. Ten years further down the road, in 1970, the American colossus, which had seemed in 1960 to tower over the planet, would appear to intelligent observers trapped in terminal decline, bogged down in Vietnam, torn by race and youth riots. And yet in 1980 a recovery would have begun. But even the most optimistic strategists of that year could hardly have anticipated the world of 1990, in which the Cold War had ended, or 2000, in which the Soviet Union had vanished into more than a dozen constituent states and China had begun to emerge as a great power. And the world of 2010, in which the United States was waging wars occasioned by horrific attacks against the homeland in 2001, would have been just as impossible to foretell.

The very idea of grand strategy, then, runs on the rocks when it confronts the power of accident, contingency, and randomness that pervade human affairs. At the writing of this book, a president who prided himself on opposing the 2003 Iraq war at the time, and claimed to have ended the war responsibly, finds himself flinging several thousand American advisers back into Iraq, against an enemy whose name was virtually unknown a year before. A Russia supposedly paralyzed by internal economic and demographic decline has wrested the Crimean peninsula by force from Ukraine, and invaded the eastern portions of that country. And North Korea, once believed to be on the verge of collapse, may be instead on the verge of building ballistic missiles tipped with atomic or even thermonuclear warheads that can reach the United States.

Grand strategy often assumes, as well, that individual leaders do not really matter—but in reality, we know that they do. A Mao, a Stalin, and a Churchill swung their respective countries in very different directions than other leaders might have done. And even at the level of figures who are considerably less remarkable, who is in charge makes a difference. One may reasonably doubt whether a President Al Gore would have ordered the invasion of Iraq in 2003; President George W. Bush did.

Finally, the concept of grand strategy confuses the big idea with important choices. Containment of the Soviet Union was, one supposes, a grand strategic concept. But adopting that policy (which is what it is—a more useful if less grand term) did not determine whether the United States would stand with its British and French allies during the Suez Crisis or undermine them, intervene in Vietnam or refrain, or open the path for military collaboration with China in the 1970s. As a practical matter—and strategy is a practical business—grand strategy offers very little guidance.

===

How, then, to think about the logic of hard power at this time when so many things seem unpredictable? How to decide what kinds of forces are required, and how to employ them? If ideas are necessary—and they are—how to formulate them without falling into the trap created by grand strategy as a concept? And finally, how to do those things when America's recent experiences of war have been, in the main, unsuccessful?

The United States should begin by discarding its current array of high-level strategy documents—"The National Security Strategy of the United States," or NSS (produced by the White House), "The National Military Strategy" (produced by the chairman of the Joint Chiefs of Staff), and "The Quadrennial Defense Review," or QDR (produced by the Department of Defense, under civilian supervision). In theory, the first two are produced annually (the NSS rarely is); the latter is, as the name implies, an exercise of appalling bureaucratic complexity that occurs every four years. The first two are anodyne, because they are largely public documents. The last is the more consequential document because it shapes budget allocations.

Strategy is the art of matching military means to political ends; a single document, produced at irregular intervals, under the auspices of the president in his role as commander in chief, would make much more sense. The QDR chugs along irrespective of world events: thus the 2000 version of the document was published shortly before the 9/11 attacks rendered it obsolete. A single document, published at least every five to seven years, but at the discretion of the administration, would make more sense. And it would surely be more effective if it had both a public and a classified version, much like other countries' white papers on defense, which offer considerably more sophisticated analyses of international politics than the American version. The French "Livre blanc sur la défense et la sécurité nationale" (White Paper on Defense and National Security), issued by the office of the president of the republic, is a worthy model.[10]

White papers and formal documents are necessary, but of even greater important is substance. The United States must begin by explicitly accepting a very high level of uncertainty in its strategic planning, by establishing the modest number of things we actually can know about ourselves and about the world around us—that American demographics will continue to be better than those of China for the next thirty years, for example. We can safely assume that radical Islamists will not be inclined to come to a peaceful accommodation with the United States or regimes allied with it. At the next rung of assumptions are those to which some modest uncertainty may be attached. China is likely to remain a unitary, slowly rising great power—but it is conceivable, if unlikely, that it could experience internal political convulsions, or suffer an economic crisis resulting from its problematic internal finances. Europe may recover some portion of its military strength, but the likelihood of its being willing and able to stand on its own against Russia, or to throw large forces into North Africa and the Middle East, is slim.

Having laid out these structural elements that are roughly predictable, a serious national strategy document would lay out the many things we just do not and cannot know—from how long the leaders of China and Russia will survive, to when the next global economic crisis will hit. Social upheavals, too, are unpredictable (if they were, they would usually be forestalled by anxious rulers). Virtually no one, after all, predicted the revolutions that spread from Tunis throughout the Arab world in 2010.

This fundamental acceptance of uncertainty, an acceptance that must be articulated to the American people, has several consequences. It should mean avoiding the phony precision of projected requirements that have long bedeviled defense planning. Even crude standards, such as the ability to fight two regional wars simultaneously (the standard first used in the Clinton administration), quickly became an exercise bogged down in minutiae. More positively, it means setting standards for the size of the defense budget that will appear to be, and in some sense are, arbitrary. For example, setting defense spending as a percentage of gross domestic product (GDP) would be a major advance. It is, let it be noted, nothing more in principle than what we repeatedly demand of our European NATO partners—2 percent of GDP to face just one threat, from Russia, rather than the multiple challenges we face.

In the past, American defense spending has fluctuated between a high of 37 percent of the economy during World War II, and a low of less than 2 percent before it. Even before the Korean War marked the true opening of the Cold War, the United States was spending nearly 5 percent in 1949. For much of the late 1950s and early 1960s—before Vietnam, and a period of great prosperity—the United States spent 8 to 9 percent of GDP on defense, and it continued to spend well over 4 percent in many of the years following Vietnam. A new, sustained target of 4 percent would hardly break the bank.[11]

The advantages of a percentage-driven budget, at least until a crisis occurs, are several: it offers some predictability to the defense acquisition system; it allows, in times of relative tranquility, greater investment in research and development to sustain a military edge; and it can be justified fairly straightforwardly. As many people save some fixed percent of their income, or set aside some other portion of their income for insurance or retirement savings—and defense spending is a form of national insurance—so, too, can a nation approach military spending.

The forthright acceptance of uncertainty has many other dimensions. A military system built around uncertainty accepts the possibility that it may have to fight very different kinds of wars. In retrospect, the failure to conduct effective military governance and counterinsurgency in the early years in Iraq stemmed from the armed forces' excessively narrow concept of war before it. Those pernicious assumptions derived in part from the orientation of the United States Army to all-out warfare that dated back to World War II, and in part from its triumphalist reading of the outcome of the first Gulf War of 1991. In that case, it was generally believed that the proper use of American power was overwhelmingly the defeat of a conventional opponent. The follow-up would be someone else's task.[12]

The wars of the twenty-first century may take many forms. Conventional conflict, including with China, most assuredly cannot be ruled out. At the other end of the spectrum, terrorism will surely continue. In between, what has been called hybrid war—blending different forms of force with subversion, sabotage, and terror—will also exist. Wars may be sudden or build up slowly; they may be protracted. One of the signal failures of American military thinking in the years before Iraq and Afghanistan was its inability to articulate doctrine, or simply prepare officers psychologically, for the possibility that a war might drag on for a decade or more.

As important as the hardware the Department of Defense buys in the next twenty years will be the intellectual formation of the men and women who lead its armed forces. It is a cliché among historians that the leaders of World War II were bred in the staff and war colleges of the interwar period, at a time when the best senior officers taught, and the best rising officers attended those institutions, and they devoted themselves to thinking about future war. Today's war colleges are much larger and less selective institutions, and often less focused on thinking about the future of war than on giving officers a basic grounding in contemporary international relations. If the strategic future is unpredictable, there must be a premium on preparing leaders, and eventually the American public, to accept many understandings of what war is. Creating the right intellectual culture for thinking about hard power should be an essential task of senior leadership rather than, as it is now, a mere afterthought for leaders preoccupied by budgetary and operational issues.

A much more concrete adaptation to uncertainty is investment in mobilization as a strategic concept. For most of American history, in fact, this was how the United States prepared for war. It was understood that the United States' peacetime forces would be supplemented, indeed swamped, by newly raised and equipped forces in war. This was rarely a smooth process, and after the First World War—in which the vast American expeditionary force was embarrassed by its need to rely on British and French airplanes, artillery, and even light machine guns—the Army and Navy invested shrewdly in mobilization planning. The Army Industrial College, created in 1924, studied these problems; the chief of staff of the Army in 1940, General George C. Marshall, ordered the rewriting of manuals and training doctrine for an army of citizen soldiers. And American industry was able to deliver an astonishing flood of equipment within two years of full mobilization. After World War II, the Army Industrial College became the Industrial College of the Armed Forces (ICAF).

There are some pockets of mobilization preparation in today's military, but they consist chiefly of plans to increase the production of key consumables (guided bombs and the like) without the usual stifling bureaucratic procedures of peacetime. ICAF became, in 2013, The Eisenhower School, and its focus turned more to acquisition than mobilization. The main platforms used by the military—its tanks, airplanes, and ships—are produced in relatively small quantities on very few production lines. Take the latest fighter introduced into American service. Three dozen were delivered in 2014, and it is with pride that Lockheed Martin informs visitors to its website that that number will double . . . in three years. The F-35 has been in development since the 1990s, and a test plane flew in 2000. By way of contrast, the B-29, the US Army Air Forces' most sophisticated bomber during World War II, went from orders for a prototype in 1940 to production in 1941. By 1946, five years later, nearly 4,000 had been manufactured, many seeing active service in the Pacific. Matters are very different today. By 1943, the Newport News shipyard could build a front-line *Essex*-class aircraft carrier in about fifteen months. Today, a carrier takes four or five times as long. World War II submarines were similarly built in a bit more than a year; today, even with remarkable advances in modular construction, they take almost two and a half times as long.[13]

A mobilization-oriented military would have plans in peacetime to build new kinds of forces rapidly and to equip them quickly. In some cases—the MRAP mine-protected vehicle discussed in chapter two was one—this has been done, but such examples are few. Bigger ideas, such as converting civilian platforms to military use (e.g., the DC-3 became the C-47 transport of World War II), are less in evidence. In our age of mass-produced unmanned aerial vehicles, that is one possibility that exists. But a mobilization-ready military would be prepared to shuck off, on short notice, assumptions about how the core units of the military should be equipped. In a mobilization-based military, it is possible that the high-end forces of peacetime, equipped with F-35 fighter aircraft, would fight alongside mass produced, improvised swarms of less sophisticated aircraft managed by contractors or newly recruited service personnel. Of course, this would require a difficult adjustment for a military used to the idea of small numbers of high-performance platforms manned by elaborately trained operators, commanded by officers who have learned their craft during a slow and careful ascent through the ranks.

The human side of mobilization is particularly important. After 9/11 there is no question that the United States government could have recruited an extraordinary range of individuals for public service in the military or intelligence community. There were no plans to do so, and no willingness, either—although there was a willingness to hire (expensive) contractors, whose incentives and outlooks are very different than those of men and women who have taken a service oath. There was no parallel to the way in which during World War II professors joined the Office of Strategic Services, business people became colonels in the Army's quartermaster corps, and small-town mayors became civil affairs officers ready to conduct the occupation of Germany and Japan.

Future war is unlikely to require the conscription of young men and women, and certainly not on the scale of the world wars. But the services can do far better at bringing in high-quality individuals, to include those with various kinds of technological and cultural expertise, giving them appropriate rank, and making use of them. It occasionally does this with surgeons and lawyers; it should do it with software engineers and anthropologists as well. To do this would require breaking the model forged in the aftermath of Vietnam: a relatively small career force that requires not only painstaking preparation for each level of command or expert operation, but also a progression that is not to be shortcut by lateral entry into the higher ranks. Rather than, as now, a reserve system that simply parallels active duty military service, the armed forces might consider programs that permit the commissioning of special talents from the civilian world directly into higher ranks (up to lieutenant colonel, say). At the very least, the government can prepare now to do this in the event of a national emergency.

The United States will fight very few, if any, of its future wars alone. For all that America's allies are used to complaining about it, and for all that American politicians berate one another about failing to tend to them, the fact is that the nation is remarkably effective at managing coalitions. For some seventy years, beginning with the grandest coalition of all, the United Nations against Germany and Japan, Americans have not only coordinated armies in the field, but shared logistical and intelligence systems. The United States built the great alliance, NATO, that held the line in the Cold War, guaranteeing it with a quarter of a million troops permanently stationed in Europe. And even when NATO did not come into play directly—during the 1991 Gulf War with Iraq, for example—NATO procedures (e.g., the assembly of a common Air Tasking Order to coordinate air operations) did.

Today, foreign officers are to be found in American headquarters, and sometimes in quite senior positions such as chief of staff in a senior command. American war colleges are filled with foreign officers; and in the field, in the air, and at sea, scores of nations are accustomed to operating alongside the United States. Even when the United States goes through acrimonious disputes with allies—think France during the Iraq war from 2003 onward—it is remarkable how quickly quarrels get patched up. By the end of the Bush administration, Franco-American cooperation over Afghanistan and Iran, to name just two instances, were close. Indeed, France has gradually come to equal and even in some cases replace Britain as a security partner in Europe.

So far, so good. In the future, however, the United States will have to readjust its alliance portfolio. Its European partners, although still robust on paper, have been cutting muscle far more than fat from their defense budgets for decades. Take Germany: a country that in 1985 spent more than 3 percent of GDP on defense and spends barely 1 percent today; a country that only ten years ago fielded 1,700 modern Leopard 2 tanks, and now has little more than 400 in its arsenal. Nowhere, however, is this more pronounced than in the case of Great Britain, America's most important military ally for over seven decades. In 1985 more than 5 percent of British GDP went to defense; today, less than 2.5 percent. Thirty years ago it fielded a military of almost a third of a million men and women; today, less than half as many. Even twenty years ago, while the post–Cold War drawdown was under way, it had a fleet with thirty-eight major surface combatants (including three aircraft carriers) and two dozen submarines. As of 2015 the still-shrinking Royal Navy had precisely half as many major surface combatants, including no carriers (although two are being built, albeit without the airplanes to fly off them), and fewer than half as many submarines.[14]

At the same time, other partners, most of them not formal allies, have been emerging. India, with which the United States had an arms' length relationship throughout most of the late Cold War, is increasingly a partner. India will never refer to itself as an ally of the United States, but the US-Indian relationship is built on the bedrock of shared values (the world's most powerful and the world's largest democracies), common interests (particularly wariness about China and radical Islam), and ever-deepening societal ties. The Indian military is large and growing; so, too, is military cooperation.

Some old allies are growing in the scale of military power. Japan has as many soldiers as it did twenty years ago; it has more combat aircraft, as many (but much better) submarines, and a slightly smaller surface fleet composed of much larger and more capable warships—more than twice as many surface warships as Britain's Royal Navy, which once dwarfed it. This is, after the US Navy, the largest and most effective navy in Asia. It has excellent technology (its Soryu-class submarines, for example) and is gradually shedding some of the inhibitions about deploying military power that it took from its World War II experience. On a lesser scale the same may be said of Australia, whose small but high-quality armed forces have repeatedly fought alongside their American counterparts throughout the first two decades of the twenty-first century.

And there are smaller allies, too. The United Arab Emirates (UAE), for example, with a tiny population but a larger defense budget than Turkey, has a small, superbly equipped military. Its special operations forces are notably effective (they served particularly well in Afghanistan), and it is willing to use them. In 2015 the UAE dispatched an armored brigade to take the fight to Iranian-backed Houthi rebels in Yemen. Or Israel: the United States helped midwife it into existence two generations ago, and it now has considerably more military potential than most European states, in terms of sheer quantity (almost twice as many combat-capable aircraft as France, for example) and much greater combat experience. Or the Colombian military, which, with American support, has created the most proficient and combat-experienced infantry in Latin America, and in large numbers too: 237,000 in the Army alone, two and a half times the size of the British Army.

To be sure, all of these numbers conceal far more complex comparisons of technology, training, and sophistication at the multiple activities that are required for the conduct of war—logistics and intelligence processing, most notably. But the raw numbers are instructive nonetheless. American statecraft should focus more attention on these rising allies and others—such as Poland, Australia, and often-overlooked Canada—in constructing the military coalitions of the twenty-first century. The true aim of military diplomacy is not primarily establishing good relationships with potential adversaries, as some believe; rather, it is consolidating the partnerships and coalitional relationships that multiply American power in pursuit of common aims. A subtle recasting of those relationships is one of the first tasks of a reordered American security policy.

There remains one final question, and that is the largest of all: when and under what conditions should the United States actually use military power? The temptation, in the wake of the unhappy outcome of the Iraq and possibly even the Afghan war, is to formulate a set of rules, stringent in their requirements for the use of force. Such an effort was attempted three decades ago as the United States emerged from its post-Vietnam despondency. Secretary of Defense Caspar Weinberger articulated his famous six rules for the use of military force in a speech on November 28, 1984, at the National Press Club.

1. The United States should not commit forces to combat overseas unless the particular engagement or occasion is deemed vital to our national interest or that of our allies.
2. If we decide it is necessary to put combat troops into a given situation, we should do so wholeheartedly and with the clear intention of winning.

3. If we do decide to commit forces to combat overseas, we should have clearly defined political and military objectives. We should know precisely how our forces can accomplish those clearly defined objectives. And we should have and send the forces needed to do just that.

4. The relationship between our objectives and the forces we have committed . . . must be continually reassessed and adjusted if necessary.

5. Before the United States commits combat forces abroad, there must be some reasonable assurance that we will have the support of the American people and their elected representatives in Congress.

6. The commitment of U.S. forces to combat should be a last resort.[15]

Upon examination, unfortunately, each of Weinberger's rules falls apart. The first is self-evidently untrue. The United States has frequently used force in cases that do not affect its survival or fundamental well-being, from interventions in Grenada to Bosnia, Haiti to Somalia. This has always been so, and there is no reason to think it will change. The term "vital national interest" is so vague that it can be expanded or contracted almost indefinitely, according to the whim of those who use it.

The second supposes that the term "winning" is clear: often it is not. Particularly in a complex political situation, the United States may decide not to use its full force to obliterate an opponent, but to compel the enemy to yield on favorable terms. The third principle, that the United States should know in advance exactly how it will achieve its ends, flies in the face of military history: no use of force is ever completely predictable; it is impossible to know "precisely how our forces can accomplish those clearly defined objectives." The fourth principle, continually readjusting the relationship between objectives and forces, is fine as far as it goes—but it neglects the reality that in war, sometimes raw determination outweighs a nice calculation of ends and means. "Reasonable assurance" of popular support again assumes too much. It is often the case that the American people lend their support to successful enterprises and turn away from unsuccessful ones. Achieve military success and public support will follow, not the other way around. Finally, the notion of combat as a "last resort" falls apart under close inspection: as Clausewitz mordantly observed, one always has the option of giving the enemy what it wants. Warfare is therefore never a last resort.

Weinberger's rules ignited a heated, if generally civil, debate with Secretary of State George Shultz. The two World War II veterans disagreed profoundly about how to employ military power. In the end, although Weinberger's rules had a real purchase with the American military, he lost the argument. His attempt to codify rules for the use of military power, however, has lingered, and after the painful experience of Iraq in particular has reemerged. And surely some general guidelines—less prescriptive than Weinberger's, and more along the lines of the reality of warfare—make sense. Herewith, then, is an alternative set of rules, almost surely to be amended by experience.

1. Understand your war for what it is, not what you wish it to be.

Carl von Clausewitz described this as the cardinal task of wartime leaders. They must, he goes on to say, neither mistake their war for, "nor try to turn it into, something that is alien to its nature. That is the first of all strategic questions and the most comprehensive." Of all the mistakes in war, perhaps the most dangerous is the reduction of thinking to axioms or catch phrases. The intellectual judgment that is most required of any president and his military advisers is understanding the concrete circumstances into which he or she will throw US forces. The wars of the twenty-first century will differ from those of the past, and from each other. If there is one lesson to be learned from America's wars from Korea through Iraq, it is that attempting to fit them into a template (particularly a template that excluded protracted irregular conflict) was a mistake.[16]

It is not enough to describe a war as a conventional conflict, or a counterinsurgency, or a counterterror campaign. It is downright dangerous to explain it by analogies: in retrospect, one of the worst mistakes of those who conducted the seemingly completely successful 1991 war with Iraq was their insistence that this war would *not* resemble the Vietnam War. By self-consciously thinking about the war as a kind of photographic negative of the Indochina conflict (very short, conventional, intense, no counterinsurgency), they paradoxically set the conditions for the protracted standoff with Saddam Hussein that culminated in a far costlier follow-on war two decades later. When, in 2003, the war resumed, American leaders did not have a good grasp on the actual circumstances of the Iraqi state and the society the United States had pulverized in the intervening years, and hence were unprepared for the protracted occupation and reconstruction that was required. Clausewitz's belief that "understanding your war" in all of its uniqueness is "the first, the supreme, the most far reaching act of judgment that the statesman and commander" have to make is surely correct. It requires a self-conscious purging of one's mind of analogies, parallels, and metaphors—hard for anyone, and especially for political and military leaders launching a war.[17]

2. Planning is important; being able to adapt is more important.

In November 1940 Winston Churchill delivered a remarkable eulogy of Neville Chamberlain, his predecessor as prime minister who died after a bout with cancer. Chamberlain had favored appeasement of Hitler; Churchill rightly and prophetically opposed it. Yet Churchill, a man of unusual prescience, observed, "It is not given to human beings, happily for them, for otherwise life would be intolerable, to foresee or to predict to any large extent the unfolding course of events. In one phase men seem to have been right, in another they seem to have been wrong." He declared Chamberlain a man of rectitude and sincerity, which he described as a kind of shield to his memory. "It is very imprudent to walk through life without this shield, because we are so often mocked by the failure of our hopes and the upsetting of our calculations."[18]

Inevitably, initial judgments will be, at best, only partly correct. Circumstances will change, and unpredictable things will happen. Part of the decision to go to war requires accepting that the future will contain surprises, because of what our opponents will do, and because we can never quite gauge our own abilities accurately. No war ever turned out remotely like what we expected: America's World War II was expected to begin against Germany—instead it opened with a Japanese surprise attack. No one saw the Korean War coming. After Korea, General Omar Bradley warned his countrymen never to engage in another land war in Asia—and in little more than a decade they did. Before 2001, what sane Pentagon planner anticipated deploying tens of thousands of American soldiers to Afghanistan? Very few wars in history last as long as planners think, cost what they expect in blood and treasure, or end up with quite the results hoped for or anticipated.

Therefore, American strategists should build in a large and explicit margin of error, in terms of the forces that may be needed, the time operations may take, and the price that may have to be paid. They must be prepared for the possibility that the war will turn into something other than they anticipated, and that it will prove longer, more difficult, or more costly than anticipated. But that cuts the other way as well: it is quite possible, as in 1991 in Iraq, that success will be swift and more complete than looked for. In that case, planners should be prepared to exploit such success as well as cope with failure. In the same vein, leaders must prepare to remold and reshape the armed forces, from tactical units to higher commands, in accordance with the war they have, rather than the war they wish they had. George C. Marshall, chief of staff of the United States Army during World War II, was no great strategist, but he was in many ways the organizer of victory, in part because he was willing to purge the senior officer corps ruthlessly, to remake organizations, and to transform training.

3. You will prefer to go short, but prepare to go long.

It is a strategic commonplace that Americans are impatient, and some have gone so far as to argue that US strategic culture should accept this as a given, and that no matter what the cost, the nation should avoid long wars. It is not in fact true: the United States has persisted in its military engagements in Korea and Europe since the middle of the twentieth century. It sustained a military force in Iraq for more than eight years, and could easily have continued to do so longer, had the administration been more determined and adroit in negotiating with its Iraqi partners, and they less feckless in their self-confidence. To commit oneself only to fighting wars lasting a few weeks or months is to fatally cripple one's ability to use force. Again, one must accept wars for what they are.[19]

The implications are cautionary. In particular, although the United States can and has done nation building through military occupation successfully before—Germany and Japan are major cases; arguably South Korea and the Philippines, minor ones—it has done so only through a willingness to engage in protracted occupation and investment of military and civilian resources. When it does so, it is a mistake to think that the burden will be shouldered by the civilian agencies of government. In practice, they are usually either inadequately resourced, or culturally and organizationally incapable of delivering what the military wants. This is not an argument per se against the use of force to assist local allies in rebuilding government and establishing control of their territory—but it does argue for caution and a willingness to craft efforts that are sustainable, both internationally and domestically, such as what Americans have shown in Colombia in its half-century war against FARC insurgents.

What is undoubtedly true, however, is that political leaders must develop support for sustained military engagements abroad. In the initial flurry of patriotism and enthusiasm, the American people will tend to support a president who takes them into a shooting war. That enthusiasm erodes over time; in the meanwhile, political leaders learn to take it for granted. That is a mistake. Particularly if casualties are expected, the American people have to be informed and persuaded that a campaign is worth undertaking. If they believe it is—the extremely aggressive use of special operations forces against al-Qaeda and similar movements being a good example—they will support a war for a very long time indeed.

4. While engaging in today's fight, prepare for tomorrow's challenge.

It can be more dangerous not to act than to act—a point often lost in contemporary strategic debates. Inaction is a choice, too, and can have perilous consequences. Even in the wake of a smashing success, there will simply be further challenges, which may be peaceful (e.g., the long-term deployment of a quarter of a million American troops to Europe in the 1950s) or violent (e.g., American protection of the Kurds and, to a lesser extent, Shia of Iraq after 1991). There will be no end states and precious few exits—only new and different problems.

This is so particularly because for the United States, unlike Switzerland, hard power is about far more than protecting its borders and citizens at home and abroad. One may argue with historians whether ours is a more dangerous period than the Cold War, a point upon which reasonable people can disagree. But surely, as we have seen in previous chapters, it is more complex. It is a world of nearly an order of magnitude more independent states than in the decades before the Cold War began; it features an array of new weapons and modes of conflict existing in parallel with old and well-understood ones; it is a world in which the flood of information and instantaneity of communication make decision making more fraught and compressed than ever before.

American military planning doctrine the divides conflict into six phases: (0) prewar preparations to "shape the environment," (I) deterrent activities to prevent war, (II) seizing the initiative through deployments if deterrence has failed, (III) dominating the enemy (probably by destroying it), (IV) stabilizing the postwar situation, and (V) handing over to civilian authorities at the end of conflict. The orderliness is absurd. And yet this conceptualization shapes how the American military approaches war. In practice nothing like so orderly a process can or does take place. A more promising approach would be, as a war winds down (and sometimes even before that), to begin looking over the horizon to the next conflict. A good example of this might be the way in which the United States Army Air Forces (which later became the Air Force) began thinking early about the requirements for a conflict with the Soviet Union, even as the Cold War took shape.[20]

5. Adroit strategy matters; perseverance usually matters more.

War is a contest of will: and although clever operations and tactics matter, they do not count as much as sheer grit, at all levels. Presidents and lance corporals alike must understand this. In the final analysis, it is often indeed the case that victory goes to the side that refuses to accept that it is defeated, and the hardest decisions are never as clear in advance as they are in retrospect. This is particularly true for the United States, whose vast resources are unlikely to be exhausted in a conflict, but whose will may. Whatever his other faults as a strategist, President George W. Bush's finest moment came in 2006 when he ordered the surge of five more brigades to Iraq, to retrieve what looked to be a sinking situation. His military advisers disagreed, warning that it would break the force if he did so. His response—that they would be more likely broken by a defeat—became something of a legend.[21]

Perseverance is a virtue taught to young soldiers; that, rather than tactical excellence, is what a young infantryman takes away from the Army's grueling nine-week Ranger course. At the higher levels it is often assumed that intellectual virtues predominate over the rawer psychological traits needed in combat, and in a way that is true. But as great chess players have long known, even in a purely intellectual activity (which war is not), determination must back up the intellect. The war leader who is brilliant but lacks steel in his or her spine will fail.

6. A president can launch a war; to win it, he or she must sustain congressional and popular support.

Although popular support for the use of force can never be guaranteed in advance, and setting aside sudden emergencies requiring executive action, any substantial use of the armed power of the United States should get support from the people's representatives in Congress. Wars always increase executive power, and that has been no exception in the wars of the twenty-first century. From vast campaigns of assassination to the deployment of thousands of troops to Iraq in 2014, US presidents have felt free to use military power without obtaining congressional consent. This is both contrary to America's constitutional norms and unwise. Sooner or later, war will take the country to a place where unity is essential: better to have that moment come when both houses of Congress—whose instinct is normally to support a president during a period of emergency—are on the record in support. Indeed, in the case of Libya in 2011 and both Syria and Iraq later, it was convenient for both Congress and the president to avoid confronting the challenge of an authorization to use military force. Such temporary avoidance of the problem, however, ended up making American policy less firm and more contentious—and as a result, less effective.

The greatest fault of both Presidents Bush and Obama in Iraq and Afghanistan was their failure to repeatedly explain to the American people why their country was waging those wars. The contrast with a wartime leader, such as Churchill, is striking. Although our attention is more often drawn to the ringing phrases in the heroic period of Britain's standing alone—"we will fight on the beaches and on the landing grounds"—what is more striking was Churchill's use of long national addresses to explain to his own country and in some measure to the world the nature of the war in which they were embarked. Aristotle, the first and greatest student of rhetoric, noted that it was an art indispensable to the conduct of war, and he was right. An earlier Greek, Thucydides, in his magnificent history of the Peloponnesian War, showed the importance and the power of speech in sustaining and directing a war. In the Cold War two very different presidents, John F. Kennedy and Ronald Reagan, sustained public support for a dangerous and protracted standoff with the Soviet Union through their eloquence. Future wartime leaders will need no less.[22]

Weinberger articulated his rules in a world in which one could plausibly believe the United States would have to use force very rarely, if at all. He spoke at one of the peaks of the Cold War, in which the United States was rebuilding armed forces that had been materially and psychologically depleted by Vietnam. The need was for armed force to balance that of the Soviet Union in a contest that would, however, most likely remain peaceful. And, of course, Weinberger was dealing with the traumatic consequences of a war utterly unlike the one that he had served in as a young man. One can forgive the lack of realism his rules revealed: a later generation, weary and apprehensive though it may be, cannot afford the same indifference to the world as it is. A checklist of criteria for using hard power is pointless. Rather, what is needed is a prudent set of reminders to guide American leaders who have concluded, however reluctantly, that violence is the least bad policy choice.

Postscript: The Eagle's Head

In early March 1946, the presidential train was chugging its way to Fulton, Missouri. President Harry S. Truman had deliberately refrained from reading an early draft of the remarks that his guest, Winston Churchill, would give at Westminster College. The president, less than a year in power, was still uncertain how far to go in confronting the Soviet Union and its dictator Joseph Stalin, and he guessed that it would be easier all around if he could claim prior ignorance about what his guest might say.

But he did wine and dine the British statesman, now leader of the opposition in Parliament. As they talked of many things, Truman pointed out the presidential seal, whose redesign he had personally supervised. "This may interest you," he said. "We have just turned the eagle's head from the talons of war to the olive branch of peace." Churchill considered for a bit and then offered a suggestion. "The head should be on a swivel so that it can turn from the talons of war to the olive branch of peace as the occasion warrants."[1]

As was so often the case in his long life, Churchill was right: the eagle's head had to be able to swivel from olive branch to arrows and back. That was a hard lesson for Americans in 1946, after they had fought a global war, albeit with considerably fewer sacrifices than their British allies. It may be a hard conclusion for Americans today to accept at the end of more than a decade and a half of protracted warfare that has cost thousands of American lives, and left tens of thousands wounded in body and spirit. It may be particularly difficult to do so when the horizon of international politics appears more murkily ominous than at any time since the end of the Cold War, a world in which it is easy to make costly mistakes, and perhaps a world where one may hope to avoid those errors by shrinking from any hazardous action. The inclination of the citizens of the Great Republic to retire from world affairs has rarely dominated their national life, but neither has it ever been wholly absent from it.

Military power is, at best, a rough and imprecise instrument, used painfully and with unpredictable results. It is not a scalpel, but a knife that can turn in its wielder's hand. Despite decades of military diplomacy and a discourse of statecraft that abstracts from the reality of the threats force embodies, military power is about the ability to crush, maim, destroy, and kill. Although it often taps some of the highest virtues of which human beings are capable—comradeship, perseverance, dedication to duty, self-sacrifice—there is nothing lovely about it. It is, however, indispensable, and at this juncture in our history, perhaps, more so than ever. As Churchill had warned three years before that train ride with Harry Truman, a failure to exercise military power for aims larger than self-defense narrowly understood could be calamitous.

Americans of the early twenty-first century face neither the roughly competitive but generally optimistic world that Theodore Roosevelt dealt with in the early twentieth century, nor yet the era of totalitarian terror in the middle of that century that his cousin, Franklin Roosevelt, and his successors helped defeat in one case and contain in another. After a period of uncertainty and doubt, particularly in the wake of the controversial and ill-conducted war in Iraq and its no less poorly conducted aftermath, one should not expect the kind of successes that Ronald Reagan's and George H. W. Bush's administrations snatched from a crumbling Soviet Union at century's end.

"As our case is new," Lincoln rightly said in his annual message to Congress in 1862, "so we must think anew, and act anew." Those words are justly famous, but perhaps more telling is Lincoln's phrase "we must disenthrall ourselves." Today, Americans disenthralling themselves means understanding that as instructive as their nation's past is with regard to understanding the uses the United States has made of power, it offers no precise guide to the future. A new generation of US statesmen will have to forge new approaches to the use of the nation's still colossal armed power, making principled and prudential judgments of a kind unlike those of previous generations.

The United States is a mature great power; for well over a century it has towered over all the nations of the earth. Today, the balance of economic strength has shifted in enduring ways, leaving the United States more first among equals than the juggernaut of the last century. But the changes go deeper than that. The very weight of America's experiences in the last century, successful and unsuccessful alike, may get in the way of a readjustment of policies and alliances; it may make difficult the supple shifts and adaptations that an adroit use of military force will require in the future.

In 1943 Churchill urged upon America its assumption of a new role in the world. That which lies before the grandchildren and great-grandchildren of those he addressed is different, in critical respects, from the role the United States took on during World War II and the Cold War. Only three years later, in that train crossing the prairie, Churchill urged upon his American host, about whom he harbored private doubts, a kind of flexibility intermingled with resolution that is still needed. In the world as it is, the day is remote when the eagle can be content merely to gaze at the olive branch.

As Churchill also knew, however, the genius of the United States lies in its ability to reinvent and reimagine itself, to tap its vast resources of talent and wealth, to bring new generations of leaders to the fore, and to act in a larger interest than that of mere selfishness. Its ability to act with good effect internationally is, moreover, inseparable from its military strength, and its ability to use that strength. Despite all of America's blunders and errors, the wars half won and the setbacks unredeemed, US military power has, on the whole, been a force for good in the world. The use of that power was a critical element—hardly the only one, but indispensable—in winning the Cold War and securing unprecedented prosperity to ourselves and others. With good judgment and careful management, it will continue to be so. We cannot assume that the world of the twenty-first century will avoid horrors as bad as, or even worse, than those of the twentieth. The better angels of human nature have not triumphed. But the record of the last century also teaches us that even in the darkest times, the proper temper of freedom remains sober optimism, and in that respect, nothing has changed.

Acknowledgments

All authors accumulate debts of gratitude, and I am most emphatically no exception. Three superb research assistants, Annie Seibert, Will Quinn, and above all Jeb Benkowski (whose labors in 2015–2016 were, like Jeb himself, Herculean) were as indispensable as they were indefatigable. An equally invaluable contribution was made by friends and colleagues who read the manuscript and commented on it at considerable length with brutal if salutary candor: Rafi Cohen, Tom Donnelly, Eric Edelman, Tom Keaney, Bob Killebrew, Dick Kohn, Mara Karlin, Tom Mahnken, Jim Mann, Tom Ricks, and Paula Thornhill. Under their bludgeonings I have not, as the poet W. E. Henley puts it, cried aloud, but I certainly have winced as they excoriated an early draft for cheap shots, unsubstantiated arguments, and leaps of logic. It's a much better book because of them.

At Johns Hopkins School of Advanced International Studies, Dean Vali Nasr and Associate Deans John Harrington, Myron Kunka, and Peter Lewis eased my path, particularly with some opportune teaching relief in the final stretch. The SAIS library staff was, as ever, terrifically responsive to numerous urgent requests. Thayer McKell kept me organized, and John McLaughlin shared not only his wisdom about the world of intelligence, but his wizardly gifts to keep me sane. My faculty colleagues at this wonderful institution have been a source of stimulation, and sometimes, as in the case of Jakub Grygiel, inspiration. I have learned much from my students over the years, and particularly those who have taken my course "The Art of Strategic Decision." I tested out on them many of the ideas contained herein.

At the end of 2006 Secretary of State Condoleezza Rice asked me to serve as counselor of the Department of State, which I did for two extremely busy and rewarding years. I owe her, President George W. Bush, and my colleagues in government much. Working for and with them was an education as rich as that of any graduate school, and it has left its mark on how I view matters strategic, including those addressed in this book. Not in government, but on its threshold, friends and colleagues in the 2012 Romney campaign and later the John Hay Initiative, and in particular Brian Hook, helped me think in very direct ways about policymaking.

Funding for research and travel came from the Smith Richardson Foundation, whose generosity I very much appreciate, as well as the personal encouragement of Nadia Schadlow and Marin Strmecki.

I will not try to name all the individuals, in the United States and abroad, who have influenced my thinking on the matters discussed herein—I am quite sure that I would be mortified at those that I left out. But let me say that old friends, such as Peter Feaver; international colleagues, such as Hew Strachan; the wise men and women of American public life, such as Andrew Marshall; experienced diplomats, such as Jim Jeffrey; generals, such as John Allen and David Petraeus; senior officials who plug away out of the limelight, such as Doug Lute and David Gordon; area specialists, such as Ashley Tellis or the staff of the China Maritime Studies Institute; and thoughtful foreign experts, such as P. K. Singh, have taught me much. This book is a product of years of ongoing conversations with them as much as it is my reflections in the privacy of my study.

My family has been, as ever, wonderfully supportive. Usefully for an author holding forth on weighty matters of national policy, my children Rafi, Miki, Becky, and Nathan have instilled in me a degree of humility. "So, Dad, you're an expert in strategic *planning*?" has been a not-uncommon refrain when things have gone awry in the Cohen household. Their spouses, Talya, Ari, and Elana, have brought them, and my wife and me, great joy. My grandchildren are not yet at a stage where they know anything about what it takes to write a book. They seem rather to take the view that Grandpa's job is to read stories and buy them ice cream, and that is fine with me. As for my wife, Judy, without her I would be lost; my gratitude to her is boundless.

Andrew Wylie helped make the writing of books rewarding as well as interesting. His encouragement and good judgment means much to me as it does to considerably more famous authors. Lara Heimert at Basic Books was a splendidly demanding yet amusing boss: she and her highly professional team have improved this book, and working with them has been a pleasure as well.

Finally, I want to thank the many soldiers, diplomats, civil servants, and others who hosted me down range, as the saying goes. I dedicate this book to them and to their brothers and sisters who since the terrors of 9/11 have exposed themselves to mortal danger on behalf of what is and will remain, whatever its passing troubles, the Great Republic.

Notes

Notes to Introduction

1. Theodore Roosevelt, "National Duties," in *Theodore Roosevelt: Letters and Speeches*, ed. Louis Auchincloss (New York: Library of America, 2004), 772.

2. On Roosevelt's military policy, see Matthew M. Oyos, "Theodore Roosevelt, Congress, and the Military: U.S. Civil-Military Relations in the Early Twentieth Century," *Presidential Studies Quarterly* 30, no. 2 (June 2000): 312–331. On US naval fleet, see Kenneth Wimmel, *Theodore Roosevelt and the Great White Fleet: American Sea Power Comes of Age* (Dulles, VA: Brassey's, 2000). Theodore Roosevelt quote, *Theodore Roosevelt: An Autobiography* (1913; repr. New York: Da Capo Press, 1985), 565.

3. Bruce Stokes, "Americans Deeply Divided on U.S. Role in World," available at http://globalpublicsquare.blogs.cnn.com/2014/07/09/americans-deeply-divided-on-u-s-role-in-world/, accessed June 24, 2015.

4. Historical statistics are available from the Office of Management and Budget, found at www.whitehouse.gov.

5. Data on expenditure drawn from Office of Management and Budget historical tables. The nominal GDP percentages is derived from Louis D. Johnston and Samuel H. Williamson, "The Annual Real and Nominal GDP for the United States, 1790–1928," MeasuringWorth, 2008. www.measuringworth.com, accessed March 11, 2016. Casualties from Nese F. DeBruyne and Anne Leland, "American War and Military Operations Casualties: Lists and Statistics," Congressional Research Service, January 2, 2015, available at www.fas.org, accessed June 24, 2015, and from the Defense Casualty Analysis System. Also see "Principal Wars in Which the United States Participated—U.S. Military Personnel Serving and Casualties," Defense Manpower Data Center, US Department of Defense, 2015, available at www.dmdc.osd.mil, accessed June 25, 2015.

6. Cyril Falls, *The Art of War* (New York: Oxford University Press, 1961), 6.

Notes to Chapter 1

1. "Anglo-American Unity," September 9, 1943, in *Winston S. Churchill: His Complete Speeches, 1897–1963*, ed. Robert Rhodes James, vol. 7, *1943–1949* (New York: Chelsea House Publishers, 1974), 6823–6824.

2. For a good overview of the period following World War II, see Steven L. Rearden, *History of the Office of the Secretary of Defense*, vol. 1, *The Formative Years, 1947–1950* (Washington: Historical Office, Office of the Secretary of Defense, 1984).

3. His first reference was in an address to a Joint Session of Congress, September 11, 1990, which may be found at www.millercenter.org. The second speech followed the conclusion of the war, on March 6, 1991, and available at the same website. Both accessed July 6, 2015.

4. Albright statement from interview, *The Today Show*, NBC-TV, February 19, 1998. Transcript on file at www.fas.org, accessed May 30, 2016.

5. Steven Pinker, *The Better Angels of Our Nature: Why Violence Has Declined* (New York: Viking, 2011), 696.

6. For anthropologists' view, see, for example, Lawrence H. Keeley, *War Before Civilization: The Myth of the Peaceful Savage* (New York: Oxford University Press, 1996).

7. Max Ehrenfreund, "We've Had a Massive Decline in Gun Violence in the United States. Here's Why," *Washington Post*, December 3, 2015, available at www.washingtonpost.com, accessed May 1, 2016.

8. For an interesting review essay, see Azar Gat, "Is War Declining—and Why?" *Journal of Peace Research* 50, no. 2: 149–157. See also Pinker, *Better Angels*, 192.

9. Pinker, *Better Angels*, 207ff. Fukuyama's argument was first published as "The End of History," *National Interest* (Summer 1989); it is more fully developed in his book, *The End of History and the Last Man* (New York: Free Press, 1992).

10. For a pioneering discussion of this idea, see Charles Perrow, *Normal Accidents: Living with High-Risk Technologies*, 2nd ed. (Princeton, NJ: Princeton University Press, 2011).

11. There are many adherents of this view, which has a long history in the American academy going back to Hans Morgenthau in the 1950s. For one of the more thoughtful writers, see the writings of Barry R. Posen, including "Pull Back: The Case for a Less Activist Foreign Policy," *Foreign Affairs* (January 2013): 1–5, and his book *Restraint: A New Foundation for U.S. Grand Strategy* (Ithaca: Cornell University Press, 2015). See also Christopher Layne, "This Time It's Real: The End of Unipolarity and the *Pax Americana*," *International Studies Quarterly* (2012): 203–213. On nuclear issues in particular, see Kenneth Waltz, "The Spread of Nuclear Weapons: More May Be Better," *Adelphi Papers* 171 (London: International Institute for Strategic Studies, 1981). For

a contemporary application of this view, see his essay "Why Iran Should Get the Bomb," *Foreign Affairs* (July/August 2012): 2–5. A more recent version of Waltz's larger argument is Zachary S. Davis, "The Realist Nuclear Regime," *Security Studies* 2, nos. 3–4 (1993): 78–99.

12. John J. Mearsheimer, "America Unhinged," *National Interest* (January/February 2014): 9–30.

13. John J. Mearsheimer and Stephen M. Walt, *The Israel Lobby and U.S. Foreign Policy* (New York: Straus and Giroux, 2007). I stand by my critique of it, "Yes, It's Anti-Semitic," *Washington Post*, April 5, 2006, available at www.washingtonpost.com, accessed July 13, 2015.

14. Joseph S. Nye Jr., "Soft Power," *Foreign Policy* 80 (Autumn 1990): 153–171.

15. Ibid., 168. See also, for example, Joseph S. Nye Jr., "Get Smart: Combining Hard and Soft Power," *Foreign Affairs* 88, no. 4 (July/August 2008): 160–163.

16. Drew DeSilver, "5 Facts About Indian Americans," Pew Research Center, September 30, 2015, available at www.pewresearch.org, accessed July 8, 2015.

17. There are a number of careful studies of this subject. See, for example, Daniel Drezner, *The Sanctions Paradox: Economic Statecraft and International Relations* (Cambridge: Cambridge University Press, 1999); Brendan Taylor, *Sanctions as Grand Strategy* (London: International Institute for Strategic Studies, 2010); Meghan O'Sullivan, *Shrewd Sanctions: Statecraft and State Sponsors of Terrorism* (Washington, DC: Brookings, 2003).

18. Regarding Iranian oil exports, see the testimony of the undersecretary of the treasury for terrorism and financial intelligence, "Written Testimony of David S. Cohen," United States Senate Committee on Foreign Relations. January 21, 2015. For expansion of Iranian centrifuge production, see Kenneth Katzman, "Iran Sanctions," Congressional Research Service, April 21, 2015, available at www.fas.org, accessed July 8, 2015.

19. See Priyanka Boghani, "What's Been the Effect of Western Sanctions on Russia?" PBS, January 13, 2015, available at www.pbs.org, accessed July 8, 2015, and Michael Birnbaum, "A Year into a Conflict with Russia, Are Sanctions Working?" *Washington Post*, March 27, 2015, available at www.washingtonpost.com, accessed July 8, 2015.

20. On financial sanctions, see Juan Zarate, *Treasury's War: The Unleashing of a New Era of Financial Warfare* (New York: PublicAffairs, 2013).

21. Stanley Hoffmann, *Gulliver's Troubles, or the Setting of American Foreign Policy* (New York: McGraw-Hill, 1968).

22. The effect of American culture is the argument of Andrew J. Bacevich's works, including *American Empire: The Realities and Consequences of U.S. Diplomacy* (Cambridge, MA: Harvard University Press, 2002). See also his *The Limits of Power: The End of American Exceptionalism* (New York: Metropolitan

Books, 2008) and *Washington Rules: America's Path to Permanent War* (New York: Metropolitan Books, 2010).

23. Lee Kuan Yew, *From Third World to First: The Singapore Story: 1965–2000* (New York: Harper Collins, 2000), 467, 573.

24. "Remarks by the President in State of the Union Address," January 24, 2012, available at www.whitehouse.gov, accessed May 31, 2016.

25. Underrating randomness/overrating competence is one of the key points made in two recent brilliant books: Nassim Nicholas Taleb, *Fooled by Randomness: The Hidden Role of Chance in Life and in the Markets* (New York: Random House, 2008), and Daniel Kahneman, *Thinking Fast and Slow* (New York: Farrar, Straus, and Giroux, 2011). "All political lives, unless they are cut off in midstream at a happy juncture, end in failure, because that is the nature of politics and of human affairs," from J. Enoch Powell, *Joseph Chamberlain* (London: Thames and Hudson, 1977), 151.

26. "*Insulation!* That was the ticket." Tom Wolfe, *The Bonfire of the Vanities* (New York: Farrar, Straus & Giroux, 1987), 55.

27. On universities, Marjorie Heins of the academic freedom and tenure committee of the American Association of University Professors, quoted in Stephanie Saul, "N.Y.U. Professor Is Barred by United Arab Emirates," *New York Times*, March 16, 2015, available at www.nytimes.com, accessed April 4, 2016. On Facebook, Chris Matthews, "China Praises Facebook's Decision to Censor Dissident," *Fortune*, January 13, 2015, available at www.fortune.com, accessed April 4, 2016.

28. John Quincy Adams, "Address on U.S. Foreign Policy," July 4, 1821, available at www.presidentialrhetoric.com, accessed July 13, 2015.

29. On self-interest, see, for example, Robert E. Osgood, *Ideals and Self-Interest in America's Foreign Relations* (Chicago: University of Chicago Press, 1953). For a contemporary view of the challenge of world order for US statecraft, see Henry A. Kissinger, *World Order* (New York: Penguin, 2014).

Notes to Chapter 2

1. I have discussed the lessons of Vietnam in *Supreme Command: Soldiers, Statesmen and Leadership in Wartime* (New York: Free Press, 2002), 184–203. On Vietnam metaphors, see R. W. Apple, "A Military Quagmire Remembered: Afghanistan as Vietnam," *New York Times*, October 31, 2001, available at www.nytimes.com, accessed December 28, 2015.

2. Rice quote from personal conversation with Condoleezza Rice, Department of State headquarters, spring 2007. On nation-building, see, for example, then candidate George W. Bush's remarks at the presidential debate in Winston-Salem, North Carolina, October 11, 2000, or his remarks to foreign journalists: "October 11, 2000 Debate Transcript," Commission on Presidential Debates, 2016, accessible at www.debates.org; George W. Bush.

"Interview with Foreign Journalists," July 17, 2001, online by Gerhard Peters and John T. Woolley, *The American Presidency Project*, 2016, accessible at www .presidency.ucsb.edu. The 2015 figure is a low estimate, derived from adding up the results of drone strikes in South Asia and Yemen, as compiled by the New America Foundation, July 29, 2015, available at http://securitydata.newamerica .net. This does not count strikes conducted in other countries, or individual terrorists targeted and killed in raids by special forces.

3. See, for example, US Senate Select Intelligence Committee, *Report of the Select Intelligence Committee About Iraq's WMD Programs and Links to Terrorism and How They Compare with Prewar Assessments with Additional Views*, September 8, 2006, 60–112, intelligence.senate.gov. For an interesting journalistic account, see Stephen F. Hayes, *The Connection: How al Qaeda's Collaboration with Saddam Hussein Has Endangered America* (New York: HarperCollins, 2004). Connections did exist; how deep and consequential they were remains a matter of debate, although surely the fears that al-Qaeda was operating at the behest of Saddam, or under his control, were misplaced.

4. *The Iraq Inquiry* ("Chilcot Commission"), Testimony of the Rt. Hon. Tony Blair, January 29, 2010, 6, available at www.iraqinquiry.org.uk, accessed July 28, 2015.

5. Bush's decision to end Saddam Hussein regime: George W. Bush, *Decision Points* (New York: Crown, 2010), 232. There have been many accounts of the decision to go to war in Iraq, to include the memoirs of senior decision-makers. One of the more meticulous is that of then undersecretary of defense for policy, Douglas Feith, who was in the boiler room of policymaking; see his *War and Decision: Inside the Pentagon at the Dawn of the War on Terrorism* (New York: Harper, 2008), 181–239.

6. On Islamic thought prior to Qutb's execution, see Lawrence Wright, *The Looming Tower: Al-Qaeda and the Road to 9/11* (New York: Alfred A. Knopf, 2007), chap. 1, "The Martyr," 7–31; see also 79–80, 108–109, and passim. On the effect of sanctions against Iraq, see "Iraq: 1989–1999, a Decade of Sanctions," International Committee for the Red Cross, December 14, 1999, available at www.icrc.org, accessed July 27, 2015. Bin Laden quote: "Bin Laden's Fatwa," Public Broadcasting Service, August 23, 1996, available at www.pbs.org, accessed July 27, 2015. A chronology of sanctions and inspections may be found at Daryl Kimball and Paul Kerr," "Disarming Saddam—A Chronology of Iraq and UN Weapons Inspections from 2002–2003," Arms Control Association, July 2003, available at www.armscontrol.org.

7. Had Al Gore won the presidency: see Frank P. Harvey, *Explaining the Iraq War: Counterfactual Theory, Logic, and Evidence* (Cambridge: Cambridge University Press, 2012).

8. On ambassadors' views, see Bernard Gwertzman and Ryan Crocker, "Iraq's Role in the Long War Against Isis," Council on Foreign Relations, September 25, 2014, available at www.cfr.org, and Josh Rogin, "Obama's Iraq

Ambassador: I Wanted Troops to Remain in Iraq," *Foreign Policy*, November 1, 2012, available at www.foreignpolicy.com, accessed April 17, 2015. Both men have given their views at length in a number of venues. On the lack of inevitability, see Emma Sky, *The Unraveling: High Hopes and Missed Opportunities in Iraq* (New York: PublicAffairs, 2015), xi.

9. Costs of War Project, Brown University, available at http://watson .brown.edu, accessed July 28, 2015.

10. See Michael Waterhouse and JoAnne O'Bryant, "National Guard Personnel and Deployments: Fact Sheet," Congressional Research Service, January 17, 2008, available at www.fas.org; see also David R. Segal and Mady Wechsler Segal, "U.S. Military's Reliance on the Reserves," Population Reference Bureau, March 2005, available at www.prb.org, accessed May 30, 2016. On the Vietnam call-up, see John D. Stuckey and Joseph H. Pistorius, "Mobilization for the Vietnam War: A Political and Military Catastrophe," *Parameters, Journal of the US Army War College* 15, no. 1 (1985): 26–38.

11. "Suicide in the Military: Army-NIH Funded Study Points to Risk and Protective Factors," National Institutes of Health, March 3, 2014, available at www.nimh.nih.gov.

12. On waivers, see Lizette Alvarez, "Army and Marine Corps Grant More Felony Waivers," *New York Times*, April 22, 2008.

13. Costs of War Project, Brown University, accessed July 28, 2015.

14. Statistics from Nese F. DeBruyne and Anne Leland, *American War and Military Operations Casualties: Lists and Statistics*, Congressional Research Service, January 2, 2015, available at www.fas.org, accessed July 28, 2015.

15. Quote from Carl von Clausewitz, *On War*, trans. Michael Howard and Peter Paret, bk. 1 (Princeton, NJ: Princeton University Press, 1982), 120.

16. There are a number of accounts about how old lessons were relearned, including Fred Kaplan, *The Insurgents: David Petraeus and the Plot to Change the American Way of War* (New York: Simon & Schuster, 2013), and Frank G. Hoffman and G. Alexander Crowther, "Strategic Assessment and Adaptation: The Surges in Iraq and Afghanistan," in *Lessons Encountered: Learning from the Long War*, ed. Richard D. Hooker Jr. and Joseph J. Collins (Washington, DC: National Defense University Press, 2015), 89–163. The issues remain contentious. See David J. Kilcullen, *Counterinsurgency* (Oxford: Oxford University Press, 2010); Bing West, *The Strongest Tribe: War, Politics, and the Endgame in Iraq* (New York: Random House, 2008) for two very different views. Of the firsthand accounts, I would single out Peter R. Mansoor, *Baghdad at Sunrise: A Brigade Commander's War in Iraq* (New Haven: Yale University Press, 2008). For the most rigorous analysis of Iraq thus far, see Stephen Biddle, Jeffrey A. Friedman, and Jacob N. Shapiro, "Testing the Surge: Why Did Violence Decline in Iraq in 2007?" *International Security* 37, no. 1 (Summer 2012): 7–40. A lively exchange with their critics followed: "Correspondence: Assessing the Synergy Thesis in Iraq," *International Security* 37, no. 4 (Spring 2013): 173–198.

17. On detainee operations, see Cheryl Benard et al., *The Battle Behind the Wire: U.S. Prisoner and Detainee Operations from World War II to Iraq* (Santa Monica, CA: RAND, 2011).

18. Leon Panetta, with Jim Newton, *Worthy Fights: A Memoir of Leadership in War and Peace* (New York: Penguin, 2014), 223–224.

19. For Hammes's views, see T. X. Hammes, "Raising and Mentoring Security Forces in Afghanistan and Iraq," in Hooker and Collins, *Lessons Encountered*, 335. The whole essay, pages 277–344, merits careful reading.

20. The best account thus far of McChrystal's operation is McChrystal's own *My Share of the Task* (New York: Penguin 2013). As for other operations, good recent accounts include Sean Naylor, *Relentless Strike: The Secret History of Joint Special Operations Command* (New York: St. Martin's Press, 2015) and Scott Shane, *Objective Troy: A Terrorist, A President, and the Rise of the Drone* (New York: Tim Duggan, 2015).

21. Discussed somewhat elliptically in McChrystal, *My Share of the Task*, 177 and passim. A much more extensive description can be found in the former director of both the National Security Agency and the Central Intelligence Agency Michael V. Hayden, *Playing to the Edge: American Intelligence in the Age of Terror* (New York: Penguin, 2016).

22. On PRTs, which have been studied by a number of institutions, see, for example, "Provincial Reconstruction Teams in Iraq," US Institute of Peace, March 20, 2013, available at www.usip.org, accessed July 31, 2015. The US Army's Peacekeeping and Stability Operations Institute and the Strategic Studies Institute have also produced valuable studies; e.g., Carter Malkasian and Gerald Meyerle, "Provincial Reconstruction Teams: How Do We Know They Work?" March 25, 2009, available at www.strategicstudies-institute.army.mil, accessed July 31, 2015. An excellent overarching review is David C. Gompert and John Gordon IV, et al., *War by Other Means: Building Complete and Balanced Capabilities for Counterinsurgency* (Santa Monica, CA: RAND, 2008).

23. See Raphael S. Cohen, "Beyond Hearts and Minds," PhD dissertation, Georgetown University, submitted May 15, 2014, available at http://repository .library.georgetown.edu, accessed July 31, 2015.

24. About the creation and use of a deputy national security adviser, see Robert M. Gates, *Duty: Memoirs of a Secretary at War* (New York: Penguin, 2014), 482 and passim.

25. About the British Army in Afghanistan, see Patrick Macrory, *Retreat from Kabul: The Catastrophic British Defeat in Afghanistan, 1842* (Guilford, CT: Lyons Press, 2002). Camp in the low ground, leave your ammunition supply outside your camp, and dawdle as you withdraw, and it is not surprising that you will be annihilated. One of the best books on the early phases of the Afghan war is Seth Jones, *In the Graveyard of Empires: America's War in Afghanistan* (New York: W. W. Norton, 2009).

26. One wishes that policymakers could have spent the time reading the works of acute students of contemporary Iraq, such as Amatzia Baram, *Building Toward Crisis: Saddam Husayn's Strategy for Survival* (Washington, DC: Washington Institute for Near East Policy, 1998) or Ofra Bengio, *Saddam's Word: Political Discourse in Iraq* (New York: Oxford University Press, 1998). Both described the tribalism of modern Iraq, and Bengio was particularly acute on Saddam's cynical turn toward radical Islamic discourse (see, in particular, pages 176–202).

27. On the death toll, see Andrew de Grandpre and Andrew Tilghman, "Iran Linked to Deaths of 500 U.S. Troops in Iraq, Afghanistan," *Military Times,* July 15, 2015, available at www.militarytimes.com.

28. "Remarks by the President at National Defense University," May 23, 2013; "Remarks of John O. Brennan, Special Assistant to the President for Homeland Security and Counterterrorism, on Ensuring al-Qa'ida's Demise," delivered June 29, 2011. Both available at www.whitehouse.gov and accessed July 31, 2015. The West Point translations of the bin Laden archive, which are being constantly updated, may be found at www.ctc.usma.edu.

29. Per Pew Research Center polls: "More Now See Failure than Success in Iraq, Afghanistan," January 30, 2014, available at www.people-press.org, accessed July 31, 2015.

30. See Whitney Kassel, "The Army Needs Anthropologists," *Foreign Policy,* July 28, 2015, available at www.foreignpolicy.com; Tom Vanden Brook, "Army Kills Controversial Social Science Program," *USA Today,* June 29, 2015, available at www.usatoday.com; Christopher Sims, "The Human Terrain System: Operationally Relevant Social Science Research in Iraq and Afghanistan," *Strategic Studies Institute,* US Army War College, December 2015, available at www.strategicstudiesinstitute.army.mil.

31. See Robert W. Komer, *Bureaucracy Does Its Thing: Constraints on U.S.-GVN Performance in Vietnam,* R-967-ARPA (Santa Monica, CA: RAND, 1972); see also Todd Greentree, "Bureaucracy Does Its Thing: US Performance and the Institutional Dimension of Strategy in Afghanistan," *Journal of Strategic Studies* 36, no. 3 (2013): 325–356.

32. "NATO Takes Control of Afghanistan Peace Mission," *Guardian,* August 11, 2003, available at www.guardian.com.

33. On the Obama administration, see the scathing memoir by Obama's first secretary of defense, Gates, *Duty: Memoirs of a Secretary at War.*

34. Regarding congressional support, the Iraq war alone: In 2002 Democratic senators, including Hillary Clinton and John Kerry, voted for the war, and such newspapers as the *Washington Post, New York Times,* and the *Economist* supported it. The congressional vote for war with Iraq was in fact far more lopsided than that of the 1991 war with the same country. Yet in retrospect, the 1991 case for war seems even starker. See also "U.S. Needs More International Backing," Pew Research Center, February 29, 2003, available at www .people-press.org/2003/02/20/us-needs-more-international-backing/.

35. Ross Douthat, "The Secret of Trump's Success," *New York Times*, December 16, 2015, available at www.douthat.blogs.nytimes.com, accessed December 28, 2015.

36. The beginning of the Third Iraq War, following the Islamic State's conquest of Mosul, increased the numbers there to 3,600 in 2015. For more details, see Amy Belasco, "Troop Levels in the Afghan and Iraq Wars FY2001–2012," Congressional Research Service, July 2, 2009, and Heidi M. Peters, Moshe Schwartz, and Lawrence Kapp, "Department of Defense Contractors and Troop Levels in Iraq and Afghanistan: 2007–2014," Congressional Research Service, July 22, 2015. Drone data from http://securitydata.newamerica.net, accessed July 31, 2015.

37. Pew Research Center, "America's New Internationalist Point of View," October 24, 2001, accessed May 31, 2016; "Beyond Red vs. Blue: Section 6: Foreign Affairs, Terrorism and Privacy," June 26, 2014, accessed July 31, 2015. Both may be found at www.people-press.org.

38. About the controversies surrounding these wars: Not just in the United States. The controversy over the British participation in the Iraq war has simmered for years. See *The Iraq Inquiry* (the Chilcot report), available at www.iraqinquiry.org.uk, which was released on July 6, 2016. The full response of former prime minister Tony Blair also merits reading; it may be found at the sites of various newspapers, including www.independent.co.uk and at http://blair.3cdn.net/7c545e7dd16bfda1c8_aqm6ii5qy.pdf.

39. Two important books on the subject of the United Kingdom are Jonathan Bailey, Richard Iron, and Hew Strachan, eds., *British Generals in Blair's Wars* (Farnham, Surrey: Ashgate, 2013), and Christopher L. Elliott, *High Command: British Military Leadership in the Iraq and Afghanistan Wars* (London: C. Hurst, 2015).

Notes to Chapter 3

1. On US spending, see International Institute for Strategic Studies, *The Military Balance 2015* (London: Routledge, 2015), 486.

2. On personnel costs, see "Trends in Military Compensation," Bipartisan Policy Center and the American Enterprise Institute, available at www.aei.org; also, "Growth in DoD's Budget from 2000 to 2014," Congressional Budget Office, November 2014, available at www.cbo.gov.

3. See, for example, Gustav Gressel, "Russia's Military Revolution, and What It Means for Europe," European Council on Foreign Relations, 2015, available at www.ecfr.eu, accessed January 4, 2016.

4. For a concise account of the history of ballistic missile defenses, see Kenneth P. Werrell, *Hitting a Bullet with a Bullet: A History of Ballistic Missile Defense* (Maxwell Air Force Base, Montgomery, AL: Airpower Research Institute, 2000).

5. On the cost of nuclear weapons, see Todd Harrison and Evan Braden Montgomery, *The Cost of U.S. Nuclear Forces* (Washington, DC: Center for

Strategic and Budgetary Assessments, 2015). For short descriptions of other countries' nuclear arsenals, one can turn to the IISS *Military Balance* or the estimates compiled by the Bulletin of Atomic Scientists. A good discussion of the nuclear debate is Evan Braden Montgomery, *The Future of America's Strategic Nuclear Deterrent* (Washington, DC: Center for Strategic and Budgetary Assessments, 2013). For another take, see Clark Murdock et al., *Project Atom: A Competitive Strategies Approach to Defining U.S. Nuclear Strategy and Posture for 2025–2050* (Washington, DC: Center for Strategic and International Studies, 2015).

6. For Russia's program, see Hans M. Kristensen and Robert S. Norris, "Russian Nuclear Forces, 2015," *Bulletin of the Atomic Scientists: Nuclear Notebook*, 1–14. For Pakistan's, see Kristensen and Norris, "Pakistan Nuclear Forces, 2015," *Bulletin of the Atomic Scientists* 71, no. 6, accessed December 30, 2015. For China's, see Kristensen and Norris, "Chinese Nuclear Forces, 2013," *Bulletin of the Atomic Scientists* 69, no. 6: 79–85. Also note "China 'Has up to 3,000 Nuclear Weapons Hidden in Tunnels', Three-Year Study of Secret Documents Reveals," *Daily Mail*, December 1, 2011, available at www.dailymail .co.uk, accessed May 31, 2016. See Phillip A. Karber, "Strategic Implications of China's Underground Great Wall," Georgetown University Asian Arms Control Project, September 26, 2011, available at www.fas.org.

7. The 2010 Nuclear Posture Review deals more with the safety of the arsenal than with its modernization, strictly speaking. Department of Defense, *Nuclear Posture Review Report 2010* (Washington, DC: Department of Defense, 2010).

8. On the second nuclear age, see Paul Bracken, *The Second Nuclear Age: Strategy, Danger, and the New Power Politics* (New York: Henry Holt, 2012), 1. About Russia's arsenal, see US Department of Defense, *Soviet Military Power 1987* (Washington, DC: US Government Printing Office, 1987), available at edocs.nps.edu; "The INF Treaty," *Report of the Committee on Foreign Relations of the United States Senate*, April 14, 1988, 56, available at http://babel .hathitrust.org; Amy F. Woolf, "Russian Compliance with the Intermediate Range Nuclear Forces (INF) Treaty: Background and Issues for Congress," Congressional Research Service, October 13, 2015, available at www.fas.org. Concerning China, see Neal Conan and Phillip Karber, "Team Ignites Debate over China's Nuclear Tunnels," National Public Radio, December 22, 2011, available at www.npr.org.

9. On North Korea's nuclear capabilities, see John Schilling, Jeffrey Lewis, and David Schmerler, "A New ICBM for North Korea?" 38 North, December 22, 2015, available at www.38north.org. As for Iran, even the International Atomic Energy Agency (IAEA), under pressure to give Iran a clear bill of health and receiving little cooperation from that country, found evidence of activities aimed at developing a nuclear explosive device. Director General of IAEA, "Final Assessment on Past and Present Outstanding Issues regarding

Iran's Nuclear Programme," December 15, 2015, available at www.iaea.org, accessed January 4, 2016.

10. But US nuclear preemption is never ruled out, either. In 2006 a former and a future secretary of defense argued for conventional preemptive attacks on North Korea's missiles were that to become necessary. Ashton B. Carter and William J. Perry, "If Necessary, Strike and Destroy," *Washington Post,* June 22, 2006, available at www.washingtonpost.com, accessed January 4, 2016.

11. Stephen Biddle, "Victory Misunderstood: What the Gulf War Tells Us About the Future of Conflict." *International Security* 21, no. 2 (Fall 1996); also Jesse Orlansky and Jack Thorpe, eds., *73 Easting: Lessons Learned from Desert Storm via Advanced Distributed Simulation Technology* (Alexandria, VA: Institute for Defense Analyses, 1992), available at www.dtic.mil.

12. For discussion of Haig, see Timothy Travers, *The Killing Ground: The British Army, the Western Front and the Emergence of Modern Warfare, 1900– 1918* (London: Allen & Unwin, 1987), 95.

13. See my own *Commandos and Politicians: Elite Military Units in Modern Democracies* (Cambridge, MA: Harvard University Center for International Affairs, 1978).

14. Size of special forces in the 1950s, see John Prados, *US Special Forces: What Everyone Needs to Know* (New York: Oxford University Press, 2015), 27. Contemporary figures from International Institute for Strategic Studies, *Military Balance 2015* (London: Routledge, 2015), 51, 229.

15. Karam Shoumali, Anne Barnard, and Eric Schmitt, "Abductions Hurt U.S. Bid to Train Anti-ISIS Rebels in Syria," *New York Times,* July 30, 2015.

16. For an excellent summary of the issue of global infrastructure, see Stacie L. Pettyjohn, *U.S. Global Defense Posture, 1783–2011* (Santa Monica, CA: RAND, 2012). On US military bases abroad, see Department of Defense, "Base Structure Report—Fiscal Year 2015 Baseline," 2015, available at www .acq.osd.mil, accessed August 4, 2015.

17. "United States Department of Defense Fiscal Year 2015 Budget Request Program Acquisition Cost by Weapon System," Office of the Under Secretary of Defense (Comptroller), March 2014, available at http://comptroller .defense.gov; also "F-35 Joint Strike Fighter Assessment Needed to Address Affordability Challenges," United States Government Accountability Office, April 2015, available at www.gao.gov.

18. Concerning the Harpoon, various sources include "3M-54 Klub," Federation of American Scientists, September 3, 2000, available at www.fas.org, accessed August 6, 2015; Lyle Goldstein, "China's YJ-18 Supersonic Anti-Ship Cruise Missile: America's Nightmare?" *The National Interest,* June 1, 2015, available at www.nationalinterest.org, accessed August 6, 2015; "AGM/RGM/ UGM-84 Harpoon Missile," Boeing, 2015, available at www.boeing.com, accessed August 6, 2015; "AGM-84 Harpoon," Federation of American Scientists, February 17, 2015, available at www.fas.org, accessed August 6, 2015.

Regarding the F-35 fighter, see Jerry Hendrix, "The Retreat from Range: The Rise and Fall of Carrier Aviation" (Washington, DC: Center for a New American Security, October 2015), available at www.cnas.org.

19. On the Kornet, see "Kornet E Anti-Tank Missile, Russia," *Army Technology*, 2015, available at www.army-technology.com, accessed August 5, 2015; also "Raytheon/Lockheed Martin FGM-148 Javelin Anti-Tank Missile Launcher," Military Factory, July 2, 2015, www.militaryfactory.com, accessed August 6, 2015.

20. On the US Army during World War II, see Alan Gropman, "Industrial Mobilization," in his edited volume, *The Big "L": American Logistics in World War II* (Washington, DC: National Defense University Press, 1997), 1–96.

21. Spenser Wilkinson, *The Brain of an Army: A Popular Account of the German General Staff* (Westminster: Archibald Constable & Co., 1895).

22. Steve Vogel, *The Pentagon: A History* (New York: Random House, 2008).

23. On the Joint Chiefs of Staff, see Edward J. Drea et al., *History of the Unified Command Plan, 1946–2012* (Washington, DC: Joint History Office, Office of the Chairman of the Joint Chiefs, 2013).

24. On Dempsey, see Veronica Stracqualursi, "Outgoing Joint Chiefs Chairman Martin Dempsey Reflects on His Toughest Day on the Job," *ABC News*, September 6, 2015, available at www.abcnews.go.com, accessed September 7, 2015.

25. By different accounting rules, personnel costs, including civilian salaries, are over half the budget. See Todd Harrison, *Analysis of the FY 2015 Defense Budget* (Washington, DC: Center for Strategic and Budgetary Assessments, 2015), and Office of the Under Secretary of Defense (Comptroller), *National Defense Budget Estimates for FY 2016* (March 2015).

26. See the sharp criticisms offered by a former president of the US Army War College, Robert H. Scales, "Too Busy to Learn," *Proceedings* 136, no. 2 (February 2010). The critiques are not new. See, for example, Williamson Murray, "The Army's Advanced Strategic Art Program," *Parameters* (Winter 2000–2001): 31–39. See also Ike Skelton, Joseph Brennan, Jack Davis, et al., *Report of the Panel on Military Education of the One Hundredth Congress of the Committee on Armed Services* (Washington, DC: US Government Printing Office, 1989), 1, and current data from the war colleges. In 1988, 864 students were enrolled full-time; in 2015, about a hundred more.

27. Carl von Clausewitz, *On War*, trans. Michael Howard and Peter Paret, bk. 2 (Princeton, NJ: Princeton University Press, 1982), 154.

28. Percentages derived from the data in International Institute for Strategic Studies, *The Military Balance, 2015* (London: Routledge, 2015).

29. On fitness, see Joe Gould, "Army Recruitment Command Boss: Overweight Youth a Growing Problem," *USA Today*, August 29, 2014, available at www.usatoday.com; "Forum Studies Bleak Recruiting Future of the

All-Volunteer Army," *U.S. Army*, October 20, 2015, available at www.army. mil; "DoD Announces Recruiting, Retention Numbers Through June 2015," US Department of Defense, August 4, 2015, available at www.defense.gov.

30. Regarding entitlements and for an interesting treatment of a much larger problem, see John Micklethwait and Adrian Wooldridge, *The Fourth Revolution: The Global Race to Reinvent the State* (New York: Penguin, 2014). About life expectancies, see Wan He and Mark N. Muenchrath, *90+ in the United States: 2006–2008* (Washington, DC: US Census Bureau, 2011), 2.

31. The best work on this subject comes from the pen of Nicholas Eberstadt. See, for example, his pathbreaking article, "World Population Implosion?" *Public Interest* 129 (Fall 1997): 3–22. On the impact of the youth bulge in the 1960s see Daniel Hart and Rebecca Lakin Gullan, "The Sources of Adolescent Activism: Historical and Contemporary Findings," in *Handbook of Research on Civic Engagement in Youth*, ed. Lonnie R. Sherrod, Judith Torney-Purta, and Constance A. Flanagan (Hoboken, NJ: John Wiley & Sons, Inc., 2010), 67–81.

32. On world population, see "World Population Prospects: The 2015 Revision" (New York: United Nations, 2015), 18ff and passim. About the impact of aging, see, among others, Mark L. Haas, "A Geriatric Peace? The Future of U.S. Power in a World of Aging Populations," *International Security* 32, no. 1 (Summer 2007): 112–147; Michael Beckley, "China's Century? Why America's Edge Will Endure," *International Security* 36, no. 3 (Winter 2011/2012): 41–78; Martin C. Libicki, Howard J. Shatz, and Julie E. Taylor, "Global Demographic Change and Its Implications for Military Power," (Santa Monica, CA: RAND Corporation, 2011); and Nicholas Eberstadt, "Growing Old the Hard Way: China, Russia, India," *Policy Review* no. 136 (April/May 2006), www.hoover.org/research/growing-old-hard-way-china-russia-india, accessed August 52015. The best book on this subject is Josef Joffe, *The Myth of America's Decline: Politics, Economics, and a Half Century of False Prophecies* (New York: W. W. Norton, 2014).

33. Ezra F. Vogel, *Japan as Number One: Lessons for America* (Cambridge, MA: Harvard University Press, 1979). Charles A. Kupchan, "The Travails of Union: The American Experience and Its Implications for Europe," *Survival* 46, no. 4 (Winter 2004–2005): 103–120.

34. "World Development Indicators," *World Bank*, 2015, available at http://databank.worldbank.org, accessed August 5, 2015; "International Comparisons of GDP Per Capita and per Hour, 1960–2011," Bureau of Labor Statistics, available at www.bls.gov, accessed August 5. 2015.

35. "World Development Indicators."

36. Data derived from United Nations Statistics Division, "Value Added by Economic Activity, at current prices—US Dollars," United Nations National Accounts Main Aggregates Database, December 2015, accessible at http://unstats.un.org/unsd/snaama/. See also Marc Levinson, "U.S. Manufacturing in

International Perspective," Congressional Research Service, April 26, 2016, accessible at www.fas.org. It should be noted that German and Japanese manufacturing went from nearly 11 and 10 percent to 7 and 6.5 percent, respectively, during the same period—proportionally, a larger drop.

37. On asset management, see "The Financial Services Industry in the United States," *Select USA* (US Department of Commerce), 2015, available at http://selectusa.commerce.gov, accessed August 3, 2015; also "Market Capitalization of Listed Companies," World Bank, 2015, available at http://data .worldbank.org, accessed August 3, 2015. As for intellectual capital, see "Statistics of the Academic Ranking of World Universities," 2015, available at www .shanghairanking.com, accessed August 5, 2015.

38. On technological theft by Russia and China, see, for example, David Alexander, "Theft of F-35 Design Data Is Helping U.S. Adversaries," Reuters, June 19, 2013, available at www.reuters.com; "China's Cyber-Theft Jet Fighter," *Wall Street Journal*, November 12, 2014, available at www.wsj.com. See also "Resilient Military Systems and the Advanced Cyber Threat," Defense Science Board, US Department of Defense, January 2013, available at www .acq.osd.mil.

39. About Japan, see Mark Harrison, "The Economics of World War II: An Overview," University of Warwick, 1998, available at www2.warwick .ac.uk. See also "The Effects of Strategic Bombing on Japan's War Economy," *The United States Strategic Bombing Survey*, December 1946, available at www .archive.org.

40. Arguments include one by none other than Alexis de Tocqueville, *Democracy in America*, trans. Harvey C. Mansfield and Delba Winthrop, pt. 3 (Chicago: University of Chicago Press, 2000), 617–638.

41. Two-thirds arguments, from Pew Research Center, "As New Dangers Loom, More Think the U.S. Does 'Too Little' to Solve World Problems," August 28, 2014, available at www.people-press.org, accessed August 5, 2015; also Pew Research Center, "Public Sees U.S. Power Declining as Support for Global Engagement Slips," December 3, 2013, accessed August 5, 2015; and Pew Research Center poll conducted February 2014, accessed August 5, 2015. Data from 2015 survey from Pew Research Center, "Do You Think Barack Obama Is Too Tough, Not Tough Enough, or About Right in His Approach to Foreign Policy and National Security Issues?" December 25, 2015, accessed January 4, 2016. Thirty-four percent said "about right"; but 58 percent, "not tough enough."

42. On proposed Chinese emigration, see Robert Frank, "Chinese Millionaires Plan to Leave in Droves: Poll," September 15, 2014, available at www.finance.yahoo.com, accessed August 5, 2015. Americans' opinion of US military: Pew Research Center, "Public Esteem for Military Still High," July 11, 2013, available at www.pewforum.org, accessed August 5, 2015.

43. Hamilton's phrase is found in *The Federalist Papers*, Number 70: "Energy in the Executive is a leading character in the definition of good government. It is essential to the protection of the community against foreign attacks; it is not less essential to the steady administration of the laws; to the protection of property against those irregular and high-handed combinations which sometimes interrupt the ordinary course of justice; to the security of liberty against the enterprises and assaults of ambition, of faction, and of anarchy." Bernard Bailyn, ed., *The Debate on the Constitution: Federalist and Antifederalist Speeches, Articles, and Letters During the Struggle over Ratification*, Part II (New York: Library of America, 1993), 346.

44. Data on American military from the SIPRI Military Expenditure Database Stockholm International Peace Research Institute, 2015, available at www.sipri.org.

45. All data sourced from IISS, *The Military Balance 2015* (London: Routledge, 2015), passim.

Notes to Chapter 4

1. On Chinese history, see Loren Brandt, Debin Ma, and Thomas Rawski, "From Divergence to Convergence: Re-evaluating the History Behind China's Economic Boom," London School of Economics, January 2012, available at http://eprints.lse.ac.uk, accessed May 3, 2015. On the murderousness of the regime, see Jean-Louis Margolin, "China: A Long March into Night," in Stéphane Courtois et al., *The Black Book of Communism: Crimes, Terror, Repression* (Cambridge, MA: Harvard University Press, 1999), 463–546. On Mao, see the biography by Jung Chang and Jon Halliday, *Mao: The Unknown Story* (New York: Alfred A. Knopf, 2005). The three-volume history by Frank Dikötter is mesmerizing reading: *The Tragedy of Liberation: A History of the Chinese Revolution, 1945–1957* (New York: Bloomsbury Press, 2013), *Mao's Great Famine: The History of China's Most Devastating Catastrophe, 1958–1962* (New York: Walker & Co, 2010), and *The Cultural Revolution: A People's History, 1962–1976* (New York: Bloomsbury Press, 2016). For basic facts on China's economy, see "China Overview," World Bank, March 25, 2015, available at http://worldbank.org, accessed June 3, 2015. For a succinct summary of the issues that China faces, see Minxin Pei, "The Twilight of Communist Party Rule in China," *The American Interest*, November 12, 2015, available at www.the-american-interest.com, accessed January 7, 2016. Strikingly, in March 2015 a much more sanguine analyst, David Shambaugh, published a provocative and even more pessimistic article, "The Coming Chinese Crackup," *Wall Street Journal*, March 6, 2015, available at www.wsj.com, accessed January 7, 2016.

2. About China's year-on-year growth, see Richard A. Bitzinger, "China's Double-Digit Defense Growth," *Foreign Affairs*, March 29, 2015, available at

www.foreignaffairs.com, accessed June 26, 2015. On China's defense budget, see Office of the Secretary of Defense, "Annual Report to Congress: Military and Security Developments Involving the People's Republic of China 2015," April 7, 2015, available at www.defense.gov, accessed June 24, 2015. Using a Purchasing Power Parity measure, however, the IISS puts Chinese defense expenditures at $314 billion, a more plausible figure. *The Military Balance 2016* (London: Routledge, 2016), 240.

3. The OSD annual report on Chinese military developments is a valuable source; so, too, is the annual *Military Balance* produced by the International Institute of Strategic Studies. For a good introduction to the Chinese military, see Peter Mattis, *Analyzing the Chinese Military: A Review Essay and Resource Guide on the People's Liberation Army* (Washington, DC: Jamestown Foundation, 2015). See as well the regular reporting by the US China Economic and Security Review Commission, available at www.uscc.gov. The latest unclassified attempt at a net assessment is Eric Heginbotham et al., *The U.S. China-Military Scorecard: Forces, Geography, and the Evolving Balance of Power, 1996–2017* (Santa Monica, CA: RAND, 2015), but see also Thomas G. Mahnken, ed., *Competitive Strategies for the 21st Century: Theory, History, and Practice* (Stanford, CA: Stanford University Press, 2012), 131–256. On the Chinese base at Djibouti, see Agence France-Presse, "Djibouti President: China Negotiating Horn of Africa Military Base," May 10, 2015, available at www.defensenews.com.

4. On China's military modernization, see *The Military Balance*, various years, and Anthony H. Cordesman and Steven Colley, "Chinese Strategy and Military Modernization in 2015: A Comparative Analysis," Center for Strategic and International Studies October 10, 2015, available at www.csis.org, accessed December 3, 2015. For an interesting examination of the limits of Chinese modernization drawing on open Chinese sources, see Michael S. Chase et al., *China's Incomplete Military Transformation: Assessing the Weaknesses of the People's Liberation Army (PLA)* (Santa Monica, CA: RAND, 2015), RR-893-USCC.

5. The best one-volume assessment of the standoff between China and the United States is Aaron L. Friedberg, *A Contest for Supremacy: China, America, and the Struggle for Mastery in Asia* (New York: W. W. Norton, 2011).

6. Concerning China's economy vis-à-vis that of the United States, see Mike Bird, "China Just Overtook the U.S. as the World's Largest Economy," *Business Insider*, October 8, 2014, available at www.businessinsider.com, accessed August 17, 2015.

7. For a useful summary, see China Economic and Security Review Commission, *Annual Report to Congress 2015*, chap. 2, "U.S.-China Security Relations," available at www.uscc.gov.

8. For a long time the PLA was studied as more a political than a military organization. This is changing with such works as Mark A. Ryan, David M.

Finkelstein, and Michael A. McDevitt, eds., *Chinese Warfighting: The PLA Experience Since 1949* (New York: Routledge, 2015), or the series of conference papers edited by Roy Kamphausen and David Lai, among others. For example, Roy Kamphausen, David Lai, and Andrew Scobell, eds., *The PLA at Home and Abroad: Assessing the Operational Capabilities of China's Military* (Carlisle, PA: US Army Strategic Studies Institute, 2010) and Roy Kamphausen, David Lai, and Travis Tanner, eds., *Assessing the People's Liberation Army in the Hu Jintao Era* (Carlisle, PA: US Army Strategic Studies Institute, 2014).

9. Quoted statements: John Grady, "Locklear: U.S. 'Shouldn't Talk Ourselves Into' Conflict with China," USNI News, March 25, 2014, available at www.news.usni.org, accessed August 17, 2015. Spencer Ackerman, "Climate Change Is the Biggest Threat in the Pacific, Says Top U.S. Admiral," *Wired*, March 11, 2013, available at www.wired.com, accessed August 17, 2015; James Cartwright, Richard Burt, Chuck Hagel, et al., "Global Zero U.S. Nuclear Policy Commission," Global Zero, 2012, available at www.globalzero.org, accessed August 18, 2015. Scott Kennedy, ed., *China Cross Talk: The American Debate over China Policy Since Normalization* (Lanham, MD: Rowman & Littlefield, 2003), 237.

10. On strategic trust, see Mike Mullen, "A Step Toward Trust with China," *New York Times*, July 25, 2011, available at www.nytimes.com.

11. See Phillip Saunders, "Will China's Dream Turn into America's Nightmare?" Jamestown Foundation, April 1, 2010, available at www.jamestown.org. "China's Military Strategy," State Council Information Office of the People's Republic of China, May 26, 2015, available at www.news.usni.org.

12. Julia Lovell's *The Opium War: Drugs, Dreams, and the Making of Modern China* (London: Macmillan, 2011) is a useful corrective to the usual account of exploitation, although there was surely plenty of that. Part of the problem was Chinese complicity in it.

13. These attitudes are now adapted to business as well. Gao Yuan, *Lure the Tiger out of the Mountains: The 36 Stratagems of Ancient China* (New York: Simon & Schuster, 1991). Far more sophisticated comparisons of Chinese and Western thought abound—see, for example, François Jullien's works, translated by Janet Lloyd, *The Propensity of Thing: Toward a History of Efficacy in China* (New York: Zone Books, 1999) and *A Treatise on Efficacy: Between Western and Chinese Thinking* (Honolulu: University of Hawaii Press, 2004). For a much easier read, any of the collections of essays by Simon Leys (the pen name of Pierre Ryckmans) is worthwhile. See, for example, *The Burning Forest: Essays on Chinese Culture and Politics* (New York: Holt, Rinehart and Winston, 1985).

14. Most military historians would concur with Ridgway's judgment that Eighth Army could have driven to the Yalu at that point—albeit at too high a price in human life to make it strategically worthwhile. Matthew B. Ridgway, *The Korean War* (Garden City, NY: Doubleday & Co., 1967), 150–151.

15. See Edward Luttwak's very shrewd critique not only of traditional texts, but of Han strategic abilities in *The Rise of China vs. The Logic of Strategy* (Cambridge, MA: Harvard University Press, 2012), 72–94.

16. On the 1979 border war, see Henry J. Kenny, "Vietnamese Perceptions of the 1979 War with China," in *Chinese Warfighting*, ed. Ryan, Finkelstein, and McDevitt, 217–240. The most authoritative recent account of Chinese thinking is Xiaming Zhang, *Deng Xiaoping's Long War: The Military Conflict Between China and Vietnam, 1979–1991* (Chapel Hill: University of North Carolina Press, 2015). A useful summary of China's extension into the South China Sea and its newest coast guard vessel may be found in the *2015 Report to Congress of the U.S.-China Economic and Security Review Commission*, 114th Cong., 1st session (November 2015), "Section 2: China and Southeast Asia," 428–447. For the pattern of Chinese behavior, see Ronald O'Rourke, "Maritime Territorial and Exclusive Economic Zone (EEZ) Disputes Involving China: Issues for Congress," Congressional Research Service, August 7, 2015, available at www.fas.org; also Peter A. Dutton, "China's Maritime Disputes in the East and South China Seas," testimony before the House Foreign Affairs Committee, January 14, 2014, available at www.usnwc.edu.

17. See Andrew J. Nathan and Perry Link, eds., *The Tiananmen Papers*, compiled by Zhang Liang (New York: Public Affairs, 2001); the best recent book on the Chinese Communist Party, and therefore on the governance of modern China, is Richard McGregor, *The Party: The Secret World of China's Communist Rulers* (New York: Harper, 2010).

18. For Chinese views of American decline see, for example, Bonnie S. Glaser, "A Shifting Balance: Chinese Assessments of U.S. Power," in *Capacity and Resolve: Foreign Assessments of U.S. Power* (Washington, DC: Center for Strategic and International Studies, 2013). On Chinese impressions of American strategic conduct, see Andrew Scobell, David Lai, and Roy Kamphausen, eds., *Chinese Lessons from Other People's Wars* (Carlisle, PA: US Army Strategic Studies Institute, 2011), particularly Dean Cheng, "Chinese Lessons from the Gulf Wars," 153–200.

19. On China's foreign policy approach, see Alastair Ian Johnston, *Cultural Realism: Strategic Culture and Grand Strategy in Chinese History* (Princeton, NJ: Princeton University Press, 1995); Michael Swaine and Ashley Tellis, *Interpreting China's Grand Strategy: Past, Present, and Future* (Santa Monica, CA: RAND, 2000); Andrew Scobell, *China and Strategic Culture* (Carlisle, PA: US Army Strategic Studies Institute, 2000); and, most important, Andrew J. Nathan and Andrew Scobell, *China's Search for Security* (New York: Columbia University Press, 2012). The global hegemony argument is made by Michael Pillsbury, *The Hundred-Year Marathon: China's Secret Strategy to Replace America as the Global Superpower* (New York: Henry Holt, 2015).

20. See Guan Guihai, "The Influence of the Collapse of the Soviet Union on China's Political Choices," in *China Learns from the Soviet Union,*

1949–Present, ed. Thomas P. Bernstein and Li Hua-yu (Lanham, MD: Lexington Books, 2010). The most dramatic optimist turned pessimist on China's prospects is David Shambaugh, "The Coming Chinese Crackup," *Wall Street Journal*, March 6, 2015, available at www.wsj.com, accessed June 1, 2016.

21. The classic view is Henry Kissinger, *On China* (New York: Penguin, 2011). For a respectfully critical review, see Jonathan Spence, "Kissinger and China," *New York Review of Books*, June 9, 2011, available at www.nybooks.com. On the mistranslation see Richard McGregor, "Zhou's Cryptic Caution Lost in Translation," *Financial Times*, June 10, 2011, available at www.ft.com, accessed August 17, 2015. The one-child policy is one example of a disastrous choice; see Mei Fong, *One Child: The Story of China's Most Radical Experiment* (New York: Houghton Mifflin Harcourt, 2016). The decision to provide free winter heating via coal for all areas north of the Huai River is another; see Yuyu Chen, Avraham Ebenstein, Michael Greenstone, and Hongbin Li, "Evidence on the Impact of Sustained Exposure to Air Pollution on Life Expectancy from China's Huai River Policy," *Proceedings of the National Academy of Sciences of the United States of America* 110, no. 32 (2013).

22. On China's use of paramilitary organizations and militias to advance its position in the South China Sea, see Andrew S. Erickson, "Tracking China's 'Little Blue Men'—A Comprehensive Maritime Militia Compendium," August 27, 2015, available at www.andrewerickson.com, accessed January 20, 2016.

23. For an example of Chinese thinking, see the observations of the editor of *People's Daily*, the Communist Party's official mouthpiece: Li Hongmei, "U.S. Hegemony Ends, Era of Global Multipolarity Begins," *People's Daily Online*, February 24, 2009, available at http://en.people.cn.

24. On antipiracy efforts, see Andrew S. Erickson and Austin M. Strange, "No Substitute for Experience: Chinese Antipiracy Operations in the Gulf of Aden," *China Maritime Studies*, no. 10 (Newport, RI: US Naval War College, 2013).

25. See "Significant Cyber Incidents Since 2006," Center for Strategic and International Studies, March 10, 2014, available at www.csis.org; "Cybersecurity Incidents," Office of Personnel Management, 2016, available at www.opm.gov; Colin Clark, "DNI Clapper IDs China as 'The Leading Suspect' in OPM Hacks; Russia 'More Subtle,'" *Breaking Defense,* June 22, 2015, available at www.breakingdefense.com.

26. For a useful summary of developments, see Ronald O'Rourke, "China Naval Modernization: Implications for U.S. Navy Capabilities—Background and Issues for Congress," Congressional Research Service RL33153, July 28, 2015.

27. On the DF-21D, see "Re-enter the DF-21D ASBM," U.S. Naval Institute, July 2011, available at http://blog.usni.org. There is, by now, a very large literature on this topic of the US protection of the Pacific. See, among others, Toshi Yoshihara and James R. Holmes, *Red Star Over the Pacific: China's Rise*

and the Challenge to U.S. Maritime Strategy (Annapolis, MD: US Naval Institute Press, 2010); Thomas G. Mahnken and Dan Blumenthal, eds., *Strategy in Asia: The Past, Present and Future of Regional Security* (Stanford, CA: Stanford University Press, 2014); Dennis M. Gormley, Andrew S. Erickson, and Jingdong Yuan, *A Low-Visibility Force Multiplier: Assessing China's Cruise Missile Ambitions* (Washington, DC: National Defense University Press, 2014); and Eric Heginbotham et al., *The U.S.-China Military Scorecard: Forces, Geography, and the Evolving Balance of Power, 1996–2017* (Santa Monica, CA: RAND, 2015).

28. On assassin's mace, see Andrew S. Erickson, Lyle J. Goldstein, and William S. Murray, "Chinese Mine Warfare: A PLA Navy 'Assassin's Mace' Capability," *China Maritime Studies*, no. 3 (Newport, RI: US Naval War College, 2009). See also Peter Dutton, Andrew S. Erickson, and Ryan Martinson, eds., "China's Near Seas Combat Capabilities," *China Maritime Studies*, no. 11 (Newport, RI: US Naval War College, 2014).

29. For detailed polling of Asian publics, see "Global Opposition to U.S. Surveillance and Drones, but Limited Harm to America's Image," Pew Research Center, July 14, 2014, available at www.pewglobal.org, accessed January 20, 2016. In eleven Asian nations, more than half of those surveyed are concerned that territorial disputes between China and her neighbors will lead to military conflict.

30. A tilt toward accommodating China is found even in Australia, where former Australian defense official Hugh White has written *The China Choice: Why America Should Share Power* (Collingwood, Australia: Black Inc., 2012). But there are leaders, such as Malaysia's former prime minister Mahathir Mohamad, who are attracted by China's "Eastern values" as opposed to those of liberal democracy. See Cheng-Chwee Kuik, "Making Sense of Malaysia's China Policy: Asymmetry, Proximity, and Elite's Domestic Authority," *Chinese Journal of International Politics* 6, no. 4 (Winter 2013), 429–467.

31. The military supremos are not entirely unnoticed; see Dana Priest, *The Mission: Waging War and Keeping Peace with America's Military* (New York: W. W. Norton, 2004). Locklear's eventual successor, Admiral Harry Harris, takes an openly tough line on China. Jane Perlez, "A U.S. Admiral's Bluntness Rattles China, and Washington," *New York Times*, May 7, 2016, available at www.nytimes.com, accessed June 1, 2016.

32. Two contemporary commentators on naval matters, who do not always agree, are Jerry Hendrix of the Center for a New American Security and Bryan McGrath of the Hudson Institute. Their articles may be found at www.cnas.org (Hendrix) and www.hudson.org (McGrath).

33. On the adoption of the F-35, see Jerry Hendrix, "Retreat from Range: The Rise and Fall of Carrier Aviation" (Washington, DC: Center for a New American Security, 2015).

34. The best translation, according to scholars I have consulted, is Sun-Tzu, *The Art of War*, trans. Roger T. Ames (New York: Ballantine Books, 1993); references are to this edition. See also "9th International Symposium on Sun Tzu's Art of War Kicks Off," *China Military Online*, August 26, 2014, available at http://english.chinamil.com.cn; Fumio Ota, "Sun Tzu in Contemporary Chinese Strategy," National Defense University, April 1, 2014; and Ralph D. Sawyer, "Sun-Tzu, Alive and Well in Contemporary China," *Military History* 24, no. 4 (2007). For an argument that Chinese strategic culture is less distinctive, and less Sun Tzu driven, see Alastair Iain Johnston, *Cultural Realism: Strategic Culture and Grand Strategy in Chinese History* (Princeton, NJ: Princeton University Press, 1995).

35. Sun Tzu, *The Art of War*, 113.

36. Victory without bloodshed, ibid., 111. Peng Guangqian and Yao Youzhi, eds., *The Science of Military Strategy* (Beijing: Military Science Publishing House, 2005), 237 and passim. A new edition has been published, but as of this writing, is not yet available in translation.

37. Michael Handel's comparison of the two thinkers is illuminating, although I do not agree with all of it. Michael I. Handel, *Masters of War: Classical Strategic Thought*, 3rd ed. (New York: Frank Cass, 2001), in particular chap. 2, "Comparing Sun Tzu and Clausewitz," 19–32. Quoted material may be found in Carl von Clausewitz, *On War*, trans. Michael Howard and Peter Paret trans., 2nd ed., book 1 (Princeton, NJ: Princeton University Press, 1984), 75, 99, 101, 112.

38. On *hsing* and *tao*, see Sun Tzu, *The Art of War*, 104.

39. See Alan Gropman, ed., "Industrial Mobilization," in *The Big L: American Logistics in World War II* (Washington, DC: National Defense University Press, 1997), 1–96.

40. Decline in US forces in the Pacific: "Active Duty Military Personnel by Service by Region/Country (Updated Quarterly)," Defense Manpower Data Center, 2016, available at www.dmdc.osd.mil; Michael Lostumbo, Michael McNerney, Eric Peltz, et al., *Overseas Basing of U.S. Military Forces* (Santa Monica, CA: RAND, 2013); "Homeports of Active and NRFA Ships," *Naval Vessel Register*, February 8, 2016, available at www.nvr.navy.mil. William J. Perry and John P. Abizaid, chairs, "Ensuring a Strong U.S. Defense for the Future: The National Defense Panel Review of the 2014 Quadrennial Defense Review" (Washington, DC: United States Institute of Peace, 2014)

41. In July 2005, PLA general Zhu Chenghu, referring to a potential conflict over Taiwan, declared that "if the Americans draw their missiles and position-guided ammunition on to the target zone on China's territory, I think we will have to respond with nuclear weapons." Alexandra Harney and Demetri Sevastopulo, "Top Chinese General Warns US over Attack," *Financial Times*, July 15, 2005, available at www.ft.com, accessed June 1, 2016.

42. On the lessons of history vis-à-vis China, see Michael I. Handel, *War, Strategy and Intelligence* (New York: Frank Cass, 1989), "Military Deception in Peace and War" and "Strategic and Operational Deception," 310–454. For a broader argument that the United States will remain the dominant super-power, see Stephen G. Brooks and William C. Wohlforth, "The Rise and Fall of the Great Powers in the Twenty-first Century: China's Rise and the Fate of America's Global Position," *International Security* 40, no. 3 (Winter 2015/16): 7–53.

Notes to Chapter 5

1. "On The Record Briefing," Department of State, September 13, 2001, accessible at http://2001-2009.state.gov, accessed August 20, 2015.

2. Regarding *war* vs. *crime*, see "What's in a Name?" *Foreign Affairs* 81, no. 1 (January/February 2002): 247–256, and "Are We at War?" published in *Survival* 50, no. 4 (August–September 2008): 247–256. On use of the term *crusade*, see, for example, Ted Galen Carpenter, "A War, Not a Crusade," CATO Institute, September 25, 2001; also Peter Waldman and Hugh Pope, "'Crusade' Reference Reinforces Fears War on Terrorism Is Against Muslims," *Wall Street Journal*, available at www.wsj.com, September 21, 2001.

3. On the use of the term *emergency*: as Raphael S. Cohen notes, the Malayan Emergency was waged chiefly by soldiers and an increasingly militarized police force. Concerning how the use of *war* inflates a situation's importance, see, among others, Gille Andréani, "'The War on Terror': Good Cause, Wrong Concept," *Survival* 46, no. 4 (Winter 2004–2005): 31–50; Bruce Ackerman, "This Is Not a War," *Yale Law Journal* 113, no. 8 (June 2004): 1871–1907; and John E. Mueller, *Overblown: How Politicians and the Terrorism Industry Inflate National Security Threats and Why We Believe Them* (New York: Simon & Schuster, 2006). Death toll from traffic accidents vs. 9/11: Jeffrey Goldberg, "The Obama Doctrine," *Atlantic* (April 2016), 82.

4. For a take on the criminality of terrorism, sharply critical of the conduct of secret war, see Charlie Savage, *Power Wars: Inside Obama's Post-9/11 Presidency* (New York: Little, Brown, 2015).

5. On defining *jihad*, see Bernard Lewis, *The Political Language of Islam* (Chicago: University of Chicago Press, 1988), 72. Olivier Roy provocatively asks, "Is *jihad* closer to Marx than to the Koran?" and contends that "the debate on what the Koran says is sterile and helps only to support prejudice"—which is a somewhat evasive response. See Olivier Roy, *Globalized Islam: The Search for a New Ummah* (New York: Columbia University Press, 2004), 41–43. Roy is particularly interesting on the modern development of Islam in a broader sociological context. See his *Holy Ignorance: When Religion and Culture Part Ways* (New York: Columbia University Press, 2010). For more about jihadis'

definition of *jihad*, see, for example, one of the most penetrating studies of the 9/11 attackers, Terry McDermott, *Perfect Soldiers: The 9/11 Hijackers: Who They Were, Why They Did It* (New York: HarperCollins, 2005).

6. The classic account of the Crusades is Steven Runciman, *A History of the Crusades*, 3 vols. (Cambridge: Cambridge University Press, 1951), although a half-century of scholarship has extended the field considerably. See, among other recent books, Thomas Asbridge, *The Crusades: The Authoritative History of the War for the Holy Land* (New York: Harper Collins, 2010); Jonathan Riley-Smith, *The Crusades: A History*, 3rd ed. (London: Bloomsbury Academic, 2014); and by the same author, *The First Crusaders, 1095–1131* (Cambridge: Cambridge University Press, 1997). On the sack of Constantinople see Jonathan Phillips, *The Fourth Crusade and the Sack of Constantinople* (New York: Penguin, 2004).

7. Brendan Nicholson, "We'll Fight Radical Islam for 100 Years, Says Ex-Army Head Peter Leahy," *Australian,* August 9, 2014, available at www.theaustralian.com.au; Dan Bilefsky and Maïa de la Baume, "French Premier Declares 'War' on Radical Islam as Paris Girds for Rally," *New York Times,* January 10, 2015, available at www.nytimes.com.

8. For the perspective of the two administrations, see "Backgrounder: The President's Quotes on Islam," available at http://georgewbush-whitehouse.archives.gov; "George W. Bush on Terrorists Hijacking Islam in Address to Joint Session of Congress" (Berkley Center for Religion, Peace & World Affairs: Georgetown University, September 20, 2001), available at http://berkleycenter.georgetown.edu; George W. Bush, "Remarks on the War on Terror in Anchorage, Alaska," American Presidency Project, November 14, 2005, available at www.presidency.ucsb.edu; Barack Obama, "Remarks on the Death of James W. Foley in Syria from Edgartown, Massachusetts," August 20, 2014, available at www.whitehouse.gov; and Barack Obama, "President Obama: 'We Will Degrade and Ultimately Destroy ISIL,'" September 10, 2014, available at www.whitehouse.gov.

9. Two French authors who are particularly interesting, if ambivalent, about the future of Islamism are Olivier Roy, cited earlier, and Gilles Kepel. See the latter's *Jihad: The Trail of Political Islam* (Cambridge, MA: Harvard University Press, 2002). The book, completed before 9/11, postulated "the decline of Islamism" (page 366), although the analysis—and subsequent events—pointed in another direction.

10. A brief account of ibn Taymiyyah's life and doctrines may be found at "Ibn Taymiyyah, Taqi al-Din Ahmad," Oxford Islamic Studies Online 2016, available at www.oxfordislamicstudies.com; a longer treatment is Victor E. Makari, *Ibn Taymiyyah's Ethics: The Social Factor* (Chico, CA: Scholars Press, 1983).

11. Qutb quoted in Lawrence Wright, *The Looming Tower: Al-Qaeda and the Road to 9/11* (New York: Knopf, 2007), 31. The entire first chapter of

this book, "The Martyr," summarizes Qutb's life and impact. On the hijackers themselves, see Terry McDermott, *Perfect Soldiers: The 9/11 Hijackers: Who They Were, Why They Did It* (New York: Harper, 2005).

12. *The 9/11 Commission Report: Final Report of the National Commission on Terrorist Attacks Upon the United States* (Washington, DC: Government Printing Office, 2004), 61, but see also pages 240–241. In addition, see Seth G. Jones, "Al Qaeda in Iran: Why Tehran is Accommodating the Terrorist Group," *Foreign Affairs*, January 29, 2012, available at www.foreignaffairs .com, accessed August 4, 2014. New releases from the trove of documents captured during the bin Laden raid support this view. See, for example, Thomas Joscelyn, "Doomed Diplomacy," *Weekly Standard*, March 2, 2015, available at www.weeklystandard.com, accessed August 25, 2015.

13. Bernard Lewis, "The Roots of Muslim Rage," *Atlantic* (September 1990), available at www.theatlantic.com, accessed August 25, 2015. See also Gilles Kepel, *The Roots of Radical Islam*, trans. Jon Rothschild (London: Saqi, 2005). The more modern embodiment of this is Tariq Ramadan, the Islamist thinker described in Paul Berman's stinging *The Flight of the Intellectuals: The Controversy over Islamism and the Press* (New York: Melville House, 2010); see also Samuel P. Huntington, "The Clash of Civilizations," *Foreign Affairs* 72, no. 3 (Summer 1993), available at www.foreignaffairs.com.

14. "Foreign Fighters in Syria Raise Fears," *National Public Radio*, December 8, 2013, available at www.npr.org, accessed August 25, 2015. A more optimistic rendering is Daniel Byman and Jeremy Shapiro, "Be Afraid. Be a Little Afraid: The Threat of Terrorism from Western Foreign Fighters in Syria and Iraq," *Brookings Institution*, Policy Paper #34 (November 2014). The critical adjective is "Western"—there are many non-Western fighters who will nonetheless make their way to the West, and attacks may be masterminded from abroad. The foreign threat was brought home to Europe by the Friday, November 13, 2015, attacks on Paris that killed 130 people and wounded hundreds more, and which were conducted by EU citizens of Middle Eastern extraction with Syrian connections. See also, among others, Michael Knights, "Iran's Foreign Legion: The Role of Iraqi Shiite Militias in Syria," *Policywatch* 2096, Washington Institute for Near East Policy, June 27, 2013, available at www .washingtoninstitute.org, accessed August 25, 2015, and Ashley Kirk, "Iraq and Syria: How Many Foreign Fighters Are Fighting for ISIL?" *Telegraph*, August 12, 2015, available at www.telegraph.co.uk, accessed August 25, 2015.

15. Percentages: "Concerns About Islamic Extremism on the Rise in Middle East," Pew Research Center, July 1, 2014, available at www.pewglobal.org, accessed August 25, 2015.

16. "Remarks by the President at the National Defense University," May 23, 2013, available at www.whitehouse.gov, accessed August 25, 2015.

17. Figuring out the size of jihadist groups is extraordinarily difficult. For a sense of the range of views, see Peter Bergen and Emily Schneider, "Jihadist

Threat Not as Big as You Think," CNN, September 29, 2014, available at www.cnn.com; Lauren Carroll, "Retired General Says al-Qaida Has Grown 'Fourfold' in Last 5 Years," *Politifact*, February 1, 2015, available at www .politifact.com; "Boko Haram—Emerging Threat to the United States," Hearing before the Subcommittee on Counterterrorism and Intelligence of the Committee on Homeland Security of the US House of Representatives, November 30, 2011, available at www.gpo.gov; Carl Bialik, "Shadowy Figures: Al-Qaeda's Ranks Are Hard to Measure," *Wall Street Journal*, September 9, 2011, available at www.wsj.com. See also Ken Dilanian, "FBI Chief: Islamic State Group Bigger Threat Than al-Qaida," July 22, 2015, available at www .yahoo.com/news/, accessed August 22, 2015. Juste quote: Jeanette Ringkøbing, "Jyllands-Postens redaktør: 'De har vundet,'" *Politiken*, February 1, 2006, available at www.politiken.dk. Translation via Google Translate.

18. "The Future of World Religions: Population Growth Projections, 2010–2050," Pew Research Center on Religion and Public Life, April 2, 1915, available at www.pewforum.org. See also "The World's Muslims: Religion, Politics and Society," Pew Research Center: Religion and Public Life, April 30, 2013, available at www.pewforum.org.

19. The jihadist slogan has been used in a number of contexts, including this al-Qaeda announcement of responsibility for the 2004 attacks on trains in Madrid. See "Full Text: 'Al-Qaeda' Madrid claim," BBC News, March 13, 2004, available at www.bbc.co.uk/news.

20. The best strike data to be found is the New America Foundation's "International Security Data Site," http://securitydata.newamerica.net, accessed August 25, 2015. Sean Naylor, *Relentless Strike: The Secret History of Joint Special Operations Command* (New York: St. Martin's Press, 2015) is a good account of the origins of JSOC and its expansion into the chief operating organization against al-Qaeda and analogous movements. For a discussion of Handel's concept in a different context, see James Holmes and Toshi Yoshihara, "The Meaning of Sea Power," *Diplomat*, December 10, 2011, available at www.thediplomat.com, accessed June 2, 2016.

21. See the account of the man chiefly responsible for these innovations, General Stanley McChrystal, *My Share of the Task* (New York: Penguin, 2013), particularly chap. 7–10.

22. "Remarks of John O. Brennan, Assistant to the President for Homeland Security and Counterterrorism, on Ensuring al-Qa'ida's Demise," June 29, 2011, available at www.whitehouse.gov, accessed August 25, 2015.

23. See the documents released by the office of the Director of National Intelligence, "Bin Laden's Bookshelf," available at www.dni.gov. See also Eli Lake and Josh Rogin, "Exclusive: U.S. Intercepted Al Qaeda's 'Legion of Doom' Conference Call," *Daily Beast*, August 7, 2013, available at www .thedailybeast.com, accessed August 25, 2015. The remarkable text of bin Laden's letter, concerning the Arab Spring, dated April 26, 2011, is at

"SOCOM 2012–0000010-HT," West Point Combatting Terrorism Center, May 3, 2012, available at www.ctc.usma.edu. The best work on the Islamic State is William McCants, *The ISIS Apocalypse: The History, Strategy, and Doomsday Vision of the Islamic State* (New York: St. Martin's Press, 2015). See also Charles R. Lister, *The Syrian Jihad: Al-Qaeda, the Islamic State and the Evolution of an Insurgency* (Oxford: Oxford University Press, 2015). Regarding the capture of Mosul, see David Remnick, "Going the Distance: On and off the Road with Barack Obama," *New Yorker*, January 27, 2014, available at www.newyorker.com, accessed August 25, 2015.

24. The Obama administration, which prided itself on distancing itself from the unsavory practices of its predecessor, found its own record on civil liberties under sharp criticism. Charlie Savage, *Power Wars: Inside Obama's Post-9/11 Presidency* (New York: Little, Brown, 2015). Scott Shane, *Objective Troy: A Terrorist, a President, and the Rise of the Drone* (New York: Tim Duggan Books, 2015), 291. See also Mark Mazzetti, *The Way of the Knife: The CIA, a Secret Army, and a War at the Ends of the Earth* (New York: Penguin, 2013).

25. For Luttwack's views, see Edward Luttwak, *Strategy: The Logic of War and Peace* (Cambridge, MA: Harvard University Press, 1987).

26. Rita Katz, "The State Department's Twitter War with ISIS Is Embarrassing," *Time*, September 16, 2014, available at www.time.com, August 25, 2015.

27. On the opinions of the Muslim world, see "Attitudes Toward the United States," Pew Research Center, July 18, 2013, available at www.pewglobal.org, accessed August 25, 2015.

28. Assistant to the President for National Security Susan Rice, quoted in *Face the Nation* transcripts, September 16, 2012, available at www.cbsnews.com; David D. Kirkpatrick, "A Deadly Mix in Benghazi," *New York Times*, December 28, 2013, available at www.nytimes.com.

29. Sky, a British civilian who though initially opposed to the Iraq war became an adviser to American forces, concluded that the victory achieved in Iraq in 2008 was thrown away. *The Unraveling: High Hopes and Missed Opportunities in Iraq* (New York: Public Affairs, 2015). See also Michael R. Gordon and Bernard E. Trainor, *The Endgame: The Inside Story of the Struggle for Iraq, from George W. Bush to Barack Obama* (New York: Pantheon, 2012), xii, 523–684.

30. On the possibility of WMD attacks, see Rolf Mowatt-Larssen, "Al Qaeda Weapons of Mass Destruction Threat: Hype or Reality?" Belfer Center for Science and International Affairs, January 2010, available at http://belfercenter.hks.havard.edu. Concerning the Egyptian chemist, see "Al Qaeda Chemist Killed in U.S. Strike: Pakistani Agents," Reuters, July 29, 2008.

31. See the discussion in Tim Naftali, *Blind Spot: The Secret History of American Counterterrorism* (New York: Basic Books, 2006), especially pages 195–198. On Abu Nidal specifically, see Faye Bowers, "A Lesson in Defeating

a Terrorist," *Christian Science Monitor*, November 15, 2002, available at www
.csmonitor.com, accessed August 25, 2015.

32. See Gregory M. Tomlin, *Murrow's Cold War: Public Diplomacy for the
Kennedy Administration* (Lincoln, NE: Potomac Books, 2016).

33. Lawrence Wright, "ISIS's Savage Strategy in Iraq," *New Yorker*, June
16, 2014. www.newyorker.com/news/daily-comment/isiss-savage-strategy-in
-iraq. The best recent work is William McCants, *The ISIS Apocalypse: The History, Strategy, and Doomsday Vision of the Islamic State* (New York: St. Martin's
Press, 2015). See also Joby Warrick, *Black Flags: The Rise of ISIS* (New York:
Doubleday, 2015).

Notes to Chapter 6

1. Dunford quote from Philip Stewart and David Alexander, "Russia Is
Top U.S. National Security Threat: U.S. Gen. Dunford," Reuters, July 9,
2015, available at www.reuters.com.

2. Defense spending data from "SIPRI Military Expenditure Database,"
Stockholm International Peace Research Institute, 2015, available at www
.sipri.org, accessed July 13, 2015.

3. Ukraine: Paul Roderick Gregory, "Russia Inadvertently Posts Its Casualties in Ukraine: 2,000 Deaths, 3,200 Disabled," *Forbes*, August 25, 2015,
available at www.forbes.com, accessed August 27, 2015.

4. See, for example, remarks by Presidents William J. Clinton and George
W. Bush in 2000 and 2001 respectively. William J. Clinton, "Remarks to the
Russian State Duma in Moscow," American Presidency Project, June 5, 2000,
available at www.presidency.ucsb.edu. George W. Bush, "Address at Warsaw
University," American Presidency Project, June 15, 2001, available at www
.presidency.ucsb.edu.

5. US policies toward Russia are documented at Department of State,
"United States Relations with Russia: After the Cold War," available at
http://2001-2009.state.gov, accessed August 27, 2015. See also James M. Golgeier and Michael McFaul, *Power and Purpose: U.S. Policy Toward Russia After
the Cold War* (Washington, DC: Brookings, 2003). On the underestimation of
Putin, see Fiona Hill and Clifford G. Gady, *Mr. Putin: Operative in the Kremlin*, 2nd ed. (Washington, DC: Brookings, 2015), 370–374. For a glimpse into
the nature of the contemporary Russian system, see Peter Pomerantsev, *Nothing Is True and Everything Is Possible: The Surreal Heart of the New Russia* (New
York: PublicAffairs, 2014).

6. On Putin's behavior, see Hill and Gady, *Mr. Putin*, 261–265, 298–300,
307–308.

7. Ceding of Ukraine to the NPT text can be found at www.msz.gov.pl.

8. On the Russian way of hybrid war, see Michael Kofman and Matthew
Rojansky, "A Closer Look at Russia's Hybrid War," *Kennan Cable*, no. 7

(Washington, DC: Woodrow Wilson International Center for Scholars, April 2015); Maria Snegovaya, "Putin's Information Warfare in Ukraine: Soviet Origins of Russia's Hybrid Warfare," Institute for the Study of War, September 2015, available at www.understandingwar.org; Alexander Lanoszka, "Russian Hybrid Warfare and Extended Deterrence in Eastern Europe," *International Affairs* 92, no. 1 (2016), available at www.chathamhouse.org; Merle Maigre, "Nothing New in Hybrid Warfare: The Estonian Experience and Recommendations for NATO," German Marshall Fund of the United States, February 2015, available at www.gmfus.org.

9. Defense spending data may be found at "SIPRI Military Expenditure Database." See also Andrew Chuter, "NATO Defense Spending Continues to Decline," *DefenseNews*, June 23, 2015, available at www.defensenews .com. The most noticeable turnaround is in Central and Eastern Europe, unsurprisingly. Alessandro Marrone, Olivier De France, and Daniele Fattibene, "Defence Budgets and Cooperation in Europe: Developments, Trends and Drivers," Instituto Affari Internazionali, Institut de Relations Internationales et Strategiques, SWP, ELIAMEP, FOI, Polish Institute of International Affairs, and Royal United Services Institute, January 2016, available at www.iai.it. On whether to aid Ukraine, see Katie Simmons, Bruce Stokes, and Jacob Poushter, "NATO Publics Blame Russia for Ukrainian Crisis, but Reluctant to Provide Military Aid," Pew Research Center, June 10, 2015, available at www.pew global.org. Germans were opposed 77 to 19 percent. On aiding NATO allies against Russia, ibid.

10. On Russia and the media, see studies by Leon Aron, "Putinformation," American Enterprise Institute, August 3, 2015, available at www.aei.org and "Russian Propaganda: Ways and Means," Statement before the Senate Foreign Relations Committee Subcommittee on Europe and Regional Security Cooperation, November 3, 2015, available at www.foreign.senate.gov. On subconventional warfare, see, for example, Amy F. Woolf, "Nonstrategic Nuclear Weapons," Congressional Research Service, February 23, 2015, available at www.fas.org; Benjamin Bidder, "Russia Today: Putin's Weapon in the War of Images," *Spiegel Online International*, August 13, 2013, available at www .spiegel.de, accessed August 27, 2015. On Russian thinking about tactical nuclear weapons, see Jacob W. Kipp, "Russian Doctrine on Tactical Nuclear Weapons: Contexts, Prisms, and Connections," in *Tactical Nuclear Weapons and NATO*, ed. Tom Nichols, Douglas Stuart, and Jeffrey D. McCausland (Carlisle, PA: US Army Strategic Studies Institute, 2012), 116–154; "The Military Doctrine of the Russian Federation," as approved by Russian Federation presidential edict, February 5, 2010 (translation available at www.carnegie endowment.org). This has subsequently been revised in 2015. References to Putin's rattling of nuclear sabers may be found in Max Fisher, "How World War III Became Possible," *Vox*, June 29, 2015, available at www.vox.com. Putin declared that he was ready to go to a nuclear alert over Ukraine. See

"Ukraine Conflict: Putin 'Was Ready for Nuclear Alert,'" BBC, March 15, 2015, available at www.bbc.com.

11. Kerry and Khamenei quotes, www.memri.org/clip_transcript/en/4838 .htm, accessed August 26, 2015.

12. On US reaction to Iranian hostility, see Robin Wright, "'Death to America!' and the Iran Deal," *New Yorker*, July 30, 2015, available at www .newyorker.com.

13. "Iran," *Amnesty International Report 2014/15*, available at www .amnesty.org, accessed August 26, 2015.

14. For a useful timeline, see Shreeya Sinha and Susan Campbell Beachy, "Timeline on Iran's Nuclear Program," updated April 2, 2015, *New York Times*, available at www.nytimes.com, accessed August 26, 2015. Fuller accounts may be found at "Iran," Nuclear Threat Initiative, available at www.nti .org, and "Nuclear Iran," Institute for Science and International Security, 2016, available at www.isisnucleariran.org.

15. Hammond ignored the anti-Israel remark. "Israel Should Be Annihilated, Iranian Official Says," *Jerusalem Post*, August 25, 2015, available at www .jpost.com, accessed August 27, 2015.

16. The full text of the Joint Comprehensive Plan of Action to defer Iranian nuclear weapons is available at www.state.gov. For a critique, see Eliot A. Cohen, Eric S. Edelman, and Ray Takeyh, "Time to Get Tough on Tehran: Iran Policy After the Deal," *Foreign Affairs* 95, no. 1 (January/February 2016): 64–76. Iran's intent to destroy Israel is in the words of the commander of the Basij militia, Mohammad Reza Naqdi: Lazar Berman, "Iran Militia Chief: Destroying Israel Is 'Nonnegotiable,'" *Times of Israel*, March 31, 2015, available at www.timesofisrael.com, accessed, August 27, 2015. As recently as late June 2016, the German intelligence service reported, "[T]he illegal [Iranian] proliferation-sensitive procurement activities in Germany registered by the Federal Office for the Protection of the Constitution persisted in 2015 at what is, even by international standards, a quantitatively high level. This holds true in particular with regard to items which can be used in the field of nuclear technology. The Federal Office for the Protection of the Constitution also registered a further increase in the already considerable procurement efforts in connection with Iran's ambitious missile technology program which could among other things potentially serve to deliver nuclear weapons." "2015 Annual Report on the Protection of the Constitution: Facts and Trends." *Bundesamt für Verfassungsschutz*, June 28, 2016, accessible at www.verfassungsschutz.de /en/public-relations/publications/annual-reports. More detailed accounts of Iranian proliferation-relevant behavior in the wake of the Iran deal may be found at the Institute for Science and International Security (see www.isis nucleariran.org) and the Wisconsin Project on Nuclear Arms Control's Iran site (www.iranwatch.org).

17. On Clapper's comments, see "U.S. Intelligence Assessment of Iran," February 9, 2016, available at http://iranprimer.usip.org; Kenneth Katzman, "Iran, Gulf Security, and U.S. Policy." Congressional Research Service, January 14, 2016, available at www.fas.org.

18. For a good overview of the North Korean nuclear program, see the Nuclear Threat Initiative's "Country Profiles: North Korea," updated August 2015, available at www.nti.org, accessed August 27, 2015. See also 38 North, the website of the US Korea Institute at SAIS, www.38north.org. On North Korea's missile testing and development program, see International Institute of Strategic Studies, *The Military Balance, 2015* (London: Routledge, 2015), 226.

19. John Schilling and Henry Kan, "The Future of North Korean Nuclear Delivery Systems," in the US-Korea Institute at SAIS's North Korea's Nuclear Futures Series (2015), available at www.38north.com, accessed August 27, 2015. In general, this website is one of the best sources for analysis of North Korean foreign and military policy.

20. On Pakistan's nuclear arsenal, see David Albright and Serena Kelleher-Vergantini, "Pakistan's Fourth Reactor at Khushab Now Appears Operational," Institute for Science and International Security, January 16, 2015, available at www.isis-online.org, accessed August 27, 2015.

21. On Pakistan's relationship with China, see Jonah Blank, "Thank You for Being a Friend: Pakistan and China's Almost Alliance," *Foreign Affairs* (online), available at www.foreignaffairs.com, accessed February 8, 2016.

22. For a withering critique of those who will the ends (deterrence) without understanding or accepting the means (the actual employment of large scale violence), see Albert Wohlstetter, "Bishops, Statesmen, and Other Strategists on the Bombing of Innocents," *Commentary* 75, no. 6 (June 1983): 15–35. Quote from Thomas Schelling, *Arms and Influence* (New Haven, CT: Yale University Press, 1966), 43 and passim.

23. Rhetoric of threats discussed in personal conversation, Professor Martin Kramer, August 1990. On "red line," see Rebecca Ballhaus, "Gates: Syria Red Line Was 'Serious Mistake,'" *Wall Street Journal*, January 15, 2014, available at http://blogs.wsj.com, and "Panetta: Obama's 'Red Line' on Syria Damaged U.S. Credibility," *Real Clear Politics*, October 7, 2014, available at www.realclearpolitics.com. This is a video of an interview with Katie Couric on Yahoo! News.

24. Again, a personal impression reinforced by numerous conversations with foreign officials in Asia, Europe, and Latin America.

25. Winston S. Churchill, *The Second World War*, vol. 3, *The Grand Alliance* (Boston: Houghton Mifflin, 1951), 607–608.

26. The influence that the United States will exert on this world will be less than it has exercised in the past twenty-five years," Raymond Aron, *The Imperial Republic: The United States and the World, 1945–1973*, trans. Frank Jellinek (Englewood Cliffs, NJ: Prentice-Hall, 1974), 328; see also pages 148ff. and his

memoirs, *Mémoires: 50 ans de réflexion politique* (Paris: Julliard, 1983), particularly chap. 23, "Henry Kissinger et la fin de l'hégémonie américaine," 607–633. On America as a hyperpower, see "To Paris, U.S. Looks Like a 'Hyperpower,'" *New York Times*, February 5, 1999, available at www.nytimes.com.

27. Overviews of American opinion can be found in the quadrennial "America's Place in the World" surveys done by Pew, as well as global assessments of the United States. Richard Wike, Bruce Stokes, and Jacob Poushter, "Global Publics Back U.S. on Fighting ISIS, but Are Critical of Post-9/11 Torture," available at www.pewglobal.org, accessed August 31, 2015. There is also a large and growing, if inconclusive, scholarly literature on credibility. See, for example, Max Abrahms, "The Credibility Paradox: Violence as a Double-Edged Sword in International Politics," *International Studies Quarterly* 57, no. 4 (2013); Sebastian Rosato, "The Inscrutable Intentions of Great Powers," *International Security* 39, no. 3 (Winter 2014/15) and succeeding issues in which a lively debate ensued.

28. A good, if somewhat dated book on how the United States accommodated Russia in the early post–Cold War years is James M. Goldgeier and Michael McFaul, *Power and Purpose: U.S. Policy Toward Russia After the Cold War* (Washington, DC: Brookings, 2003).

29. David Lerman, "U.S. Training Yields Only 60 Syria Rebels So Far, Carter Says," *Bloomberg Business*, July 7, 2015, accessed August 31, 2015. See also "General Austin: Only '4 or 5' U.S-Trained Syrian Rebels Fighting ISIS," ABC News, September 16, 2015, available at www.abcnews.com.

30. For the official report of one of the original political warfare organizations of World War II, see David Garnett, *The Secret History of PWE: The Political Warfare Executive, 1939–1945* (London: St. Ermin's Press, 2002). On the use of propaganda, see, for example, Laura A. Belmonte, *Selling the American Way: U.S. Propaganda and the Cold War* (Philadelphia: University of Pennsylvania Press, 2008); Max Boot, "Political Warfare," *Policy Innovation Memorandum* 33 *Council on Foreign Relations* (June 2013), available at www.cfr.org; William Rosenau. *Waging the 'War of Ideas* (Santa Monica, CA: RAND, 2006); Susan L. Gough, "The Evolution of Strategic Influence," US Army War College, April 7, 2003, available at www.fas.org.

Notes to Chapter 7

1. Barry Posen, "Command of the Commons: The Military Foundations of U.S. Hegemony," *International Security* 28, no. 1 (Summer 2003): 5–46.

2. On "milieu goals," see the discussion in Arnold Wolfers, *Discord and Collaboration: Essays on International Politics* (Baltimore: Johns Hopkins University Press, 1962), 73–74.

3. Anne Clunan and Harald A. Trinkunas, eds., *Ungoverned Spaces: Alternatives to State Authority in an Era of Softened Sovereignty* (Stanford, CA:

Stanford University Press, 2010). The point in this book is that in actuality "ungoverned space" is usually run by substate actors—it is not absolutely ungoverned. See also Robert Jackson, *Quasi-States: Sovereignty, International Relations and the Third World* (Cambridge: Cambridge University Press, 1990) on the impact of decolonization. Angela Rabasa, Steven Boraz, Peter Chalk, et al., *Ungoverned Territories: Understanding and Reducing Terrorism Risks* (Santa Monica, CA: RAND, 2007) takes a more systematic and conventional look at ungoverned areas as a refuge for terrorists.

4. Ronald Robinson and John Gallagher with Alice Denny, *Africa and the Victorians: The Climax of Imperialism* (London: St. Martin's Press, 1961). The Gallagher-Robinson thesis, as it became known, engendered a robust academic debate that continues to this day. See, among others, William Roger Louis, ed., *Imperialism: The Robinson and Gallagher Controversy* (New York: New Viewpoints, 1976).

5. On the history and current interpretations of the right to protect, see Charles Homans, "Responsibility to Protect: A Short History," *Foreign Policy*, October 11, 2011, available at www.foreignpolicy.com; Alex J. Bellamy, "The Responsibility to Protect and the Problem of Military Intervention," *International Affairs* 84, no. 4 (2008): 615–639; Robert A. Pape, "When Duty Calls: A Pragmatic Standard of Humanitarian Intervention," *International Security* 37, no. 1 (Summer 2012): 41–80. A lively correspondence exchange followed this last article.

6. See "The World Factbook: Timor-Leste," Central Intelligence Agency, 2015, available at www.cia.gov.

7. See two books by thoughtful practitioners, Paddy Ashdown, *Swords and Ploughshares: Bringing Peace to the 21st Century* (London: Weidenfeld & Nicolson, 2007) and Ashraf Ghani and Clare Lockhart, *Fixing Failed States: A Framework for Rebuilding a Fractured World* (Oxford: Oxford University Press, 2008). See also Francis Fukuyama, *State-Building: Governance and World Order in the 21st Century* (Ithaca, NY: Cornell University Press, 2014).

8. The best overall source on the Syrian tragedy is the *Syrian Observatory on Human Rights*, www.syriahr.com. The UN High Commissioner for Refugees (UNHCR) also has valuable statistics, www.unhcr.org.

9. For a searing critique of Libya intervention, see Alan Kuperman, "Obama's Libya Debacle," *Foreign Affairs* 94, no. 2 (March 2015), available at www.foreignaffairs.com; a more measured account is Christopher M. Blanchard, "Libya: Transition and U.S. Policy" (Washington, DC: Congressional Research Service, March 4, 2016); the most comprehensive look thus far is Christopher S. Chivvis and Jeffrey Martini, *Libya After Qaddafi: Lessons and Implications for the Future* (Santa Monica, CA: RAND, 2014), available at www.rand.org. On the looted arms that fell into very bad hands indeed, see C. J. Chivers, "Looted Libyan Arms in Mali May Have Shifted Conflict's Path," *New York Times*, February 7, 2013, available at www.nytimes.com, accessed September 1, 2013.

10. About Yemen, see Yara Bayoumy and Mohammed Ghobari, "Iranian Support Seen Crucial for Yemen's Houthis," Reuters, December 15, 2014, available at www.reuters.com, accessed September 1, 2015.

11. For specifics on the split in American opinion, see "A Decade Later, Iraq War Divides the Public," Pew Research Center, March 18, 2013, available at www.people-press.org, accessed February 23, 2016.

12. A classic statement of the case against externally assisted development is Peter T. Bauer, *Reality and Rhetoric: Studies in the Economics of Development* (Cambridge, MA: Harvard University Press, 1984); his essay, "Foreign Aid: Abiding Issues," in Peter T. Bauer, *From Subsistence to Exchange and Other Essays*, by Peter T. Bauer (Princeton, NJ: Princeton University Press, 2000) reinforces the point. A more recent case by a Zambian-born, Harvard- and Oxford-trained economist is Dambisa Moyo. *Dead Aid: Why Aid Is Not Working and How There Is a Better Way for Africa* (New York: Farrar, Straus and Giroux, 2009). In a similar vein, see Simeon Djankov, José García Montalvo, and Marta Reynal-Querol, *The Curse of Aid* (Washington, DC: World Bank, 2007).

13. For a short synopsis of the US Navy in the 1800s, see John Dull, *American Naval History, 1607–1865* (Lincoln: University of Nebraska Press, 2012), chap. 5, "Trade Protection and the War with Mexico, 1815–1861," 65–81. On this phase of America's confrontation with Iran, see David Crist, *The Twilight War: The Secret History of America's Thirty Year with Iran* (New York: Penguin, 2012), 235–379.

14. On US Navy Freedom of Navigation Operations (FONOPS), see "Freedom of Navigation Program Fact Sheet," US Department of Defense, March 2015, available at www.policy.defense.gov; "Freedom of Navigation Report for Fiscal Year 2014," US Department of Defense, March 23, 2015; Thomas B. Fargo, "Walking the Talk in the South China Sea," in C. Christine Fair and Mark W. Frazier, eds. *Asia Policy* 21 (January 2016), 59–65.

15. The annual report "Piracy and Armed Robbery Against Ships" from the International Chamber of Commerce International Maritime Bureau is a valuable source of data, available at www.imo.org. The 2014 report, for example, shows that attacks declined from 445 globally in 2010 to 245 in that year.

16. See Ronald O'Rourke et al., "Changes in the Arctic: Background and Issues for Congress," Congressional Research Service, January 19, 2016; Heather Conley and Caroline Rohloff, "The New Ice Curtain: Russia's Strategic Reach to the Arctic" (Washington, DC: Center for Strategic & International Studies. August 2015); Pavel K. Baev, "Russia's Arctic Illusions" (Washington, DC: Brookings. August 27, 2015); Andrew Erickson and Gabe Collins, "China's New Strategic Target; Arctic Minerals." *Wall Street Journal,* January 18, 2012, available at http://blogs.wsj.com; Caitlin Campbell, "China and the Arctic: Objectives and Obstacles," U.S.-China Economic and Security Review Commission, April 13, 2012, available at www.uscc.gov; Gwynn

Guilford, "What Is China's Arctic Game Plan?" *Atlantic*, May 16, 2013, available at www.theatlantic.com.

17. United Nations Office for Outer Space Affairs, www.unoosa.org; and Satellite Industry Association, www.sia.org are two useful websites for basic data on space. The Federation of Atomic Scientists Space Policy Project, www.fas.org/spp/, is extremely useful on military-related issues.

18. NASA, "Space Debris and Human Spacecraft," September 26, 2013, available at www.nasa.gov.

19. Full text of the Outer Space Treaty is to be found at www.history.nasa.gov.

20. For an excellent short summary of the uses of outer space, see John M. Collins, *Military Geography for Professionals and the Public* (New York: Brassey's, 1998) chap. 7, "Inner and Outer Space," 137–152. The American military's approach to space is summarized in International Institute for Strategic Studies, *The Military Balance 2015* (London: Routledge, 2015), 13–16.

21. For three of the better recent books on cyberwarfare, see Adam Segal, *The Hacked World Order: How Nations Fight, Trade, Maneuver, and Manipulate in the Digital Age* (New York: PublicAffairs 2016), and Thomas Rid, *Cyber War Will Not Take Place* (Oxford: Oxford University Press, 2013); on the other side, Joel Brenner, *America the Vulnerable: Inside the New Threat Matrix of Digital Espionage, Crime, and Warfare* (New York: Penguin, 2011). For a skeptical treatment of cyberwarfare as a threat, see Rid, *Cyberwar Will Not Take Place*, as well as Erik Gartzke, "The Myth of Cyberwar: Bringing War in Cyberspace Back Down to Earth," *International Security* 38, no. 2 (Fall 2013): 41–73. A more worried version is Joel Brenner, *Glass Houses: Privacy, Secrecy, and Cyber Insecurity in a Transparent World* (New York: Penguin, 2011); recent journalistic accounts include Fred Kaplan, *Dark Territory: The Secret History of Cyber War* (New York: Simon and Schuster, 2016). Some particular cases are: Andreas Schmidt, "The Estonian Cyberattacks" in Jason Healey, ed. *The Fierce Domain–Conflicts in Cyberspace, 1986–2012.* (Washington, DC: Atlantic Council, 2013); David Hollis, "Cyberwar Case Study: Georgia 2008," *Small Wars Journal*, January 6, 2011, accessible at www.smallwarsjournal.com; Jon R. Lindsay, "Stuxnet and the Limits of Cyber Warfare," *Security Studies* 22 (2013), pages 365–404; Kim Zetter. "NSA Acknowledges What We All Feared: Iran Learns from US Cyberattacks," *Wired*, February 10, 2015, accessible at www.wired.com.

22. James Kraska and Michael Monti, *The Law of Naval Warfare and China's Maritime Militia International Law Studies* 91 (2015), available at http://stockton.usnwc.edu, accessed September 4, 2015.

Notes to Chapter 8

1. On the need for a stronger military, see *Ensuring a Strong U.S. Defense for the Future: The National Defense Panel Review of the 2014 Quadrennial*

Defense Review (Washington, DC: US Institute of Peace, 2014). The NDP was cochaired by former secretary of defense William Perry and retired four-star general John Abizaid, and included senior Republican and Democratic officials. Given the events of recent years, even greater increases in force structure and end strength are probably required.

2. Quote from People's Republic of China, Ministry of Defense, "Chinese Military Strategy," May 2015, available at www.news.usni.org.

3. Putin quotes from Vladimir V. Putin, "A Plea for Caution from Russia," *New York Times*, September 11, 2013, available at www.nytimes.com, accessed September 6, 2015.

4. On the importance of credibility, see Stephen Brooks, John Ikenberry, and William Wohlforth, "Don't Come Home, America: The Case Against Retrenchment," *International Security* 37, no. 3 (Winter 2012/13).

5. For a longer discussion of the simultaneity trap, see my eponymous essay in the *American Interest*, February 9, 2016, available at www.the-american-interest.com.

6. "X" (George F. Kennan), "The Sources of Soviet Conduct," *Foreign Affairs* (July 1947), available at www.foreignaffairs.com.

7. Maurice Druon, *The Poisoned Crown*, trans. Humphrey Hare (New York: HarperCollins, 1957), 95–96.

8. Quote from Isaiah Berlin, "Political Judgment," in *The Sense of Reality: Studies in Ideas and Their History*, ed. Henry Hardy (New York: Farrar, Straus and Giroux, 1996), 45.

9. Definition of *grand strategy*: Edward Mead Earle, "Political and Military Strategy for the United States," *Proceedings of the Academy of Political Science* 19, no. 2 (January 1941): 7. A good overview of its large and growing literature may be found in Hal Brands, *The Promise and Pitfalls of Grand Strategy* (Carlisle, PA: US Army War College Strategic Studies Institute, 2012); he makes the case for it in *What Good Is Grand Strategy?: Power and Purpose in American Foreign Policy from Harry S. Truman to George W. Bush* (Ithaca, NY: Cornell University Press, 2014).

10. Available on many websites, for example, www.ambafrance-ca.org.

11. Office of Management and Budget, "Historical Tables, Table 3.1, Outlays by Superfunction and Function: 1940–2020," available at www.whitehouse.gov, accessed September 6, 2015.

12. The memoirs of Colin Powell, *My American Journey* (New York: Random House, 1995), are an unintentionally revealing depiction of the mind-set of senior army leadership determined never to repeat Vietnam.

13. Concerning F-35s, see "Four Things to Know About F-35 Production Ramp-Up," June 16, 2015, available at www.f35.com, accessed September 6, 2015.

14. These statistics are taken from different editions of the authoritative *Military Balance* produced each year by the International Institute for Strategic

Studies. I have, in particular, used the 1995/1996, 2004/2005, and 2015 editions.

15. Caspar W. Weinberger, "The Uses of Military Power," remarks prepared for delivery to the National Press Club, November 28, 1984, available at www.pbs.org, accessed September 6, 2015.

16. On being a cardinal task, see Carl von Clausewitz, *On War*, trans. Michael Howard and Peter Paret, bk. 1 (Princeton, NJ: Princeton University Press, 1982), 88.

17. See my discussion of the 1991 war with Iraq in *Supreme Command: Soldiers, Statesmen, and Leadership in Wartime* (New York: Free Press, 2002), 188–203.

18. "Neville Chamberlain," November 12, 1940, in *Winston S. Churchill: His Complete Speeches*, ed. Robert Rhodes James (New York: Chelsea House Publishers, 1974), vol. 6, *1935–1942*, 6307–6308.

19. For a particularly eloquent argument for short wars, see Samuel P. Huntington, "Playing to Win," *National Interest* 3 (Spring 1986): 8–16. "If we are going to win, we have to win quickly" can be found on page 14.

20. On the six phases of war, see Chairman of the Joint Chiefs of Staff, *Joint Operation Planning*, Joint Publication 5-0, August 11, 2011, iii–38ff. and passim.

21. On the surge decision, see Michael R. Gordon and Bernard E. Trainor, *The Endgame: The Inside Story of the Struggle for Iraq, from George W. Bush to Barack Obama* (New York: Pantheon, 2012), 267–311.

22. I discuss Churchill in my chapter on the prime minister in *Supreme Command*; see, in particular, page 132.

Notes to Postscript

1. Clark Clifford with Richard Holbrooke, *Counsel to the President: A Memoir* (New York: Random House, 1991), 102.

Index

Eliot A. Cohen is the Robert E. Osgood Professor of Strategic Studies at Johns Hopkins University's School of Advanced International Studies (SAIS). The prize-winning author of several books, including *Supreme Command* and *Conquered into Liberty*, Cohen lives in the Washington, DC, area.

©Kaveh Sardari